A BASEBALL ALBUM

GERALD SECOR COUZENS

Lippincott & Crowell, Publishers

New York

Grateful acknowledgment is hereby made for permission to reprint the following:

"How Baseball Began" by Dr. Harold Seymour. Reprinted by permission of Dr. Harold Seymour.

"Baseball's Other Self: Cricket" by John Fowles. First appeared as "Making a Pitch for Cricket" in *Sports Illustrated*. Copyright © 1973 by J. R. Fowles, Ltd. Reprinted by permission of Wallace & Sheil Agency, Inc.

"John Pappas Tries Out for the Mets" from *Assignment: Sports* by Robert Lipsyte. Copyright © 1970 by Robert M. Lipsyte. Reprinted by permission of Harper & Row, Publishers, Inc.

"Ty Cobb's Wild Ten-Month Fight to Live" by Al Stump. Reprinted by permission of Al Stump.

"The Silent Season of a Hero" by Gay Talese. Reprinted by permission of Gay Talese.

"The Kid's Last Game" by Ed Linn. First appeared in *Sport* magazine. Copyright © 1961 by Edward Linn. Reprinted by permission of The Sterling Lord Agency, Inc.

"Outdoor Kabuki" from *The Chrysanthemum and the Bat* by Robert Whiting. Reprinted by permission of Dodd, Mead and Company, Inc.

"The Dilution of Memorable Events" by Leonard Koppett. Reprinted by permission of *The Sporting News*, St. Louis, Missouri.

Grateful acknowledgment is hereby made to the following for permission to use photographs on the pages listed:

Commissioner's Office, New York, N.Y.: 221
Library of Congress: 11, 34, 39, 46, 164 (top), 177, 180, 219 (bottom), 230 (top)
Louisville Slugger: 80 (bottom)
National Archives: 168, 205
National Baseball Hall of Fame and Museum, Inc.: 5, 19, 25, 51, 54, 59, 72, 76, 80 (top), 84, 86 (bottom), 94, 103, 118, 127, 138, 159, 187, 194, 199, 219 (top), 224, 227, 230 (bottom), 234

All other photographs by the author.

FIRST EDITION

Designed by C. Linda Dingler

U.S. Library of Congress Cataloging in Publication Data

Couzens, Gerald Secor.
  A baseball album.

  1. Baseball—United States—History—Addresses, essays, lectures. I. Title.
GV863.A1C65   796.357'0973   79-25044
ISBN 0-690-01864-9
ISBN 0-690-01883-5 pbk.

80 81 82 83 84 10 9 8 7 6 5 4 3 2 1

For my mother and father,
who first brought me to the Little Field

CONTENTS

ACKNOWLEDGMENTS

This book wouldn't have been possible if it weren't for the help of the following people: Jack Redding, chief librarian at the National Baseball Hall of Fame and Museum, who was of immense help in offering suggestions and ideas; Jim Benagh, whose advice and notes and whose book *Incredible Baseball Feats* were of great assistance; Jay Acton, who originally went to bat for me and kept me in the game; Frank Gentile, who offered all the casework when times got difficult; Brian Cox, my editor; and of course my wife, Elisa, who was with me through it all.

Baseball changes so little,
it renews itself each year without effort,
but always with feeling.

—Roger Angell

ORIGINS

This Year in Baseball

1845: Alexander J. Cartwright, "The Father of Modern Baseball," codified baseball playing rules.

1846: Cartwright's home team, the New York Knickerbockers, lost to the New York Nine club 23–1, in the first recorded baseball game; Elysian Fields, Hoboken, New Jersey.

1849: Baseball uniforms introduced for the first time by the Knickerbocker Club of New York.

1858: Englishman Henry Chadwick published the first rule book for baseball and headed the rules committee of the National Association of Baseball Players, founded that year.

1859: Williams College lost to Amherst College in the first official collegiate baseball game.

1862: William Cammeyer opened Union Grounds in Brooklyn, the first enclosed facility constructed specifically for baseball and the home grounds of the Mutuals.

1864: Alfred J. Reach, of London, England, was paid $1,000 to play for the Philadelphia Athletics in the National Association. This is considered to be the first instance of player salary.

1867: William "Candy" Cummings, pitching for the Excelsior club of Brooklyn, first used the curveball on a regular basis. "The greatest change ever made in the National Game was the introduction of what is known as curve pitching" (Cap Anson).

1869: The Cincinnati Red Stockings were the first professional team. More than 4,000 fans turned up to greet them on their return from an undefeated eastern tour. They presented the team with a 1,600-pound iron bat inscribed with the names of the nine starting players and two substitutes.

1871: Box seats were introduced at Union Grounds in Brooklyn. Now for an extra 25 cents a spectator could sit in a more protected and private area.

1874: The Philadelphia A's and the Boston club toured England and Ireland for a series of baseball and cricket matches, the first foreign tour by baseball teams.

1875: Joseph Borden threw the first no-hit game in the major leagues on June 28, leading Philadelphia to a 4–0 victory over Chicago. But it wasn't until after his death on October 14, 1929—the same day that the A's beat the Cubs to win the Series—that he was credited with the feat. Because of baseball's unsavory reputation, Borden had pitched under the name Nedrob (Borden spelled backward), and later no one would believe he was the man who did the pitching in 1875.

1876: The National League was formed on February 2 in New York City. Boston defeated Philadelphia 6–5 in the league's first game.

1882: Richard Higham, a National League umpire, was the first umpire ever suspended for aiding gamblers betting on the outcome of baseball games.

1888: A. G. Spalding, owner of the Chicago White Stockings, left with a group of players on baseball's first globe-trotting exhibition, a trip that Spalding hoped would bring international popularity to the sport.

1894: On Memorial Day, Boston infielder Link Lowe, became the first player in the majors to hit four home runs in one game.

1896: Charles Hinton, Princeton University professor, invented the first baseball pitching machine.

1897: Baltimore Spider outfielder Willie Keeler hit safely in 44 consecutive games.

1901: Chicago played Cleveland in the rival American League's first official game.

1903: Boston, with Cy Young pitching two victories, defeated Pittsburgh 5 games to 3 to win the first World Series.

1904: Montford M. Cross was Philadelphia's full-time shortstop and played in 153 games this season. His .182 batting average is still the lowest ever recorded in the history of the game for a starting player.

1909: On August 19, in a game between the Red Sox and Cleveland, Cornelius Ball of Cleveland performed the major leagues' first unassisted triple play.

1910: Former semipro player, U.S. President William Howard Taft, threw out the first ball at the Washington Senators baseball opener, setting a precedent that lasted as long as there was a team in the nation's capital.

1916: On June 2, Cleveland players became the first to wear numbered uniforms when they appeared on the field with numbers stitched on their shirt-sleeves in a game against Chicago.

1917: In Chicago, Jim "Hippo" Vaughn, pitcher for the Cubs, and Fred Toney, the Cincinnati pitcher, engaged in the only double no-hitter in the major leagues. In the tenth inning the roof fell in on Hippo; a single, a dropped ball, and baserunning by Olympic sprint sensation Jim Thorpe brought in the winning runs for Cincinnati and a loss for Vaughn.

1920: The major leagues outlawed the use of the spitball pitch.
Leon Cadore of Brooklyn and Joe Oescheger of Boston pitched a 26-inning 1–1 standoff that was called because of darkness.

1921: Baseball's first commissioner, Judge Kenesaw Mountain Landis, brought in to clean up baseball following revelations coming out of the "Black Sox" scandal.

1924: The New York Giants and the Chicago White Sox returned from an unsuccessful European trip that attracted as many paying customers in Dublin, Ireland, as there were players on the field.

1933: Spectators numbering 47,500 watched in Chicago as the American League defeated the National League 4–2 in baseball's first All-Star Game.

1935: President Franklin D. Roosevelt pressed a button in the White House, and lights went on in Cincinnati's Crosley Field, allowing 20,000 spectators to watch Cincinnati beat Philadelphia in baseball's first night game.

1936: Ty Cobb, Babe Ruth, Christy Mathewson, Honus Wagner, and Walter Johnson were the first players selected for the Baseball Hall of Fame.

1941: In a night game against Cleveland on July 17, Joe DiMaggio's record-setting 56-consecutive-game hitting streak was ended.

1944: Joe Nuxhall, a fifteen-year-, ten-month-, eleven-day-old pitcher from Hamilton, Ohio, became the youngest player in the history of the major leagues when he took the mound for Cincinnati in a game the Reds were losing 13–0. His five walks, wild pitch, two singles, and five runs allowed in only two thirds of an inning led to his disappearance from baseball for eight years. He later went on to win 135 games, making the National League All-Star team on two occasions.

1947: Jackie Robinson, the first black player in modern times and Brooklyn's second baseman, wins Rookie-of-the-Year honors.

1950: The great Grover Cleveland Alexander, the lanky pitcher who led the Phils to their first pennant in 1915 and still leads the National League for pitching 437 complete games, was found in a Saint Paul, Nebraska, flophouse, dead from alcoholism at the age of sixty-three.

1956: Don Newcombe had 27 pitching victories for the Dodgers and became the first winner of the Cy Young Award, an award given annually to the best pitcher in the major leagues.

1959: Harvey Haddix, a pitcher for the Pittsburgh Pirates, had a perfect game going on May 26 against the Milwaukee Braves. A throwing miscue in the thirteenth inning, a sacrifice bunt, a walk, and a three-run homer ended one of baseball's most fantastic pitching efforts.

1961: Playing in Yankee Stadium on October 1, Yankee outfielder Roger Maris sent Tracey Stallard's pitch into the bleachers for his 61st home run, breaking Babe Ruth's season record of 60, set in 1927.

1962: The New York Mets, baseball's newest team, had a disastrous first season. Playing with castoffs from other teams, players out of retirement, and walk-ons, the Mets lost a record 120 games. No other team in history has lost so many.

1968: Saint Louis Cardinal Bob Gibson won the first of his two Cy Young awards by establishing 1.12 as the best ERA ever for a pitcher. Gibson went 22–9 and drove the Cards to the pennant. In the opening game of the Series against the Tigers, he set a Series record by fanning 17 batters.

1969: The Mets were simply amazin'. With Jerry Koosman's two pitching victories, the Mets shocked the Orioles 4–1 to win the Series and become the first expansion team to perform the feat.

1972: A thirteen-day-long player strike, the first in the major leagues, set back the opening of the season by more than a week. The issue of the players' pension fund was finally settled, but some teams ended up missing eight games in the abbreviated season.

1976: After twenty-two years in the major leagues, Hank Aaron retired from the game with a record 755 career home runs, the most ever hit.

1978: The Los Angeles Dodgers became the first team in organized sports to top the 3-million-spectator mark for one season. Helped by promotional giveaways, good weather, and a fine Dodger team, 3,347,845 paying fans clicked through the turnstiles.

The controversial New York Yankees, beset by internal troubles, staged the most dramatic comeback in the history of American sports. Trailing the division-leading Boston Red Sox by 14 games on July 19, the Bronx Bombers won 52 of their next 73 games to tie Boston for the division title; they beat the Sox in the special play-off game and beat the Royals for the American League crown. In the World Series against the Dodgers, after being down by two games, the Yanks stormed back to win the next four games and win the Series, one of the most thrilling in Series history.

100TH ANNIVERSARY

*You are cordially invited
to participate in the celebration of
Professional Baseball's 100th Anniversary
at the
Centennial Dinner
honoring
Baseball's "Greatest Players Ever"*

*Monday Evening, July 21, 1969
(Eve of the 1969 All-Star Game)
Sheraton-Park Hotel, Washington, D. C.*

Subscription: $35 per Person   Tables of Ten

*Cocktails 6:00 p.m.   Dinner promptly at 7:00 p.m.
Formal Dress   Ladies welcome*

*R.S.V.P.
Please use enclosed card*

*Please make checks payable to
Baseball Centennial Dinner*

Baseball Centennial Dinner Invitation

"No more rounders!" That feverish cry came from the surely overexuberant and most likely wine-sotted dinner guests gathered one night in 1889 at Delmonico's Restaurant, the fashionable dining spot in New York City. The revelers were members of Albert G. Spalding's troupe that had just returned from one of baseball's longest world tours. It was at this gathering that the germinating seeds of the Abner Doubleday/Cooperstown baseball naissance hoax were first dropped.

In "How Baseball Begin," Dr. Harold Seymour, the noted baseball historian, lays bare the myth and shows how baseball, our "national game," actually came to be. Says Professor Seymour, "To ascertain who invented baseball would be equivalent to trying to locate the discoverer of fire."

How Baseball Began

by Dr. Harold Seymour

Baseball in the United States is both a sport and a business. It is also an important social institution in our complex American society. Recognized as the "national game," it has become a symbol of America in much the same way that the Olympic Games are associated with Greece or cricket with England. Baseball even has a mythology of its own. Part of that myth enshrines its origin. Traditionally, baseball is accepted as a home-grown product; but actually it is no more indigenous to the United States than the automobile or the idea of mass production in factories. The fact that baseball, too, had its inception abroad bolsters a truth frequently overlooked or ignored—that most inventions, ideas, and institutions seldom are the work of one individual in one country.

The myth concerning the origin of baseball began to take shape in the spring of 1889 at famous Delmonico's in New York City, where some three hundred people, including such public figures as Mark Twain and Chauncey M. Depew, gathered to fete the squad of professional baseball players, headed by Albert G. Spalding, just returned from their world tour.[1] Organized baseball had just approached the end of a decade of financial success and increasing popularity in America; and Spalding, then president of the Chicago Club and also head of a thriving sporting goods business, had felt the time opportune for spreading the gospel of the American national game abroad. He therefore had headed a band of professionals, consisting of his own club and a picked group of all-stars from the rest of the National League, on a globe-circling exhibition trip which

1. New York *Clipper*, April 13, 1889.

included stops at Honolulu, Australia, and the Pyramids, and a game in England with the Prince of Wales among the spectators.

At the banquet, one of the speakers, Abraham G. Mills, fourth president[2] of the National League, perhaps made over-exuberant by the occasion, said he wanted it distinctly understood that "patriotism and research" had established that the game of baseball was American in origin. His audience greeted this pronouncement with enthusiastic cries of "No rounders!" Thus, according to the New York *Clipper,* the English claim that America's national game was a descendant of the English game of rounders was "forever squelched."[3]

The "research" to which Mills referred is somewhat obscure. Perhaps he had in mind the assertions of John Montgomery Ward, a prominent player and lawyer, who had stated unequivocally the previous year that baseball did not spring from rounders, but was a product of the "genius of the American Boy."[4]

But this question as to the birthplace of the game had become a subject for controversy only recently. Prior to the decade of the eighties, rounders had been generally accepted as the ancestor of baseball.[5] However, after the Civil War, organized teams had attained importance, and baseball evolved from a simple, primitive game into a popular show business. It had gained prestige not unmixed with American pride in having a "national game." Consequently, its devotees found it increasingly difficult to countenance the notion that their favorite sport was of foreign origin. Pride and patriotism required that the game be native, unsullied by English ancestry—even if the rounders theory could be disproved by no stronger weapons than shouting and incantation.

Nevertheless, the rounders idea somehow was not to be "forever squelched." The doctrine persisted, although without clinching evidence. The issue was unresolved for years until brought to focus in an article which appeared in *Spalding's Guide for 1903,* written by the first great baseball sports writer, the "Father of Baseball" and the leading advocate of the rounders argument, Henry Chadwick.[6] He had always pleaded rounders, claiming that he had played the game in England as a boy, and that early American "town ball" was very similar to it.[7] Two conspicuous features common to both games, Chadwick pointed out, were the use of four posts for base stations and putting runners out

2. Mills was not the third president, as generally claimed. After the death of William A. Hulbert, the League's second president, in 1882 A. J. Soden of the Boston Club succeeded to the office for a brief interval preceding the administration of Mills. *Spalding's Official Base Ball Guide for 1883* (New York: 1883), 97. (Published annually 1877–1939 under various titles, but hereinafter referred to as *Spalding's Guide.*)

3. New York *Clipper,* April 13, 1889.

4. John M. Ward, *Baseball: How to Become a Player* (Philadelphia: 1888), 21.

5. *Beadle's Dime Base-Ball Player* (New York: 1871), 71. Also see Charles A Peverelly, *The Book of American Pastimes, Containing a History of the Principal Base-Ball, Cricket, Rowing, and Yatching Clubs of the United States* (New York: 1866), 338; and Newton Crane, *Baseball* (London: 1891), 2.

6. *Spalding's Guide for 1903,* 5–6.

7. Henry Chadwick, *The American Game of Base Ball: How It Is Played* (Philadelphia: 1888), 7.

by throwing the ball at them—"soaking" or plugging," as it was called.

Thus challenged, Spalding, the champion of the American theory,[8] suggested settling the question once and for all. A blue-ribbon commission was appointed consisting of seven men of "high repute and undoubted knowledge of Base Ball" and including two United States Senators. The committee itself supplied the window-dressing while A. G. Mills, the chairman, did what actual work was done. After collecting testimony over a period of three years,[9] consisting of recollections but no solid documentary evidence, Mills wrote and presented a report, dated December 30, 1907, to the effect that (1) baseball originated in the United States, and (2) the first method of playing it "according to the best evidence obtainable to date" was devised by General Abner Doubleday at Cooperstown, New York, in 1839.[10]

The remarkable part of the report was the dragooning of Doubleday and Cooperstown on the sole basis of the recollections of one Abner Graves, one-time citizen of Cooperstown. His statement was recorded in a press release issued by the commission before its final report which was entitled "The Origin of Baseball"[11] Graves described a game of town ball in progress between pupils of Otsego Academy and Green's Select School when

... Doubleday then improved Town Ball, to limit the number of players, as many were hurt in collisions. From twenty to fifty boys took part in the game I have described. He also designed the game to be played by definite teams or sides. Doubleday called the game Base Ball, for there were four bases in it. Three were places where the runner could rest free from being put out, provided he kept his foot on the flat stone base. The pitcher stood in a six foot ring. The ball had a rubber center overwound with yarn to a size somewhat larger than the present sphere, and was covered with leather or buckskin. Anyone getting the ball was entitled to throw it at a runner between bases, and put him out by hitting him with it.[12]

Thus it was that a decision laid down by what has been called "an oecumenical council of baseball hierarchs"[13] became the basis of an American myth

8. Significantly, Spalding contradicted his own assertions in his *Guide for 1878*, 5, where he stated that Englishmen who watched Americans playing baseball "accused them of playing rounders" and were not far out of the way since "the game unquestionably thus originated."

9. This material was destroyed in a fire at the American Sports Publishing Company, Warren Street, New York City, in 1911. Robert W. Henderson, *Ball, Bat and Bishop* (New York: 1947), 182.

10. Francis C. Richter, *Richter's History and Records of Baseball* (Philadelphia: 1914), contains the text of the Commission's report.

11. A copy of the release is in the Abraham G. Mills Papers in the New York Public Library. Other Mills Papers and eight volumes of his Correspondence are in the National Baseball Hall of Fame and Museum in Cooperstown, New York.

12. "Statement of Abner Graves, Mining Engineer of Denver, Colorado, April 3, 1905," in the Abner Doubleday Papers, Cooperstown, New York.

13. Rollin L. Hart, "The National Game," *Baseball Magazine*, II (Boston: August 1909), 42. The hand-picked commission was made up almost entirely of men who were, at one time or another, very prominent in organized baseball, including the two senators. They were Abraham G. Mills, Nicholas E. Young, Alfred J. Reach, George Wright, James E. Sullivan, Arthur P. Gorman, and Morgan G. Bulkeley.

which persisted and continues to live down through the years. The average "fan" who knew or cared anything at all about the beginnings of the game he watched was under the impression that an inspired, spontaneous act by Abner Doubleday created it.[14]

Yet it is by no means certain that he ever was in Cooperstown. He was born in Ballston Spa, New York, and attended school at Auburn.[15] If he did enroll at Green's Select School at Cooperstown, he certainly was not a schoolboy there in 1839, as Abner Graves claimed, since he had matriculated at West Point the previous autumn.[16] It may well be that Doubleday had played ball with Graves and others; but if he had any significant or unusual connection with the game it is not revealed in local histories[17] or in Doubleday's writings.[18] It should be noted, too, that Abraham G. Mills had known Doubleday for years, dating from their association as soldiers in the Civil War; yet Mills never mentioned anything about Doubleday's alleged contribution to baseball prior to the publication of the Graves statement. For instance, why did not Mills take the obvious opportunity to proclaim Doubleday's supposed role while addressing that glittering company at Delmonico's on the origin of baseball?

The climax in the perpetuation of the Doubleday story came with the approach of 1939 when the major leagues made elaborate preparations to commemorate the "centennial" of the game. Large and impressive plans were formed for appropriate ceremonies at Cooperstown—and indeed carried out. A

14. The tale found its way into print also. See for example Ralph Birdsall, *The Story of Cooperstown* (New York: 1917), 224, wherein the writer states that the "solemn form of procedure" (of the commission) "placed the matter beyond doubt." Louis C. Jones, in *Cooperstown* (New York: 1949), 60–61, equivocates, saying that recent historical evidence "appears to be uncontrovertible"; yet he continues to maintain that Graves' testimony "stands unimpaired." Writers Program of the Iowa W.P.A., "Baseball! The Story of Iowa's Early Innings," *Annals of Iowa*, XXII (Des Moines: April 1941), 626, credited Doubleday and praised the "initiative" that later made him a business leader. Even the *Dictionary of American Biography* (New York: 1944), V, 391, states that Doubleday "created baseball." The *Encyclopedia Britannica* (Chicago: 1948), III, 1661, the *Encyclopedia Americana* (New York: 1948), III, 302, and *Collier's Encyclopedia* (New York: 1949), III, 214, have accepted the new evidence. *Compton's Pictured Encyclopedia* (Chicago, 1948), II, 53, takes a middle ground. More recently, Hy Turkin and S. C. Thompson, *The Official Encyclopedia of Baseball* (New York: 1951), 375, concede that most unbiased probers have been forced to acknowledge the claims of recent historical research. Nevertheless, these authors, along with baseball officials, continue to propagandize Cooperstown as a baseball "shrine"; and, since Cooperstown is irrevocably associated with Abner Doubleday, this is an indirect means of perpetuating the myth.

15. *Dictionary of American Biography*, V, 391–392.

16. *Ibid.*

17. For example, Robert B. Coffin, *The Home of Cooper and the Haunts of Leatherstocking* (New York: 1872); James F. Cooper, *The Legends and Traditions of a Northern County* (New York: 1921).

18. *Chancellorsville and Gettysburg* (New York: 1882); *Gettysburg Made Plain; A Succinct Account of the Campaign and Battles, with the Aid of One Diagram and Twenty-Nine Maps* (New York: 1909); *Reminiscences of Forts Sumter and Moultrie in 1860–61* (New York: 1876). Doubleday, in recalling his boyhood, makes no mention of interest in baseball:

"You ask for some information as to how I passed my youth. I was brought up in a book store and early imbibed a taste for reading. I was fond of poetry and art and much interested in mathematical studies. In my outdoor sports I was addicted to topographical work and even as a boy amused myself by making maps of the country around my father's residence which was in Auburn Cayuga Co N.Y. (sic)." Abner Doubleday to Dear Sir (?), November 20, 1887, Doubleday Papers, Cooperstown, New York.

Baseball Hall of Fame was dedicated, a pageant portraying the historical highlights of the sport was presented, and an all-star contest between teams composed of baseball's all-time great players was played. All this was accompanied by the usual publicity build-up and fanfare.[19]

The United States Government lent its seal of approval when the Post Office authorized a special baseball stamp marking the event.[20] However, it did so not because of Doubleday, whose claims admittedly were "questionable," but because the date was "universally recognized in sport circles as marking the centennial"[21]—a rather nice point. Doubleday's picture was cautiously omitted, and a sandlot scene substituted as the central motif with a house, barn, church, and school in the background.[22]

Less fortunate, or perhaps more gullible, was a legislative committee of the State of New York charged with studying the situation. This committee held a public hearing at Cooperstown, August 7, 1937, at which representatives of the local chamber of commerce and of the local committee dealing with the problem appeared. According to the official report of the State legislature, "It was put in evidence that Cooperstown, New York, is the birthplace of baseball..." and the State committee recommended "that a centennial be properly celebrated at Cooperstown, New York, on the home site of the first game, the inauguration of baseball being the proud heritage of New York."

The committee went on to advocate that the event be "advertised and publicized in the pamphlets of the Conservation Department of the State of New York, and by road signs erected under its supervision...." Finally, it was urged that the State of New York "appropriate...Ten Thousand ($10,000)... to be used in advertising and generally furthering the baseball...celebration."[23]

So it was that the Doubleday myth was crystallized and enshrined in concrete form by organized baseball. Actually, the entire edifice, which had always rested upon the flimsy foundation of an elderly man's memory of events sixty-eight years after they supposedly occurred, was constructed and sanctioned in the face of timely and unimpeachable evidence, published in the midst of cen-

---

19. An illustration is *Cooperstown National Base Ball Museum* (New York: n.d.). A more recent example is John Durant, *The National Baseball Hall of Fame and Museum* (Cooperstown, New York: 1949).

20. *Postal Bulletin*, LX (Washington: May 17, 1939), No. 17694.

21. Letter of R. S. Black, Third Assistant Postmaster General, April 15, 1939, in Robert W. Henderson, "Baseball: Notes and Materials on Its Origins" (New York: 1940), 55.

22. *Postal Bulletin*, LX (May 17, 1939), No. 17694.

23. *State of New York Report of Joint Legislative Committee to study the Situation Concerning the Inaugural Baseball Game and the Growth of the Sport*. Legislative Document 73 (Albany: 1938). Evidently the Congress of the United States, too, has fallen prey to this story. In its recent investigation, it concludes that baseball "is a game of American origin." "Organized Baseball; Report of the Subcommittee on the Study of Monopoly Power of the Committee of the Judiciary," *House Report* No. 2002, p. 228, 82d Congress, 2d Session (Washington: 1952).

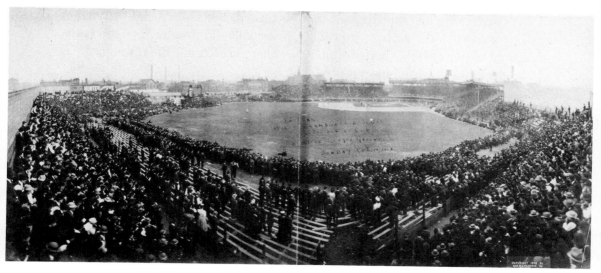

1906 World Championship Game (Chicago White Sox vs. Cubs)

tennial preparations, that Abner Doubleday had had little or nothing to do with the birth of the game; but rather, that it had sprung from rounders.[24] Adding to the difficulty, Bruce Cartwright reiterated an earlier claim that evidence in his possession showed his forebear, Alexander Cartwright, to have been the founder of baseball.[25] Although embarrassed and chagrined, baseball officials, having already committed themselves, especially financially, to Doubleday, proceeded according to plan, while sports columnists either pointed out the discrepancy or got around it as gracefully as possible.[26]

Broadly speaking, no single person invented baseball. The game was the result of an evolutionary process over a long period of years. It is known that the ball was used from earliest civilization; and the evidence is overwhelming that it was familiar as far back as ancient Egypt and adjacent lands where the ball represented the idea of fertility.[27] And of course the Greeks were thoroughly familiar with ball play. It would be difficult to present a stronger argument for ball games than that to be found in Galen's treatise, entitled "Exercise with the Small Ball." E. Norman Gardiner, classical scholar, paraphrases this document as follows:

The best of all exercises . . . are those which combine bodily exertion with mental recreation, such as hunting and ball-play. But ball-play has this advantage over hunting that its cheapness puts it within reach of the very poorest, while even the busiest man can find time to do it. Moreover it can be practised with any degree of violence or moderation, at all times and in all conditions. It exercises every part of the body, legs, hands, and eyesight alike, and at the same time gives pleasure to the mind. In contrast with athletic exercises, which make men slow or produce one-sided development, ball-play produces strength and activity, and therefore trains all those qualities which are most valuable for a soldier. Finally, it is free from dangers . . .[28]

To ascertain who invented baseball would be equivalent to trying to locate the discoverer of fire. But we are here concerned with what has direct bearing

24. Robert W. Henderson, "Baseball and Rounders," *New York Public Library Bulletin*, XLIII (New York: April, 1939), 303–314. Aside from Henry Chadwick's protests, the first substantial debunking of the Doubleday myth was provided by Will Irwin, "Baseball: (I) Before the Professionals Came," *Colliers*, XLIII (May 8, 1909), 12.

25. Frank Menke, *The New Encyclopedia of Sports* (New York: 1947), 91; Bruce Cartwright to Will Irwin, July 6, 1909, in Doubleday Papers.

26. For example, the New York *Sun*, June 10, 1939, admitted the hoax, but said baseball as an American institution required a legend, so the public would therefore go ahead and take part in the "innocuous conspiracy." Fred Lieb, sports writer assigned to prepare a feature article on the centennial, admits he faked the story although he knew of the discrepancies in the Cooperstown myth. Frederick G. Lieb, *The Baseball Story* (New York: 1950), 15.

27. John A. Krout, *Annals of American Sport, Pageant of America Series*, XV (New Haven: 1929), 114. Also Henderson, *Ball, Bat and Bishop*, 19. The Russians also claim that baseball originated from one of their ancient village games called lapta. New York *Times*, September 16, 1952, quoted a Soviet magazine, *Smena*: "It is well known that in Russian villages they played lapta, of which beizbol is an imitation. It was played in Russian villages when the United States was not even marked on the maps."

28. E. Norman Gardiner, *Greek Athletic Sports and Festivals* (London: 1910), 187–188.

on the development of baseball in America, and there is sufficient evidence to indicate that various simple bat-and-ball games were indulged in by the settlers from the first.[29] For example, the Dutch of New Netherland played "stool ball," thought to be the forerunner of cricket.[30] Even in Puritan New England the play spirit was not as dead as commonly supposed. Ball playing there was sufficiently prominent to be forbidden by Governor Bradford of Plymouth.[31]

Possibly the first record of an American baseball game is that mentioned in the journal of George Ewing, a Revolutionary soldier, who tells of playing a game of "base," April 7, 1778, at Valley Forge.[32] Early familiarity with a game called baseball is understandable, for as early as 1744 John Newbery published in London *A Little Pretty Pocket-Book*, containing a rhymed description of "base-ball" along with a small picture illustrating the game.[33] Newbery, a farmer's son, accountant, patent-medicine dealer, and printer, not only was one of the first publishers of children's books, but also tried to please children as well as to improve them—a new and good idea for that time.[34] This, like other children's books which followed it, was extremely popular and widely known[35]—evidence that a game called baseball was familiar to English boys. The book was republished in New York in 1762, in Philadelphia in 1786, and again at Worcester, Massachusetts, in 1787.[36] Therefore a ball game called baseball was familiar to Americans much before 1839, the year that Doubleday is credited with christening the game with that name.

The link between baseball and the English game of rounders is no less strong. A compilation of children's games by William Clarke called *The Boy's Own Book: A Complete Encyclopedia of All the Diversions, Athletic, Scientific and Recreative* appeared in London in 1828. A number of editions were published, but the important one is the third, which appeared in 1829. It had a description of the game of rounders.[37] That same year, 1829, the first American edition of the volume, likewise containing the rules for rounders, was printed.

29. Charles M. Andrews, *Colonial Folkways; Chronicles of American Life During the Reign of the Georges; Chronicles of America Series*, IX (New Haven: 1921), 109.

30. Esther Singleton, *Dutch New York* (New York: 1909), 290.

31. William Bradford, *Bradford's History "of Plimouth Plantation"* (Boston: 1898), 135.

32. George Ewing, *The Military Journal of George Ewing* (Yonkers: 1928), 35, 47. Cited by Henderson, "Baseball and Rounders," 311.

33. Much of this portion of the discussion, including the relationship between baseball and rounders, is based upon Henderson, "Baseball and Rounders," 303–314, who published his evidence after the preparations for the Cooperstown ceremonies had been inaugurated.

34. Lady Violet B. Carter, "Childhood and Education," in Sir Ernest Barker (ed.), *The Character of England* (Oxford: 1947), 215.

35. *Idem*.

36. Henderson, *Ball, Bat and Bishop*, 135.

37. The game was known variously in England by the names base-ball, feeder, and rounders. The latter name came to be the most commonly used. The first London edition of *The Boy's Own Book* omits rounders. A copy of the second edition has not been located. Copies of the first and the third London editions are in the Cleveland Public Library.

From this source we learn that rounders, a favorite game of western England, was played on a field on which were placed four stones or posts from twelve to twenty yards apart in a diamond-shaped pattern. The number of contestants was not specified; those on hand merely divided into two equal groups. The "out" side scattered about the field more or less haphazardly without taking up set positions, except for the "pecker" or "feeder" (pitcher), who gently tossed the ball a short distance to the "striker" (batter) from a fixed position also marked by a stone or post. The striker, if successful in meeting the ball, ran the bases clockwise as far as he could progress, depending upon the circumstances. Outs were registered when the striker did any of the following: (1) missed three swings (three-strikes rule), (2) hit the ball behind his position (one foul out), (3) had his batted ball caught, or (4) was struck by a thrown ball while attempting to negotiate the bases. The "in" side continued until each of its members had been put out, when the side which had been in the field had its innings.[38]

So much for the game of rounders as such. The great significance of these rules is that five years after they were published in the United States they were reprinted by a Boston company which, in a book entitled *The Book of Sports*, by Robin Carver, reproduced them practically verbatim, changing only the title from "Rounders" to "Base, or Goal Ball" because, as he said, those were "the names generally adopted in our country."[39] By means of this minor alteration English rounders became American baseball.

Again in 1835 a Providence, Rhode Island, firm published *The Boys and Girls Book of Sports* which likewise contained the rules for rounders as they appeared in *The Boy's Own Book* of 1829, merely substituting "Base, or Goal Ball."[40] Furthermore, in 1839 yet another sporting book appeared, *The Boy's Book of Sports: A Description of the Exercises and Pastimes of Youth*, published in New Haven. Instead of merely copying previously published rules on baseball, it tried to revise and clarify those already known. In doing so, it introduced for the first time the provision that the bases, laid out to form a "diamond," be run in counter-clockwise fashion.

In the late eighteenth and early nineteenth centuries many references to ball games having been played are to be found, particularly in diaries and memoirs. Some of these were written at the time, but many are memories of older men recalling boyhood days and are therefore not as reliable as the contemporary accounts. Nor is it always certain which game of ball was played. Neverthe-

---

38. William Clarke, *The Boy's Own Book* . . . (Boston: 1829). The second American edition appeared in 1834, published in Boston by Monroe and Francis; in New York by C. S. Francis.

39. Henderson dramatized the similarity by placing the texts of the same rules from each book in parallel columns in "Baseball and Rounders," 307; Henderson, *Ball, Bat and Bishop*, 154–157.

40. A photostatic copy is in the New York Public Library.

less the evidence is that simple ball games were well known and played in the settled communities along the seaboard, especially in New York and the New England States.[41] Certainly by the first decades of the nineteenth century, ball games were a common sight on the village greens and vacant fields or pastures as well as on college campuses.

So popular was ball in Worcester in 1816 that it was prohibited in the streets;[42] and according to Thurlow Weed, people in Rochester, New York, busy and industrious as they were, found time for recreation. There, in 1825, a baseball club of fifty members, ages eighteen to forty, met every afternoon during the ball season to play on their eight to ten acres of ground. Weed even lists the best players, among whom were some of the leading citizens.[43] In his journal written in 1835, Cyrus Parker Bradley, born in 1818, admits he never got over his boyhood love of playing and often was told "how ridiculous it was to come from the society of antiquarians and politicians and play ball with boys of six. But it is natural to me, infected by their mood, by my early life."[44] The mass of boys indulged in playing "goal" in Bangor, Maine, according to Albert Ware Paine in his journal of 1836, recorded when he was twenty-three years old.[45] And in Rhode Island ball play was performed even on Sunday.[46]

A diary entry by a Princeton student in 1786 alludes to playing "baste ball" on the campus: "A fine day, play baste ball in the campus but am beaten for I miss both catching and striking the ball."[47] At first, however, colleges discouraged students in the practice of ball playing. At least Princeton did, passing laws in 1787 against ball games on the ground that such were "low and unbecoming gentlemen" and constituted "great danger to the health by sudden and alternate heats and colds and as it tends by accidents . . . to disfiguring and maiming those who are engaged in it. . . ."[48] Gradually it was found that student disorder and mischief decreased when surplus energy was worked off in games. At Bowdoin in 1824, ball games were initiated by the authorities themselves as a method of reducing sickness. The recommendation was well received and proved beneficial if we can take the word of Henry Wadsworth Longfellow, then a student. He wrote that ball playing

. . . communicated such an impulse to our limbs and joints, that there is nothing now heard of, in our leisure hours, but ball, ball, ball. I cannot prophesy with any degree of

---

41. For examples, see below.
42. Jennie Holliman, *American Sports, 1785–1835* (Durham, North Carolina; 1931), 64.
43. Thurlow Weed, *Autobiography* (Boston: 1884), 203.
44. Cyrus P. Bradley, "Journal of Cyrus P. Bradley," *Ohio Archaeological and Historical Society Publications*, XV (Columbus, Ohio: 1906), 211.
45. Lydia A. Carter, *The Discovery of a Grandmother* (Newtonville, Massachusetts: 1920), 198, 240.
46. James B. Angell, *The Reminiscences of James Burrill Angell* (New York: 1912), 14.
47. Varnum L. Collins, *Princeton* (New York: 1914), 207.
48. Ibid., 208.

accuracy concerning the continuance of this rage for play, but the effect is good, since there has been a thoroughgoing reformation from inactivity and torpitude.[49]

Williams Latham, a student at Brown from 1823 to 1827, discussed his ball-playing experience there, explaining that sports were still unorganized; and that while ball games took place at Brown he did not enjoy them as much as he had at Bridgewater because only six or seven played on a side; hence much time was wasted running after the ball. He also complained of the pitching style because they "did throw so fair ball, they are afraid the fellow will hit it with his bat-stick."[50] Likewise, at Harvard, where he finished in 1829, Oliver Wendell Holmes played ball.[51] The same was true of George F. Hoar, who played various ball games during his boyhood in the 1830s and, after he entered Harvard in 1842, continued to engage in "the old-fashioned game of base." Hoar specified that chief among the games he played as a boy were four-old-cat, three-old-cat, two-old-cat, and base, games which, as he pointed out, were not very scientific.[52]

These various ball games had common characteristics. They were all simple, some more so than others. All appealed to the same elementary satisfaction derived from projecting one's power by swatting and throwing an object hard and for distance, or the excitement of the race to arrive safely on the base ahead of the ball. The simplest of these early games was barn ball,[53] limited to two players and requiring the smooth side of a building with some level ground in front of it. One boy threw the ball vigorously against the wall; the other, having taken his position about a dozen feet from the wall, struck at the rebounding ball with his bat. Upon connecting he ran to the wall and tried to return before his opponent recovered the ball and hit him with it. Naturally, they took turns, switching about after the batter was retired, so that each boy had his innings.

Apparently out of the desire to make participation of more boys possible, more advanced variations—the games of "old-cat"—were improvised.[54] The simplest version of these, "one-old-cat," was derived from the old English game of "Tip Cat," wherein a wooden "cat," like a spindle, was placed on the ground, then tipped in the air and struck with a stick.[55] "Old-cat merely substituted a ball for the stick. "One-old-cat" had a batter, pitcher, and two bases. The batter hit from one base, ran to the other, and returned if possible until the ball was

49. Henry W. Longfellow, in a letter to his father, April 11, 1824, in Samuel W. Longfellow (ed.), *The Life of Henry W. Longfellow*, I (Boston: 1891), 51.
50. Williams Latham, "The Diary of Williams Latham, 1823–1827" (unpublished) quoted in Walter C. Bronson, *The History of Brown University, 1764–1914* (Providence: 1914), 245.
51. Krout, *Annals of American Sport*, 115.
52. George F. Hoar, *Autobiography of Seventy Years*, I (New York: 1903), 52.
53. A good description is given in William Clark, *Boys and Girls Book of Sports* (Providence: 1835), 17, 18. (A photostatic copy is in the New York Public Library.)
54. Robert W. Weaver, *Amusements and Sports in American Life* (Chicago: 1939) 96–97.
55. Henry Chadwick, "Scrap-books, 1858–1902," 26 volumes in New York Public Library.

caught either on the fly or on one bounce. The number of lads could be increased by playing "two-, three-, or four-old-cat," which meant simply adding to the number of bases and batsmen. As the number of players increased, the opportunity and necessity for more team play presented itself.

For yet larger numbers of players, the game variously called "town-ball," "round-ball"—and later "Massachusetts ball" (to distinguish it from "the New York game")—was devised. These were the Americanized versions of English rounders and were played by large groups ranging anywhere from twelve to twenty or more on a side. Regulations varied since there were no uniform rules; hence each community had its own particular variations—just as present-day sand lot players generally add their own touches to the official rules. One side batted around until each of its players was put out; then the other aggregation had its turn.[56]

The frontier, however, did not nourish sport. The immediate battle to subdue the wilderness was too pressing to permit leisure for games. Labor and work, because they were essential, were glorified. The tendency, therefore, was to combine them with play whenever possible.[57] Necessary work and needed sport frequently were synonymous. Barn-raisings or corn-huskings, required tasks, were converted into festive frolics as well. Likewise hunting and fishing were work; but the thrill of sport was not entirely absent. Such pure "sport" as was practiced on the frontier was rugged, boisterous and even brutal, like wrestling and eye-gouging. Only when communities became more settled, enjoyed a degree of leisure, and cleared fields or village commons, did ball playing sprout and flourish; and even then sport was impeded by a lingering puritanism which frowned upon frivolity or pleasure.[58]

In New England the belief remained that "play is folly rather than wisdom in a child; and he will soonest be an adult who puts on the adult's gravity," according to a well-known pedagogue of that section. He candidly relates how, due to his own youthful training in this belief, he made a practice, when a teacher, of cheating the pupils of as much time as possible from the fifteen minutes allotted to them at noon for sports. He continues apologetically: "I had not learned so fully as I have since done, that sports are as indispensable to the health of both the bodies and minds of children as their food, their drink, or their sleep. . . .[59]

56. For more detailed descriptions see *The Base Ball Player's Pocket Companion: Containing Rules and Regulations for Forming Clubs, Directions for Playing the "Massachusetts Game" and the "New York Game," from Official Reports* (Boston: 1859), 20–22. Copies in the Cleveland Public Library and Racquet and Tennis Club in New York City.

57. John A. Krout, "Some Reflections on the Rise of American Sport," *Proceedings of the Association of History Teachers of the Middle States and Maryland*, XXVI (Philadelphia: 1929), 86.

58. Weaver, *Amusements and Sports in American Life*, 1–2.

59. William A. Alcott, *Confessions of a Schoolmaster* (Andover, 1839), 81–82.

Travelers noted the legal restrictions upon amusements; and one remarked upon the "hard precocity" of American youths who entered college at the age of fourteen and left at seventeen with degrees to commence business careers, with no interval to attain either gracefulness or health—"Athletic games and the bolder field sports being unknown."[60] Enjoyment was associated with guilt—as illustrated by the Yankee who said he was "going to town, probably git good and drunk, and Lord how I'll hate it!" This attitude only slowly disappeared; as late as 1862 churchmen succeeded in having ice skating banned in Brooklyn;[61] and of course the fight to legalize Sunday baseball took much longer.

In the South, ball playing was carried on, but not to the extent it was in the North.[62] The pattern of Southern sport tended to be formed by the dominant planter group, whose influence far exceeded its number. The result was an inclination toward aristocratic pastimes like fox hunting. Yet ball play was not as completely foreign to that section as generally thought. A case in point is Moses Waddell's famous school in South Carolina, where students found relaxation in ball games from the stern classical curriculum.[63]

Such simple, crude ball games as those described were played on a local, neighborhood basis and were admirably suited to the young, primarily rural America of the period. Few had great wealth or leisure. Playing sites were plentiful and convenient. Only the rudest preparation was necessary—laying "goals" or bases by driving sticks into the ground or placing flat rocks at approximate distances. Equipment requirements were minimum both in amount and cost. Any stout stick, wagon tongue, ax or rake handle made a capital bat; and a serviceable ball could be had by winding yarn around a buckshot or chunk of india rubber and then sewing on a leather cover, perhaps cut to size by the local shoemaker, to prevent unwinding.[64] No other paraphernalia were needed. Availability of ample space, a negligible amount of inexpensive equipment, and the simple structure of the games made for popularity and wide participation. In short, the various ball games were adapted to their surroundings and in fact mirrored them.

Another feature of early nineteenth-century ball was the fact that it was overwhelmingly a participant's game. Relatively few watched; and the promot-

60. Allan Nevins, *American Social History as Recorded by British Travellers* (New York: 1923), 115, 250.

61. "When Wholesome Sport Was Taboo," *The American City,* LII (New York: October, 1937), 87.

62. Holliman, *American Sports, 1785–1835,* 67.

63. Colyer Meriwether, *History of Higher Education in South Carolina, with a Sketch of the Free School System* (Washington: 1889), 39.

64. *Porter's Spirit of the Times* (New York), December 27, 1856. Also see William H. Venable, *A Buckeye Boyhood* (Cincinnati: 1911), 126, and James D'W. Lovett, *Old Boston Boys and the Games They Played* (Boston: 1906), 129. A ball of this early period is exhibited at the Baseball Hall of Fame and Museum, Cooperstown, New York.

The Sandlot Kid by Victor Salvatore, Cooperstown, N.Y.

er who sold baseball games as entertainment was not to appear until a later day when American society became urbanized. This meager attendance at games and their non-commercial character are reflected in the paucity of detailed information and lack of descriptions of games in the press of the day. For example, even in 1843, an advertisement announcing the forthcoming publication of a "new and comprehensive" weekly sporting paper listed more than twenty sports it would cover, such as racing, hunting, shooting, fishing, rowing, pedestrianism, pugilism, "cricketing," skating, swimming, billiards, etc., but omitted any intent to report on ball playing.[65]

The same applied to a leading theatrical and sports journal of the day, which contained lengthy indices of items pertaining to cricket during the 1840s, whereas baseball was disregarded.[66] Furthermore, the absence of team play in any real or highly developed sense is to be noted; doubtless this was due to the fiercely individualistic atmosphere of a society in flux, which lacked any permanent stratification, and in which democracy was the byword. Sufficient sophistication for highly developed team play was lacking in America prior to the Civil War.

The simplicity, informality, and absence of organization in the game, plus the fact that it was not given headline attention in the contemporary press, enhanced the recreative values of ball playing, so that even the ascetic though progressive schoolteacher William A. Alcott, confessed: "Our most common exercise was ball playing. In this, I was not very expert; but I believe I had all the healthful advantages which pertain to it, notwithstanding. It is really an excellent sport."[67]

Noted English novelist John Fowles, author of *The French Lieutenant's Woman, The Magus, Daniel Martin* and others, is an unabashed cricket fan. Fowles knows sports and their roots, as well as participles and tenses, and in the following piece he compares two cultures and their sporting preferences. He does a fine job of pointing out the intrinsic similarities between baseball and one of its progenitors, cricket.

Perhaps it's true that if it weren't for the War of Independence the United States and England would be more amenable to trying each other's game. Read on!

65. *Spirit of the Times; A Chronicle of the Turf, Field Sports, and the Stage* (New York), May 6, 1843.

66. *Ibid.* (1840s), *passim.*

67. Alcott, *Confessions of a Schoolmaster*, 295.

Baseball's Other Self: Cricket

by John Fowles

*It was not very wonderful that Catherine . . . should
prefer cricket, baseball, riding on horseback, and running
about the country at the age of fourteen, to books. . . .*
—Jane Austen, *Northanger Abbey* (1818)

What is human life but a game of cricket?
—The Duke of Dorset (1777)

Britain and America were created, as every serious historian knows, just to see how profoundly two cultures sharing a common language can fail to understand each other. Nowhere is that more clearly demonstrated than in the malignant mutual travesty that concerns our respective summer games. You smugly know we English are impossible because of our attachment to the incomprehensible ritual of cricket; we smugly know you Americans will never grow up because of your seriousness over a game we reserve for beach picnics. You don't even call it by its proper name, which is rounders. One plays rounders with a moribund tennis ball and any old bit of wood for a bat. Every decent Englishman knows that, and that "baseball" is sheer Yankee gall—trying to hide a stolen patent under a new trade name. Of course, every decent American, who equally knows baseball was handed straight from God to Abner Doubleday at Cooperstown in 1839, will spit on such a foul imputation.

Alas, poor truth. Chauvinists from either side who go to bat for the kind of view above can be retired to the bench very fast indeed by any dispassionate historian. There is hard textual evidence that baseball was played in England, *and under that name,* well back into the 18th century. But Americans can take heart. The farther back one goes, the closer the two games seem to interweave and the plainer it becomes that we are dealing with a pair of twin brothers. It is not at all certain which is the senior sibling. My own guess is that the shadowy father, the *Ur*-game, was a good deal more like his emigrant son Baseball than the introverted child who stayed at home.

They say an intrepid British secret agent once peered out of a Siberian forest at the hallucinatory sight of a meadow of white-clad figures disporting themselves before an English village—thatched cottages, ancient pub and all the rest. But our man guessed in a flash what he had stumbled on: a KGB spy school designed to counter the most fiendish of all British cover-blowing techniques—the request for a brief rundown on the finer points of cricket.

Faced with the same task I know exactly how those would-be Soviet espionage aces must have felt. I can only pray that the basecricketballese I have had to resort to does give some idea of our game. I am not, however, going to get into one grisly swampland where many brave essayists have met a tragic end: explaining the detailed rules. All Americans need understand is that whatever the obvious superficial differences between the two modern games, they are both about *precisely* the same things: pitching and batting, catching and fielding, running and tagging bases. What is fascinating indeed is this remarkable similarity at heart and the considerable differences in present-day ethos and practice, and what that paradox has to say about our two nations.

The first reference to the two games' common ancestor, club ball, is in a 13th century illuminated manuscript. Many variations of club ball developed (hockey and golf among them), and descriptions of the earliest forms are speculative. One version has it that the bases were just holes in the ground and that the striker could only be caught out or tagged out if a fielder hit the running striker with the ball or "popped" it into a base hole before the striker could reach sanctuary. The ball was tossed or bowled underhand, which is why we still, very misleadingly, call our cricket pitchers "bowlers." As in preleague baseball, the pitcher was merely a feeder, and under the striker's command.

What seems to have happened is that this archetypal version of the game went across the Atlantic with the early settlers before an important series of innovations became general in the mother country. The "living fossil" descendant in England is rounders. Visiting Americans who see it played here by boys (and girls) must not think it is some crass British notion of how baseball is played. What they are really watching is the fluid and very delightful game that every 17th and 18th century American must have known—as "old-cat" or "town ball"—before it was coded into baseball. We've all here played rounders when we were children, and one reason we can't get on with baseball is simply that the ferocious professionalism and strict rules of the developed American game seem to us (in our ignorance) like an elephant trying to imitate a chickadee. In rounders you tend to make as many bases as fancy pleases, and the diamond becomes very polyhedral. But the two games are identical in principle.

Grass seems to have been a vital factor in the divergence of the two senior sports. In southern England an early fondness grew for having an upright mark for the pitcher to aim at behind the home plate. Two variants appeared: in one the mark was a tree stump; in the other, played on the short-turfed and treeless hills we call downs in Kent, Sussex and Hampshire, the shepherd boys would set up the movable gate, or wicket, they used in their sheep pens. We retain a memory of this medieval division between "woodland" and "downland" cricket[1] in our name for the three basemarker sticks of today's game—still called with equal frequency the "stumps" or the "wicket."

Two more specific characteristics of cricket now arose. The presence of a home-plate marker instead of a hole in the ground led to a new method of putting the batter out: if the pitcher made a strike on the marker, the man with the bat was done for. As time went on, the marker became a thin planted stick, then two sticks and finally a third. In order to know if the side of one of the outer sticks had just been snicked by a pitch, two crosspieces (called "bails") were balanced on top. That gives us the 28-inch-tall, nine-inch-wide, three-stick target of modern cricket.

The second characteristic we owe to the fact that it was the hill shepherds' version of the game that eventually conquered the woodland kind. A feature of many English villages was a central and well-grazed common pasture, the "village green," whose short turf could passably reproduce the downland conditions. One may guess that the shepherd boys had already learned that on short grass the bounced pitch pays handsome dividends, which in turn argues that the pitchers in their game were not content merely to "feed" the batters. But this made nonsense of the old rule of three chances only at hitting, which baseball still retains. In cricket that sank without trace, and ever since our batters have stayed in for as long as they can avoid being put out actively—having their stumps hit by a pitch, being caught on the fly, tagged off base, and so on. Mere failure to connect or to score is no crime.

Exactly when these developments took place we do not know, but cricket seems to have risen from an obscure peasant and children's pastime to general sport in the late 17th century. It was helped on by Cromwell's Commonwealth, when many royalist sympathizers had to lead an idle country life. The first publicly recorded match took place in 1697, the first written laws date from 1744, the first mention of the game in America comes in 1751 (at New York). We know that by that time the bounced pitch was becoming universal, and the hostile role permitted the pitcher—not adopted by baseball until the late 19th century—was also general.

Seventeenth century American settlers, on the other hand, can not have had much time—in the case of the Puritans, no time at all—for frivolous games. Furthermore, they lacked the indispensable fields of short turf; if they pitched at all, one imagines it must have been high over the rough grass.

It seems logical to infer from all this that since the kind of conditions that dictated the haphazard, makeshift nature of the early medieval sport also ap-

---

1. *"Cricket,"* first clearly recorded in 1598, means a small stick—or bat.

plied in colonial America, baseball is the more genuinely "antique" version of the ancestral game. It is cricket, especially in the period 1740–1840, that metaphorically emigrated and became the newfangled of the two sports. If we forget this today it is because the game's basic principles were laid down in that period and it remains at heart an 18th century gentleman's invention, with a characteristic (compare the "rules" of formal dueling) avoidance of direct body-to-body contact.[2] Baseball was of course codified later, and so in that sense seems more modern. Cricket is allied to the fencing rapier, to country squires, to amateurism; baseball to the pugilist's bare-knuckle fist, to a non-caste society, to professionalism. . . .

The advent of the bounced pitch and the consequent need for one strip of really good "true" turf explains another peculiarity of cricket: the two-base system. Instead of a diamond, things were reduced to the batting and pitching boxes with the best turf between them. Runs are made only between these two boxes. To distribute wear and tear on the turf, home plate and mound are reversed after every six pitches from any one direction, so the catcher (in cricket, the "wicket-keeper"—and the only fielder allowed gloves, by the way) and the nine other fielders have to change position or ends. This constant switch round explains why there are three stumps at either end of the batting "track." The bowlers themselves can also change ends, but not in any two consecutive six-pitch spells. In general a cricket pitcher works from one end until he is tired or shown to be ineffective, and another pitcher takes his place. He won't come from the bullpen though, since substitutes and reliefs are forbidden in cricket except in cases of genuine injury—and even then they can't bat or pitch, only field.

The two sets of base marker "stumps" (mound to home plate, in effect) are 66 feet apart, against baseball's 60 feet six inches. This antediluvian common measure is much closer than it already looks, since the cricket batter stands in front of his plate and the pitcher "bowls" from in front of his. The actual flight distance of the ball from hand to bat therefore remains very similar to baseball, as does the speed of the fastest pitches in both games—around the 100-mph mark. Even the two balls are nearly identical in size and weight, a baseball being fractionally larger but lighter than its hard, leather-covered cricket equivalent.

Cricket runs are scored up and down this two-base line. There are always two batters on the field. The in-play man faces the pitcher, beside whom stands the out-of-play batter. If the in-play batter makes a scoring hit, he runs to the

2. A running cricket batter cannot be obstructed or touched in any way; tagging is strictly confined to hitting the base stumps with the ball. On the other hand, cricket pitchers can legitimately aim at the batter's body—and pistol the hell out of him.

Walter Johnson Coca-Cola Advertisement

mound end, while his out-of-play colleague runs down to the in-play hitter's position—and becomes the hitter for the next pitch, if only one run was possible. When the pitching switches ends, whichever batter happens to be at the new home-plate end is in play.

Another important difference in cricket batting is that there is a 360° fair-ball zone—no foul lines. A hit is good to any part of the ground. The two batters can score as many runs (one for each switch of bases) as they like. In practice more than three such actually run runs are rare. This is because a hit that crosses the ground limit is given an automatic score without running—four runs if it goes over on the bounce, six if it carries on the fly. During a five-day international match a thousand runs or more will often be scored by the end of the game (in which each team normally has two innings, though the batting team can "declare" an inning closed short of completion if it thinks it has amassed the runs it needs).

The differences from baseball grow and grow as we come into the 20th century, but I wanted to stress this extraordinarily close kinship in certain fundamentals. In their deepest imagery both sports are about protecting property against attack (in cricket slang the home-plate stumps are even known as the "castle") and the corollary need to go out and raid to survive. In both games there is a delicious ambivalence of assault and defense, of slipping through siege lines, of setting traps and ambushes, making false sacrifices; in both games the same marked stress on physical courage and agility, on impudence, stealing, conning, bluffing, risking. In both games a recurrent and deliberately manufactured personal crisis: a confrontation of pitcher and batter with everyone else temporarily in the wings, just nurses and assistants around the surgeon and his patient—though that is a very bad analogy, since the surgeon means to kill here. The bullring, matador and beast, is a better parallel.

I like the various forms of football in the world, but I don't think they begin to compare with these two great Anglo-Saxon ball games for sophisticated elegance and symbolism. Baseball and cricket are beautiful and highly stylized medieval war substitutes, chess made flesh, a mixture of proud chivalry and base—in both senses—greed. With football we are back to the monotonous clashed armor of the brontosaurs.

Baseball is a highly extrovert game, very easy to like fast—accessible, in a word, just as Americans themselves are outgoing in comparison with the English—and cricket, please note, is quintessentially English, *not* British. There is only one Welsh major league team and none at all from Scotland or Ireland. Cricket never appealed to the Celtic temperament, perhaps because it is so in-turned and self-absorbed, so indifferent to pleasing the public. It is almost as if the English decided to invent a national secret instead of a mere game. As with our political constitution, the unwritten rules count almost as much as the written ones. Throwing a small, hard missile at or near another man is too dangerous an activity if there is not, besides printed laws, an unspoken convention as to when honest hard play becomes dishonest intent to murder. This mysterious ethos of fair playing conduct, what's cricket and what isn't cricket, has crept deep into the English soul. It can't be defined in general; you can only say it was or it wasn't present in a specific situation. An area where it is very often lacking these days is in really fast pitching, but I will come to that later.

Another strange element in cricket is what a modern art critic might call its aleatory side. Aleatory art is where at least part of the creation is left to pure chance. No two cricket grounds in the world, for instance, are quite alike. There is no fixed dimension to the outer boundaries of the field. Even at major league level many grounds have easy sides to hit to, and hard ones. Some have slopes. Some are fast, others slow, depending on the type of grass grown, how close the groundsman cuts it, on weather conditions. The wildest dice of all are rolled by the weather. The nature of the bounced delivery means the state of the turf is all-important. As a rough rule lack of rain means hard turf, which suits the batter. If rain has softened the turf, it helps the pitcher. In a game lasting several days, the turf may suddenly grow fierce from docile, or *vice versa*. Since its quality in general deteriorates through a long match, in cricket the first side at bat is not a matter of who is visiting but is decided by the toss of a coin. Sometimes winning the toss virtually decides the game before it is started—yet one more element of hazard.

But nothing in cricket must seem stranger to Americans than the almost total absence of the coaching and management apparatus of baseball. Even the international teams travel with only a tour manager (to handle arrangements and publicity) and a masseur and scorer. The kingpin is very much the captain on the field. He makes *all* the tactical decisions through a game. He will also be on the team selection committee, and his voice will carry the most weight. The players effectively coach themselves. They may ask an old pro for some friendly advice, but that is all. Nor are our teams in any sense owned; they are picked and paid by elected amateur committees. This *laissez-faire* atmosphere extends right down to the individual player. A fielding captain will use his available pitchers as he pleases, but once he is at work the pitcher will pitch in general according to his own hunches and experience. He may occasionally confer with his captain and the catcher, but he is expected to formulate his own strategy. The same goes for the batters.

This comparative freedom from management and commercial pressures brings one great benefit to cricket: a surprising democracy of status among all players of the game. There are, broadly speaking, four main layers of skill. At the bottom—but only in skill, not in importance—is village cricket, with games lasting just one afternoon, four hours or so. Above that is amateur club cricket, with members drawn from a town or district or sometimes from all over the country. Their matches last a day, six hours of play. Above that is professional county cricket, equivalent to major league baseball, where three-day matches are played. On top of the pile are the "test," or international, matches that run (and sometimes sleep) for five days. But there are two other important cricket reservoirs. One is at colleges and universities. The other is in the working-class North of England, where they play to a short-duration formula called League cricket.[3] The League teams will usually have only one professional, who coaches the best local talent and also takes the star role on the field.

The glory of this complex structure is that players in all categories mix much more often than in any other sport. Oxford and Cambridge play the professional county teams, adult club sides play high schools. Many players still of class but past their professional days will happily play on club and even village teams. There is no contempt, in other words, for the bush leagues. The advantage for promising young players is enormous, since the best exponents of the game are not locked away, figures to be glimpsed on TV or from the sidelines of a major ground, but are actually there to play with or against.

By the time I was 18 I had pitched against a lot of professionals and even some international players—including two captains of England and one of the finest cricketers of all time, the West Indian Learie Constantine.[4] My second pitch to the great man he mis-hit straight to a fielder and was caught out for a "duck"—a zero. Producing that easy pop-up was the climax of my cricketing career. I don't know what the equivalent would have been for an American high-schooler—striking out Willie Mays, perhaps. Anyway, I can still see every inch of the flight and bounce of that pitch.

But the point is that the underlying philosophy of cricket makes such experiences far from rare. The assumption is that the senior players have a kind of duty to help the junior and less good ones. This means that baseball and cricket are not national games in quite the same way. The one is now a highly professional popular entertainment, the other is more of a widely practiced folk art. This readiness to accept very different levels of skill on the same field works, needless to say, only if the better players are prepared to be indulgent. On that

---

3. Recently and very successfully adopted by our major leagues—so successfully indeed that the standard three-day match may well disappear soon.

4. Later Lord Constantine, the first black man ever to sit in our House of Lords, in recognition of his brave and lifelong fight off the cricket field for racial justice. He was a trained lawyer, but in many other respects—not least in his dazzling speed and athleticism—he recalls baseball's immortal, Jackie Robinson.

same day I had Constantine's scalp, it so happened he was pitching when I had to go to bat. He was as famous for his fastball as for his batting. Until I appeared he had been bowling at half-speed, but as I came to the box I saw to my horror that he was pacing out his long run-in for real business. He duly bounded in, like a black jaguar, and delivered. I never saw the ball, just heard it hit the catcher's gloves. I did see Constantine with his hands on his hips, grinning at me. There was a laugh round the ground. A sense of proportion had been restored. But from then on he went back to his half-speed pitches, the ones he knew I had at least some chance of handling.

As in baseball, cricket batters seem cast by spectators as the heroes and the pitchers as the villains, which says something about Anglo-Saxon love of property. I was very much on the villains' side when I played myself, and I am going to pass quickly over the art of cricket batting. But one or two important differences from baseball need to be noted. Cricket batters are not, of course, more skilled than their baseball analogues,[5] but they do have a much more complex technique to learn. There are the great differences in turf brought about by preparation and mowing practices and the weather—huge adaptations of method are sometimes called for. Secondly, the flat blade of the cricket bat makes it a much more precise instrument for finding the holes between fields. Thirdly, the all-round strike zone means there is a whole armory of scoring strokes to be learned that deflect the ball *behind* the catcher. Since the batter can also receive a limitless number of pitches as long as he isn't put out, and since also a number of those pitches will be aimed straight at his body, there is in addition an elaborate defensive technique. The art of waiting out pitches is also much more vital in our game.

One last difference from baseball is this: Since no substitutes are allowed, each man on the team of 11 has to bat in a full inning, and this includes the pitchers. There is no fixed batting order. Each captain can change it as he likes, even in mid-inning, but almost invariably the specialist lead-off men, whose main task is to tire out the opening pitchers, are followed by the big run-scorers; then comes the "tail," the specialist pitchers who seldom last long at bat but who traditionally follow a death-or-glory line and slug wildly at every pitch. Once in a while luck will run with them, and there is nothing a cricket crowd loves more.

Since the cricket ball is a shade harder than a baseball, if it hits you—even at far slower speeds than the fast men pitch—it hurts. The batter therefore wears hardened shoes or boots and strapped-on protective pads from ankle to

5. But pro baseball fielders, let me add in passing, are much more skilled than *their* cricket analogues—especially in throwing.

above the knee. Above that he often wears thigh pads beneath the white pants. Also beneath the pants he will wear a "box"—a metal shell over the genitals supported on a G-string. Above the waist the only protection is on his hands—gloves with rubber spikes or pads over the fingers. This still doesn't prevent broken phalanges from being a commonplace accident every season.

So, armored a little like a medieval knight, he stands at the batting line and looks down toward the pitching end. He sees three men there. One is the umpire behind the far stumps. The second is his temporarily-out-of-play fellow batter. The third is the bowler, standing some way behind the other two—sometimes 40 yards or twice the pitching distance—and waiting to make his run-in for the delivery.

The cricket bowler's arms must be straight from shoulder to wrist as he delivers.[6] The ball doesn't have to bounce before it reaches the bat: even a baseball trajectory is perfectly legal, but the flat face of the cricket bat makes such pitches easy meat. Bowlers come in three main kinds; fast, medium, and slow, but the offensive is almost invariably begun by the fast men. True fast bowlers of international caliber are rare, since the top speed requires a very special combination of strength and pitching action—having one without the other is no good. The best of the century was Harold Larwood. His run-up to the pitching line had the violent and yet smooth acceleration of a champion long jumper. To describe the tremendous speed of pitch he could achieve in terms of bullets or cannonballs is somehow misleading—the arrow leaving the full-drawn six-foot bow gives a better impression. Watching such bowlers on their great days is a little like watching a hungry leopard attacking a series of tethered goats: very near indeed to sadism.

I hope I have by now corrected any namby-pamby impression the word "bowling" may give Americans. Facing a fast bowler is not a job for fainthearts. The cricket batter may have some of the armor of a knight, but he is, so to speak, on a stuffed horse. Some technically excellent players have never been able to face this unfair form of joust, and to most fast bowlers the faintest hint of a yellow streak is like a gold vein to a prospector—it won't go unexploited.

One mistake many Americans make is to suppose bowlers always aim at the stumps. This isn't so at all, and perhaps especially with fast men. Their tactics are given away by the special fielder-placements they use. Most of the fielders are clustered behind the batter and alongside the catcher. They are there to catch snicks off the edge of the bat, and to get these snicks the bowler will frequently aim wide of the stumps. Other fielders will often be stationed at what

6. Originally underarm, the delivery was allowed to be made from shoulder level in 1835 and then as high as one liked in 1864—against the same kind of angry protest from the batters as baseball pitchers were to hear in their sport a decade later.

may seem suicidally[7] close proximity to the batter—down to six or seven feet on occasion—to pick up easy flies from another kind of fast pitch, the "bumper." The bumper is bowled at maximum speed but deliberately "short" of a good length—good length being the normal optimum point of bounce from the bowler's point of view. The result with fast men is a pitch that rises viciously chest or head high. The intention is naked: to scare the batter physically.

There is not much the batter can do against a good bumper except put his faith in his reflexes and the lightning dodge away. If he tries to block the ball with his bat, he risks popping up a fly to the greedy hands a few feet away waiting for just such an offer. However, there is one offensive move against this cricketing beanball—a hit that is nearest to a baseball batter's pull to left field. We call it the hook. Hooking requires a first-class eye and a lot of courage; if you miss, you may end up with a broken nose or a mouthful of loose teeth.

One of the unwritten rules concerns this kind of pitch. The bumper is not used against inexpert batters (the other side's specialist pitchers) who form the tail of the inning. Occasionally one is let fly against such a lamb, and the unforgivable occurs: he is laid out flat. But the most unforgivable of all is when a fast bowler "bumps" a batting fast bowler from the other team. The ensuing situation is about as genteel as a Mafia fall-out.

The next category of bowlers, the medium pacers, are experts with the curveball. The ability to "swing" pitches with the cricket ball is something of a mystery. In its fresh state the ball has polished leather sides, which produce the most curve—so much so that the use of a new ball is strictly regulated. The pitching team gets one at inning commencement, but then no replacement until at least another 480 pitches have been made. The curve is also very dependent on air humidity—the damper the better—and on wind direction and force. But the real key is how the equatorial stitched seam of the cricket ball is held. A very ancient—illegal and universal, like the spitball—trick of the swing bowler is to lift up the seam with his nails so that it offers more air resistance and bite when it hits the turf. The second part of the bowler's art lies here: what happens when the curveball strikes the grass. Experts cannot only curve the ball either way in flight but can make it angle either way on the bounce. The batter is faced with two very fast decisions—which way the ball will move in the air and which way again when it bounces in front of him. It may curve right and then break and cut farther right, or angle back left, and the same with a left curve.[8]

In general this type of bowling is the hardest to score runs off. Many of

7. The most famous fielding casualty in the game's history was Frederick, Prince of Wales. A cricket fanatic, he died in 1751 as a result of taking a hard hit in the side.
8. The first cricket bowler to have both curves was an American—the Philadelphian J. B. King, who could have made any international team of his era. The Gentlemen of Philadelphia, incidentally, played major league cricket here as late as 1908.

our curveball bowlers are monuments of monotonous accuracy—fine for teams who want to steal their way up the standings, but hardly conducive to entertainment.

It is the third type of cricket bowler, the slowball expert, who has far and away the subtlest skills. He has to depend entirely on cunning, the mind of the fox. His two weapons are spin and flight. For spin the ball is flipped with the fingers, and often by a wrist flick as well, as it leaves the hand. When it hits the turf the imparted spin on the ball makes it move left or right of the flight line just like the English the cue can give a billiard ball. On a certain kind of turf, either softened by rain (a "sticky wicket"[9]) or turned to dust by too much sun (a "crumbling wicket"), this movement can be bewilderingly sharp. "Flight" is the ability—one of the hardest techniques to learn—to trick the batter over exactly where the ball will bounce. The effect of a well-flighted pitch is this: the batter thinks he knows precisely where the ball will land in front of him and starts out on an apparently easy half-volley drive along the ground. At the last split second he realizes he's been fooled—the ball is going to bounce short. But it is too late to stop his swing.

The Indians toured England in the summer of 1971 and gave us a rare opportunity to see a world-class quartet of slow bowlers at work. Such bowlers are a liability on a percentage-playing team, since they can be hit over the horizon if they pitch badly. Very few national teams these days have the courage to use them often. The Indians did, and won the series. The finest of their snake charmers was a small bearded Sikh named Bedi, who has the picturesque habit of wearing a different-colored turban for each day of a match. I think if any visiting American had dropped in on one of the India-England matches and seen Bedi in action, he really would have given up on cricket. He would quite rightly have assumed the English team contained the best batters in the country—and what did he see? A bizarre mini-rajah taking three or four lazy strides, then pitching balls at the kind of speed that would disgrace an arthritic grandmother, balls which her 10-year-old granddaughter could clearly have slammed every time into the cricket equivalent of the bleachers. Yet here was the cream of England poking and prodding, missing and scrambling as if bewitched. Invitation after invitation to swing, and not a run scored—most of the time not even attempted.

Bedi's magic can be explained. It was based on miraculous accuracy. The slower the pitching speed, the smaller the area of optimum bounce becomes. At Bedi's snail-like pace he was down to the equivalent of infallibly hitting a din-

---

9. "Wicket" is used not only to describe the base sticks but also the turf between them. The commonest word for this turf, however, is the pitch—one of the many linguistic traps for the American. With us a "fast pitch" means a turf giving a fast bounce, not a fastball.

ner plate at 18 yards' distance—remarkable enough, even without all the other tricks of spin, flight, pace variation and angle of delivery arm that he employed. He never quite pitched the same ball twice, even in the longest spells, though to an American they would have seemed identical. Bedi was a perfect example of cricket's only too frequent unwatchability to all but other cricketers. For the neutral *cognoscenti* it was like being in the presence of a superb sitar player; for English patriots it was like watching children, your own children, locked up in a cage with a king cobra; for the rest, alas, Bedi must have seemed a final proof that cricket was invented in a lunatic asylum by an incurable catatonic.

Bedi leads me to one advantage, a fortune of history, that cricket has over baseball: the fact that it is played as well at the highest level by a number of other countries (all former parts of the defunct British Empire) as it is at home in England. Much more important in international competition than the prestige of winning is the esthetic broadening in style and technique that results. Each of the major cricketing countries contributes a special approach, a spirit, a mood.

The Australian approach is in a sense the most Americanized—the most free of unnecessary frills and graces, the most pragmatic. Australians play a little harder to win—on top form, a shade nearer the ruthless machine than anyone else. The other five major cricketing countries are India, Pakistan, South Africa (at present boycotted), New Zealand and the West Indies. The South Africans and the New Zealanders play the game more or less in the aggressive Australian mold. The Indians and Pakistanis are more temperamental—and perhaps especially when they are touring over here, since our climate doesn't suit their style of play. They need sunshine and hard ground. The Pakistanis have more panache, the Indians more subtlety.

But beyond any doubt the greatest contribution to the modern game has come from the smallest of the six countries—the West Indies. They have given to cricket something of what the American Black South brought to the history of music—a kind of élan, a new rhythm and vitality, an athletic grace, a joy and exuberance beyond the compass of any white race. For a start, they are born gamblers, which means that whenever a West Indian is near the action there is an indefinable heightening of tension. Their finest batters have a very characteristic wristy strike, slashing and explosive, and like the finest black jazz players seem always to have something in hand over the best of their white rivals. A great Caribbean "bat" will show an acuteness of timing, a ferocity of attack, that is incomparable. Purists sometimes complain that they lack the classical elegance of the best English masters and the no-nonsense practicality of the Australian-run machines, but for sheer spectator pleasure they are in a class of their own, and in any case one might as well blame them for their inspired unortho-

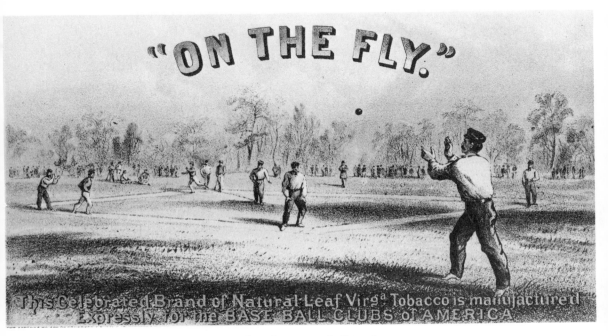

Early Tobacco Baseball Card

doxy as criticize a calypso for not being a Beethoven sonata. Many West Indian players have either settled here or come over for the summer to play in our major leagues, and English cricket is now unthinkable without their presence.

One happy result of all this is that the West Indians' cricketing popularity has helped the underprivileged position of their large community in this country. It is not only the way they play but the way they watch. West Indian spectators have as little inhibition as American baseball fans in telling the players—their own or the other side's—what they think. They have stood the English style of watching—silence broken by a polite clap—on its dull old head. A good shot they bellow for; a glorious shot they stand up and dance to.

A few years ago I was at a famous London cricket ground, the Oval, for the last day of a historic match between the West Indies and England—historic because for the first time the West Indies were close to beating England in the home series. The ground was packed solid with immigrants and native Londoners. There came a point in the final inning when it seemed the West Indies batting might collapse. The then most dangerous fast bowler in the world was the Englishman John Snow, who on the field had a fair share of the temperament of an angry young bull. The West Indian batter facing him was a little man named Rohan Kanhai, about half Snow's size. Snow began to hurl bumpers, bouncing them lethally up round Kanhai's head. Since bumpers pass high over the stumps and are dangerous in a putout sense only if the batter tries to meet violence with violence, the proper strategy for Kanhai at that fragile state of the match was to duck down out of the way and wait the storm out. He did that a few times. Then Snow charged up and pitched what was evidently meant to be the bumper to end all bumpers—a thunderbolt straight between the eyes. This time Kanhai made an extraordinary midair leap to get up to the height of the ball and took a full baseball swing at it. It was the swiftest human reaction I have ever seen, totally improvised and totally without elegance, for after he made contact he fell flat. Meanwhile, the ball was sailing high over the ground limit for the cricket version of a homer—a six-run score.

I doubt if Goliath has ever been more comprehensively slain. The whole crowd, white and black alike, roared its recognition. Every white spectator there knew it was a shot only a West Indian would have had the speed or the flair—or the madness—to attempt. The match was a formality after that. I watched the unique sight of working-class Londoners, not exactly the spearhead of the movement for racial equality in this country, loving the West Indians and all they stood for—and willing them on to the victory they eventually gained. When that came about, for a few unforgettable moments there was no color, no hate, no suspicion; just a common humanity.

And yes, in sad fact we still don't give the West Indians equal rights in our society, whatever lip service we pay to the race laws. Nevertheless, I like to think that what happened that day belongs to a real future. And I've left out one small detail. When Kanhai hit that unhittable pitch, Snow had for a moment the incredulous eyes of a steer poleaxed out of the blue. But then he did something rare in stricken Goliaths. He raised his hands and clapped. I think that's a better ending than the one in the Bible, and it will help me to a final definition. Those sullen and malevolent bumpers Snow kept pitching were not cricket; but that spontaneous clap was.

SPRING TRAINING

The National Weather Vane

He is a physically fit, well-tanned man with a head cold and a runny nose.
—Description of a major league ball player one week after his return North from spring training.

Spring training has become the national weather vane—better than the fabled groundhog anyway—baseball's way of telling the freezing northerners that warm weather, birds, and budding trees will soon be on the way. The short, snow-filled days that fill the calendar from December to February will soon give way to the sound of balls, bats, and the cry of "Play ball!"

The origins of spring training can be traced back to the Cincinnati Red Stockings' undefeated season of 1869. Undefeated teams have a way of sparking in their competitors a means of exacting revenge. In this case, it was the embarrassed Chicago White Sox who wanted to get back at the Red Stockings, so team officials went about trying to find ways of getting their team in mid-season playing form by the time opening day rolled around. It was finally decided that a warm-weather training site was needed, where the players could meet several weeks prior to the opening of the season for early drills. Team manager Tom Foley was placed in charge of the operation, and so he took his team to New Orleans for their spring practice sessions.

When Foley's White Sox beat the Reds two times that following season, other National Association teams quickly saw the merits in spring training and decided to do likewise in subsequent years. Charleston, South Carolina; Hot Springs, Arkansas; and Jacksonville, Florida, became popular spring training sites, as well as New Orleans.

Professional baseball players became instant hits with some southern townspeople, who were proud to have a ball club working out in their midst.

Once, while encamped in Columbus, Georgia, the Reds received engraved invitations to attend a triple hanging in a nearby town. No player had the courage to take up the prison warden's bizarre offer.

By the 1920s, Florida became the most popular spring training grounds. Warm weather and hospitable people who opened their arms to the northern ballplayers made the Sunshine State a permanent fixture on a team's preseason agenda. Of course, not everyone was satisfied with Florida, and so teams looked elsewhere too. In 1912 the Yankees left the mainland and adventured to the island of Bermuda for spring training. But because of the hard coral ground and unpalatable food, they happily returned to Florida the following spring. Bill Terry, the New York Giants manager from 1932 to 1941, also wanted a change from the Florida routine. In his second year at the helm of the club, he took his team to Los Angeles for spring workouts. Terry regretted his choice very quickly when the City of the Angels was rocked by an earthquake that sent the players scrambling for the open spaces and pleading for a return to Florida.

Although spring training is mainly a time for the veteran players to work off their banquet-circuit bellies, it is also the time when managers have a chance to look over the minor-league and free-agent talent that has assembled with the regulars. In the few warm weeks under the Florida sun, managers mull over which young man can help the club in some way, now, or in the future.

For all the John Pappases, spring training is a time of hope, an attempt to fulfill a lifelong dream—to make it with a big-league team. Many don't ever make it. The reasons are innumerable: too old, too slow, can't hit, can't field, position already filled, bad attitude. But then, some don't even try out. You can find these men in your local bar, living off the glory of a good high school season many years ago when bird dogs once raved about their long-ball hitting or fine glovework.

The following story is not about one of these dreamers who never tried out for the big leagues. It is about someone who in 1962 did make the effort, and although he failed was a better man for trying.

John Pappas Tries Out for the Mets
by Robert Lipsyte

John Pappas appeared on the second day of spring training. He was thin and pale, and he looked about seventeen years old. He said he was twenty-one and that he had come to St. Petersburg, Florida, to be a pitcher for the New York Mets. Nobody knew what to do with him.

The Strobridge Lithograph (1887)

In any other major league clubhouse that spring, the equipment manager or the assistant trainer or maybe even the bat boy would have heaved John Pappas out the door. But this was the second day of the Mets' very first spring, and no one was sure enough of his own job to make a decision about someone else. So Pappas just stood quietly in the hushed, green-carpeted clubhouse, his sneakers under one arm, his glove under the other.

Out on the field, a collection of hopeful strangers was trying to sort itself into a team. Rabbit-quick rookies made impossible leaping catches—always when the coaches weren't looking—and the older players, some of whom had once been stars with other teams, tried to sweat themselves down into shape for the long season ahead. The borderline players worked hardest of all, running extra laps around the outfield, taking long turns in the batting cage, and chattering "Attaboy, baby, show him the hummer, good hands, chuck it in there," because Casey Stengel, manager of the Mets, had a reputation for favoring players with spirit and hustle. The borderline players knew if they didn't make it with this brand-new team they would probably slide right on out of the major leagues.

Pappas stood for a long time in the clubhouse, politely but firmly telling anyone who asked that he had no intention of budging until someone from the Mets gave him a tryout. Finally, a tall sad-faced man came out of a side office and looked into Pappas' steady brown eyes. He introduced himself as John Murphy, an official of the new club.

"Where are you from?" asked Murphy.

"New York City," said Pappas.

"When was the last time you threw a ball?"

"Last Sunday, in New York," said Pappas.

Murphy's eyes narrowed, and he smiled, a triumphant little smile. "It snowed in New York last Sunday."

Pappas nodded. "Yes sir. But not underneath the Triborough Bridge."

Murphy's eyes widened. He motioned Pappas to a wooden bench in front of the lockers and sat down beside him. The young man said he had bought four regulation National League baseballs and pitched them at a painted square on a concrete wall under the bridge. After he was satisfied, he ran for several miles in a nearby park. Then he packed for spring training.

He had arrived in St. Petersburg at three o'clock that morning, he said, after his first airplane trip. It was also the first time he had ever been more than a hundred miles from his parents' home in Astoria, Queens.

Murphy listened and nodded and pulled at his long, sad face. Then he stood up. "We're not holding tryouts here, John." He pointed through the open clubhouse door to the practice ball fields. "There would be a million guys out there if we were."

"I don't see a million guys out there," said Pappas seriously and softly. When Murphy shot him a hard glance to see if he was being smart, Pappas looked down at his black pointy shoes.

Murphy sighed. "You play high-school ball?"

"My high school didn't have a team, Mr. Murphy, but I played Police Athletic League ball. I don't remember which precinct."

"Did anyone ever say you were professional material?"

"No, sir."

"Do your parents know you came down here for a tryout?"

"No one knows, Mr. Murphy."

Murphy sat down again, and his voice became gentle. "Do you go to school?"

"I was going to City College at night, but I stopped going to classes. And I quit my job. I was working in a furniture store. I told my mother I was coming down for a week's vacation and then I'd look for another job."

Almost wearily, Murphy said, "This is not a tryout camp."

Pappas took a deep breath. "Mr. Murphy, I don't have much experience, and I'm willing to spend a few years in the minors. But I think I can pitch, and I want to find out now. I want to succeed in the world, and I can do it if I set my mind to it."

"Of course you can," said Murphy, "but there are many ways to succeed in the world besides major league baseball."

"I'm going to stay here until someone looks at me pitch," said Pappas, running a bony hand through his black pompadour. "If they tell me I'm no good, I'll just finish my vacation and go home and set my mind to something else."

Murphy stared at Pappas for a long time. "Okay, John," he said. "You get yourself a catcher and a place to throw and call me up and I'll come over and look at you."

They shook hands, and Pappas, smiling now, bounded out of the clubhouse. "Thanks, thanks a lot," he called back over his shoulder. "I'll see you soon."

Murphy watched him go, then shook his head at us and walked back into his office. Another newspaperman turned to me and said, "That's a flaky kid for you. I don't know why Murphy wastes his time."

"What do you mean flaky?" I said. "He might really have it; he might be a star. And who says Murphy could tell from one tryout?"

"Johnny Murphy was once a great relief pitcher for the Yankees," said the other newspaperman, "and I think you're a flaky kid, too."

The weather was erratic in St. Petersburg that week, sometimes cool, almost always windy. John Pappas ran in the mornings near his motel and found youngsters to catch his pitching. Three days after he first showed up, a local newspaper arranged for Pappas to use a nearby high-school ball field, and Murphy promised to drive out to watch him pitch. Murphy said he would even bring a professional catcher.

The morning of his tryout Pappas returned to the Mets spring-training camp at Miller Huggins Field and found a seat in the sun on the grandstand. A little less pale now, but still thin and tense, he sat in a crowd of elderly tourists and pensioners and watched the Mets work out. I sat with him for a little while. He pointed at four young Met pitchers who were taking turns throwing for batting practice.

"That could be me," he said.

At 3:38 P.M. on February 23, 1962, John Pappas had his chance. While a dozen newspapermen and photographers watched, he strode onto a scruffy pitching mound and put everything in his slight body behind the baseballs he threw at Bill Whalen, a young catcher from the Mets' camp. Pappas threw for fifteen minutes in silence. He was wild, and he wasn't very fast.

At precisely 3:56 P.M. Murphy walked out to the mound and put his arm around Pappas' thin shoulders. "All you have is guts, son," he said.

They shook hands. Murphy thanked Pappas for giving the Mets a chance to look him over. Very kindly, he told Pappas to forget about professional baseball. Maybe if he were only fifteen years old it might make sense to keep at it, but at twenty-one he had too far to go and too much to learn.

Pappas thanked Murphy for giving him a tryout. He said he was satisfied and now he was going back to New York.

"I always would have wondered," said Pappas, "but now I know. I just wasn't good enough. Now I'll look for something else, some other way of being somebody."

The ball field slowly emptied, and soon there was just Pappas, and two or three of the younger newspapermen who had secretly hoped that this thin, sallow, round-shouldered young clerk would turn out to have an arm like a bullwhip, a live fastball that hummed, and a curve that danced in the sun. I think we were more disappointed than he was, and we were talking mostly for ourselves on the ride back to town, telling Pappas that there were other ways to succeed in the world besides major league baseball and that he was way ahead of the game; after all, how many men actually get a chance to try out, to find out once and for all? Pappas nodded and agreed and smiled and thanked us for our encouragement.

It was dusk when we reached his motel. The last time I saw John Pappas he was framed in the car window, and he said: "You know, I'm sorry they didn't give me a chance to hit. I'm not a bad hitter. And I play the outfield too."

CATCHERS

A Special Breed

In Memoriam
James F. McGuire (The Deacon)
For His Twenty-Five Years Behind the Plate
1884–1906

It has been accurately stated that winning baseball teams never have bad catchers and that losing teams never have good ones. This observation rings true, because after the pitcher in importance on the team is the catcher.

The catcher must remember the offensive weaknesses and strengths of every batter in the league and relay this information to his pitcher. Squatting more than two hundred times a game behind the plate through the cold northern springs and sweltering summer afternoons, a catcher must be ready and able to throw out any player trying to steal; he also has to withstand furious football-like charges at home plate that will break both the spirit and bones of weaker men.

The catcher is a special breed of baseball player. Throughout the annals of baseball much credit has been heaped upon the almighty pitcher, while the much maligned and ignored catcher has toiled away in relative obscurity. But ask any pitcher, any successful manager, and he will tell you that without his regular catcher, team victories would be scarce.

The Tools of Ignorance

The regular catcher in early baseball was considered a foolhardy man, for who else would want to risk physical injury just for the sake of helping the home team win a ball game? With the high risk of injury inherent in the position, it was the least sought after by young players. No one aspired to be a catcher. The manager assigned you to the position and you "became" one.

Catching equipment was slowly introduced to the game by men who obviously feared for their lives. This protection, inappropriately labeled "the tools of ignorance" by catcher haters, greatly aided the men behind the plate. Not only did the new equipment make them more physically secure, but it added a new-found strength that assured ball teams their catcher would budge from the plate only with the application of extreme external pressure.

The Mask

Team captain Fred Thayer first offered a modified fencing mask to teammate Jim Tyng, who wanted to quit as catcher for the Harvard University team in 1876 because he feared injury. Before Thayer's "invention," catchers would use only a rubber guard in the mouth to prevent the ball from dislodging their teeth. As the game progressed, stiff wire was added to the modified fencing masks, making them look more like bird cages than pieces of athletic apparatus. Present-day masks of lightweight alloys and thick foam-rubber padding are marked improvements over the first models; they help make the catcher's stay behind the plate both comfortable and safe.

The Mitt

Gloves were shunned by all players in early baseball because it was not considered virile or manly to wear them. At first, flesh-colored gloves with the fingertips exposed were introduced. Some men took to wearing two gloves, one on each hand, with a piece of raw meat in the glove to cushion the numbing effect the ball had on the palms. In 1891, A. G. Spalding received a patent for a catcher's mitt. His pillowlike piece of equipment allowed the catcher for the first time to move in behind the batter with assurance that he would be able to trap or stop most pitches.

The Chest Protector

In 1884 a sheepskin chest protector, the first type of protection used for the catcher's midsection, was introduced by Jack Clements, catcher for the Pittsburgh Keystones. Subsequent models were stuffed with cotton or inflated with air.

Shin Guards

Red Dooin, the Philadelphia Phillies catcher and later their manager, was the first to introduce shin guards to the profession in 1906. He got the idea from

Evolution of a Cat-cher by H. C. Megerle

English cricket players, who knew better than to play a ball game with exposed legs. Unlike his cricket contemporaries, Dooin was embarrassed to wear the shin guards in public, so he wore them underneath his uniform leg. The following season Roger Breshnahan, the Irish-born catcher of the New York Giants, decided to bare his Dooin-inspired shin guards to the public. On April 7, 1907, in a game at the Polo Grounds, he wore them for the first time outside his uniform and was almost laughed off the field by the uncomprehending fans. Dooin and Breshnahan were trailblazers, and soon other catchers started to wear the "unmanly" devices and no longer had to be afraid of spike wounds, discarded bats, or foul tips.

Catching Records

Most Lifetime Games: 1,918 by Al Lopez, from 1928 with the Brooklyn Dodgers to 1947 with the Cleveland Indians.

Most Games in One Season: 160. Randy Hundley first signed with the San Francisco Giants as an eighteen-year-old "bonus baby" in 1960 worth $110,000. Hundley was a disappointment for the Giants and didn't start to produce until later in his career. In 1968, playing with the Chicago Cubs, Hundley missed only two games in the 162-game season.

Most Base Runners Caught Stealing in a Game: 6 by Wally Schang of the Philadelphia A's in a game on May 12, 1915. Schang also holds the unenviable American League record of committing the most errors in a catching career. From 1913 to 1931, Schang was guilty of 218 miscues.

Most Errors in an Inning: 3. Ed Sweeney, New York Yankees, July 10, 1912; John Peters, Cleveland Indians, May 16, 1918; Andy Seminick, Cincinnati Reds, July 16, 1952.

Most Men Thrown Out in One Inning: 3. Leslie Nunamaker had a thirteen-year career in the majors spent with the Red Sox, Yankees, Saint Louis, and Cleveland. He had a memorable game for the Red Sox on August 3, 1914. In one inning the twenty-four-year-old rifle-armed catcher threw out three runners who tried to steal base.

Baseball's First Superstar Was a King

Mike "King" Kelly was baseball's first player of genuine superstar caliber. Off the field he attracted attention wherever he went, and people packed the ball parks whenever he was in town for a game. Kelly was a baseball innovator, and some claim that as a catcher he was the first to introduce the use of finger signals for communicating with the pitcher on the mound. At one time he held the record for rounding the bases in the amazing time of 15 seconds, and in 1887 he used this natural speed to steal 84 bases, tops in the National League that season.

Kelly started his baseball career in 1878 with Cincinnati. He quickly moved to Chicago for a six-season stay with Cap Anson and Company. Then, in a move befitting a front-page story, Kelly jumped to the Boston team in 1891 for the unheard-of sum of $15,000. Of this, $10,000 had to go to Chicago to pay for the loss of their star, and the exorbitant sum of $5,000 went to the King for his first year's salary. Local reporters were stunned. One noted that Kelly's salary would be one and a half times the salary of a U.S. Supreme Court Justice and about five times that of state governors.

"It will be remembered," one wrote, "that for his salary, Mr. Kelly works but a few months in the summer season."

Mike Kelly loved his work, and fans would cheer madly whenever he was on base. This cheering inspired him to even greater heights. His "Kelly Spread," an early forerunner of the hook slide, was his secret weapon and also the source of songbird Maggie Cline's hit tune "Slide, Kelly, Slide."

King Kelly was a lifetime .313 hitter and also adept at playing all positions. Most of his time and money, however, was frittered away on clothes and in perpetuating a fine lifestyle befitting a man of his stature. Acclaimed by many to be the world's best-dressed male, Kelly tried to live the role. On one occasion he arrived at the ball park in a carriage pulled by a team of milk-white horses. When the throng of admiring fans came to greet him at the entrance to the park, they quickly unhitched the carriage and pulled it into the park themselves. Truly a ride fit for a King!

Unfortunately, the King had one bad vice. His penchant for drink was great and soon overcame his desire to play ball. His skills eroded faster than could be imagined, and he found himself scrounging for a team. He ended his baseball days in Yonkers, New York, working as that city's Eastern League team manager. It was quite a fall.

On a return trip to Boston during the off-season, Michael Joseph Kelly, still the pride of the Irish but weakened significantly by his drinking bouts, contracted pneumonia and was rushed to the hospital in bad condition.

"I think this is me last slide," he said to the friends at his bedside. Then he moved on to that other ball field. At the age of thirty-seven, the King had been struck out by high living. Long live the King!

The following playing advice comes from King Kelly's book *Play Ball . . . Stories of the Ball Field*, which first appeared in 1888. *Play Ball* is a fine example of the late nineteenth-century sports writing—ghosted no doubt—and when you compare it with modern "how-to" books, the differences become strikingly apparent. As you will see from the example below, one thing is certain: in the nineteenth century, as in the twentieth, learning baseball through participation rather than through reading is much more fun. Reading it now, one has to chuckle at its moralistic overtones, but in its day, Kelly's "boy friends" took it all quite seriously. *This* was the way to success.

"Now, to my boy friends, and I hope I have many, I will give a few simple rules about the game: First, if you wish to become a good ball player, you must study hard, and go to school regularly. You must learn your lessons well and obey your teachers. When school is over, go out and begin a ball game. Do not play with a soft ball. It is just as good to have a good hard one. It won't hurt you any more than the soft ball. When you see it coming to you hard, do not go out of the way, but rather go towards it. The harder that it comes into your hands the least will be the damage. If you make an error, do not feel badly about it. Just make up your mind that you are going to do better the next time. Practice running and especially how to make a good, quick start. Never close your eyes when you see a ball coming. Just keep them open and say to yourself, 'Well, here is a friend of mine coming. I'll stop him before he can do any harm.' . . .

"Never run into another player with the intention of hurting him. Never get angry and never fight. Be manly, and only resort to fighting when you must do it to protect yourself. Boys, I'm a pretty old boy, and I only forgot once in my life. That one was absolutely forced on me. Make up your mind that it's much better to run than to fight. But if you run hard, and the other fellow is a better runner than you are, stop. Stop suddenly. Don't lose any wind. Just turn around and give him a good, sound thrashing. When it's all over, say that you are willing to shake hands with him. Then go home and tell your mother and father all about it."

INFIELDERS

Tinker to Evers to Chance

These are the saddest of possible words:
  Tinker to Evers to Chance.
Trio of Bear Cubs and fleeter than birds,
  Tinker to Evers to Chance.
Ruthlessly pricking our gonfalon bubble,
Making a Giant hit into a double—
Words that are weighty with nothing but trouble—
  "Tinker to Evers to Chance."
  —Franklin P. Adams

The immortal double-play combination of Joe Tinker at shortstop, Johnny "Crab" Evers at second, and Frank Chance at first was one that caught the fancy of New York newsman Franklin P. Adams, an ardent yet disappointed Giant supporter whose dreams of Giant success were continually being dashed by the Chicago Cubs. Tinker, Evers, and Chance led the Cubs to National League pennants in 1906, 1907, 1908, and 1910 and helped them win the World Series from Detroit in both 1907 and 1908. During the years when the Cubs swept the three straight titles, the feared double-play combination only completed less than 54 double plays, a figure that is easily doubled by present major-league units.

First baseman Chance was one of baseball's greatest players at that position. When he came to the Cubs in 1898, he was only an average catcher but a man who loved being behind the plate nonetheless.

By mid-season 1905, Chance was the regular first baseman and also manager of the Cubs, a title that earned him the nickname "Peerless Leader." In 1906 under Chance, the Cubs won a record 116 games and started on the road to dominance that came to distress F. P. Adams in New York.

Chance left the Cubs in 1912 and later managed the New York Highlanders (New York Yankees to you modern folk) for two seasons (1913–14) and later

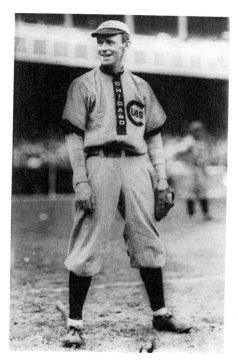

Johnny Evers

Joe Tinker

Frank Chance

the Red Sox in 1923. At six feet one inch and 195 pounds, Chance was solidly built during his active playing years, but poor health quickly took the best out of him after he left the game. He died in Los Angeles in 1924 just six days after his forty-seventh birthday.

Frank Chance lived with, managed, and played with Crab Evers and Joe Tinker, which was a difficult thing to do since after 1909 neither Evers or Tinker said a word to each other. It was their mutual hatred of each other that probably added a bit of zip to their double plays.

Evers and Tinker used to be the best of friends—until one fateful day in 1909. Crab Evers took a cab to the ball field by himself, not asking any of his teammates to join him. When later asked by an irate Tinker why he hadn't invited anyone to go with him in the cab, Evers answered by punching his overinquisitive fielding partner. The two men were finally separated, each one threatening to do the other in. They parted as enemies and agreed vehemently never to speak to each other again.

Crab Evers lasted with the Cubs until 1913, serving that final year as playing manager of the team. He then latched on with the "Miracle Braves" of Boston the following season, playing for the amazing team that went from dead last in mid-July to take the World Series title in four games from Connie Mack's Philadelphia A's.

Joe Tinker left the Cubs to manage the Cincinnati Reds in 1913 but came back to take over the Cubs in 1916. Charles Taft, the Cubs' new owner, figured he might as well give the last member of the illustrious double-play trio a try at the Cubs helm.

Taft's noble experiment did not work too well. The Cubs slumped to fifth place that year, and Tinker soon left for the sunshine of Florida to manage in the minor leagues for the next few years.

By 1938, Joe Tinker had lost a bit of his old spark. Diabetes had claimed one of his legs, and he spent his days tending to affairs at a billiards parlor he operated in Florida. As with most former big-leaguers, Joe Tinker's heart was still with baseball. When he was invited to Chicago to participate in a radio show, he readily agreed.

Johnny Evers stayed with baseball in one capacity or another after his playing days with the Cubs. He managed the Cubs again in 1921 and then took over the crosstown rival Chicago White Sox three seasons later. In the early 1930s he became involved with the Albany (New York) minor-league team, where he served as the general manager. He was in a weakened condition and bound to a wheelchair when he was invited to do a radio show in Chicago about the Cubs. But baseball was his life, so he went.

They faced each other across the room in the radio studio. Time had been unkind to both Evers and Tinker. In a short span of twenty-five years, both had lost the use of their legs. Their hair was graying. Both were in their fifities, a time when they should be enjoying the fruits of their earlier life. Instead, it was misery and a lot of suffering.

After staring at each other momentarily, the two bitter foes embraced and cried in each other's arms. After a span of too many years, the two men set out to renew a friendship that had once been the strongest on the championship Cub team.

> These are the saddest of possible words:
> Tinker to Evers to Chance.

In 1946, the three men of Adams' famous verse were inducted into the Hall of Fame, and their three bronze plaques now hang with the other 130 immortals of baseball.

> Words that are weighty with nothing but trouble—
> Tinker to Evers to Chance.

Unassisted Triple Plays . . .

The rarest feat in baseball is an unassisted triple play: one defensive player causing three outs in one inning. Oddsmakers give this a 15,000-to-1 chance of occurring. The odds that this could ever happen in the World Series are even steeper, but in Cleveland in 1920, infielder Bill Wambsganss pulled one off in the fifth inning of the fifth game against the Brooklyn Dodgers.

The last player to perform an unassisted triple killing was Washington Senator player Ron Hansen. Hansen was a sure-gloved twenty-two-year old rookie when he broke in with the Baltimore Orioles in 1960. He led all American League shortstops with 325 putouts that year, and in addition to smacking 22 home runs and knocking in 86 runs, Hansen capped off the great year by being selected Rookie of the Year in the American League.

In subsequent seasons, Hansen set numerous fielding records. In one doubleheader in 1965, he handled the ball 18 times in the first game, which went to extra innings. In the nightcap he got his hands on the ball 7 more times, making this the most ever for a shortstop in the history of baseball. In 1961, 1964, and

Ron Hansen

1968, Hansen also led the American League in double plays for shortstops.

Perhaps the highlight of Hansen's career came when he was with the Senators in 1968. The Cleveland Indians were in the nation's capital for a night game on July 30. With two runners on base early in the first inning, José Azcue, the Indians' Cuban-born catcher, came to bat. He lashed into a pitch and sent it straight for the glove of Ron Hansen. Out Number One.

Quick-thinking Hansen then tagged Dave Nelson who was caught off second base. Out Number Two.

Hansen spotted outfielder Russ Snyder retreating to first base and he ran him down. Out Number Three.

A 15,000-to-1 shot had come through. For his special accomplishments Hansen received a standing ovation from the fans and then followed it up by striking out four times in the game, just one short of the major-league record.

Hansen drew his own form of revenge for the apparent lack of appreciation on the part of the Senators management for his triple play. He got a double and a single and drove in the winning run *against* the Senators in his first game with the Chicago White Sox, the team he was traded to just three days after his triple killing!

... And the Men Who Made Them

1909: Shortstop Neal Ball of the Cleveland Indians in a game against Boston on July 19 in the second inning.

1920: Bill Wambsganss, Cleveland second baseman, hit only .154 in the Series against the Dodgers but made up for it with the only unassisted triple play in World Series history. It came in the fifth inning of the October 10 game in Cleveland. The Indians went on to win the game 8–1 and take the Series 5 games to 2.

1923: First baseman George Burns of the Boston Red Sox collared Cleveland in the second inning of a September 14 game.

Shortstop Ernie Padgett of the Boston Braves was in only his second game in the major leagues on October 6. His career would end in 1928 with one home run to his name in 271 games, but he will always be remembered for his fourth-inning play against Philadelphia in early autumn. Padgett snared Walter Holke's line drive for the first out, tagged second to get Out Number Two from Cotton Tierney, who had strayed too far from base; and ran down Cliff Lee, who couldn't get back to second on time, for Out Number Three.

1925: Forest Glenn Wright was in his second season with Pittsburgh at shortstop. In his rookie year, 1924, he led all National League shortstops in assists with 601, and the following season he joined the elite by making his unassisted triple play in the May 7 game against the Saint Louis Cardinals.

1927: Shortstop James E. Cooney was better known as "Scoops" to his Chicago Cub teammates, and if it weren't for his unassisted triple play against Pittsburgh on May 30, he might have faded out of the majors almost unknown. He played in only 33 games that season for the Cubs, and in 18 games two years later with the Boston Braves, his sixth and final club in his eight-year major-league career.

First baseman Johnny Neun's triple play came only hours after Scoops Cooney had performed the feat against the Pirates. The Tiger's first sacker had to react fast or would have had his head taken off by Cleveland outfielder Homer Summa's line drive. Neun grabbed the ball, touched first to catch Charlie Jamieson off base, then ran to second to get Glenn Myatt, who by this time was rounding third and on his way to home. The ball game was over and the Tigers won 1–0.

Triple plays are rare, and to witness one is a special treat. Tris Speaker, Hall of Fame outfielder, was on the field when three of them occurred! In 1909, his team was victimized by Neal Ball's play. In the World Series of 1920, his teammate Bill Wambsganss pulled the trick when he was managing Cleveland. And in 1923 he was again victimized by the play when George Burns of the Boston Red Sox performed the feat against Speaker's Cleveland Indians.

Fred Merkle

To Merkle: To fail to arrive.
—Early American definition now faded from use

Many thought of Fred Merkle as one of the most knowledgeable men in modern baseball. But throughout most of his career, which lasted from 1907 to 1926, Merkle was labeled, among other things, "bonehead," "ignorant," and "stupid." The fans held him responsible for the Giants' losing the National League pennant in 1908, and they would never let him forget it. Whether the charges are justified is still being debated seventy years after the fact. Historians tend to agree that the names he was called and the way he was pilloried unmercifully by the press were unjust in light of the facts. Fred Merkle was a victim of circumstance, a young man at the wrong place at the wrong time who thought more of protecting his life than of protecting a run.

Fred Merkle had a more-than-average IQ. He was one of the Giants' best chess players (Christy Mathewson held the checkers title), and he was the trusted adviser to none other than John McGraw, one of the greatest tacticians in the history of baseball. Throughout the fiasco, McGraw stood behind his player, but the press and the angry fans were looking for a scapegoat. Fred Merkle was the man. The following season, John McGraw saw fit to give this same "bonehead" a raise in salary and the starting position at first.

The incident that clouded Merkle's career came in 1908 during the Giants' pennant drive in late summer. Fred Merkle was in his second season with the team. The Giants had last been in the World Series in 1905, defeating the Phillies 4–1 for the title. New York fans were hoping for another chance at the Series following the Giants' subsequent two-season drought. With this 1908 squad they had reason to hope. The Giants were only a few games away from clinching the title at the end of the season.

The Chicago Cubs came to the Polo Grounds in late September for a three-game series that would decide the eventual winner in the National League. The Cubs had beaten the Giants in the first two games, and on September 23 in their third game they were tied 1–1 in the bottom of the ninth. Fred Merkle was on first base, while teammate Moon McCormick was on third waiting to be knocked home for the game-winning run. Giant rooters turned their eyes to shortstop Al Bridwell, the man in the batter's box. The stadium grew silent. Down at the field's edge anxious fans pushed close, ready to storm the field in time of victory to salute their team.

Al Bridwell smashed the ball to center field, and the game-winning run crossed the plate. The Giants had done it, they were the National League champs. The fans came storming out on the field.

But then it happened. As the jubilant throng rushed onto the infield, Fred Merkle, a mere nineteen-year-old newcomer from the backwoods of Wisconsin, panicked when he saw the onrushing hordes and instead of going all the way to second base to complete the play, he ran for the safety of the clubhouse. Alert Cub second baseman, Crab Evers, a student of the game's technicalities, frantically called for the ball from center fielder Solly Hofman; but Hofman's throw landed in the wildly cheering infield mob. At this time, Floyd Kroh, who had been watching the happenings from the sidelines where he was guarding the Cubs' watches and wallets, ran onto the field and fought a Giant fan for possession of the ball. Kroh finally succeeded in getting the ball to Evers, who quickly touched the base and claimed an out. Evers' play, so he claimed nullified McCormick's run because Merkle had failed to arrive at second base and complete the play. Umpire Hank O'Day agreed with Evers and called for extra innings.

Although touching second base is clearly mandated in the rule book, in practice it was rarely enforced in these times. That is, until Merkle, of course. It became impossible to resolve the situation on the field. Irate fans, shouting managers, and disbelieving Giants stormed about. Since the field could not be cleared and the game could therefore not be continued, Umpire O'Day declared the game a 1–1 tie, and a replay to decide the National League title was ordered by League President Harry Pulliam.

The Giants lost this play-off 4–2 and Merkle was roasted again. When the Cubs went on to defeat a weak Detroit Tiger team 4–1 and win the Series, the Giant fans really became incensed and seemed to decide then that they would never let Merkle forget his mistake.

Fred Merkle stayed with the Giants until 1916, when he was traded to the hated Brooklyn Dodgers. He finally ended his career in 1926 with the Yankees. Al Bridwell, whose hit had scored the noncounting winning run for the Giants, said some years later, "It would have been better for Fred Merkle if I had struck out." He was right.

Lou Gehrig

Today I consider myself the luckiest man on the face of the earth.

—Lou Gehrig, July 4, 1939

Lou Gehrig played seventeen seasons for the New York Yankees until he was cut down by amyotrophic lateral sclerosis, a rare and crippling disease more common halfway around the globe than within the confines of Yankee Stadium. Lou Gehrig, the Pride of the Yankees, was just a few days short of his thirty-eighth birthday.

I never knew Lou Gehrig, never saw him play. Nor did I ever see the movie about his life, *Pride of the Yankees.* I'm sure the teenage boys playing ball on the garbage-littered Manhattan street where he was born don't even know that Gehrig ever lived there. If they were to guess, most likely they would probably think Gehrig was the name of a singing group.

Fred Merkle

Lou Gehrig

Gehrig's apartment house—no. 409—is no longer there, replaced instead by a commercial laundry; but on the gray-brick wall where his doorway once was, a rubber ball whizzes by the stickball batter and bangs off the painted strike zone. The embarrassed boy mutters to himself and gets ready for the next pitch. Young Lou Gehrig would have sent the ball flying off the fourth-floor fire escape.

It was an overcast Sunday afternoon, just a few short weeks after the 1979 baseball season had opened. The Yanks were at home, less than two miles away from where Gehrig was born, and 35,000-plus were on hand at the ball park to cheer/hoot a former Yankee pitcher who had returned to the stadium to play ball with his new team and to push his bestselling book about his former teammates. It has been forty seasons since Lou Gehrig last played at Yankee Stadium. It's more modern now, and I don't think Gehrig would recognize the place. The Yankees, a team that was once synonymous with the character of Lou Gehrig—determined and dignified—have changed. They have won twenty-one American League crowns and fourteen World Series titles since Gehrig's career came to an end. Somehow, I feel a closer affinity to yesterday's memories and the teams of Gehrig than to today's triumphs. Perhaps it was simpler in Gehrig's time. Then it was just man against man, without the interference of hype, agentry, or incessant player dictums of "I'll go where I can get the most money." Sadly, things have changed in sports, just like Lou Gehrig's old neighborhood.

In his prime Lou Gehrig was called the Iron Man. When regular first baseman Wally Pipp became ill and took himself out of the game June 1, 1925, young Lou Gehrig, then in his first full season with the Yankees, was sent in as Pipp's replacement. Gehrig remained at first base for a major-league record 2,130 consecutive games. When he finally removed himself from the game in Detroit on May 2, 1939, he was never the same again. The bothersome lumbago that had forced him to snap his consecutive-game streak was later correctly diagnosed to be what is now universally called "Lou Gehrig's disease," an incurable disintegration of the spinal cord.

Lou Gehrig played on the same team with the great Babe Ruth, and for this reason many of his amazing baseball feats have not received as much notice. Gehrig was a quiet man and didn't like to draw attention to himself. The naturally garrulous and flamboyant Ruth was just the opposite and could make sports copy just by catching three fish on an off-day fishing trip.

In 1927, Gehrig was selected Most Valuable Player, the same year the Yanks crushed the Pittsburgh Pirates 4–0 in the Series. Four years later he won the award again, and again in 1934 and 1936. In the 1928 sweep of the Series from the Cardinals, Gehrig blasted a World Series record of four consecutive home runs. Two of them came during a 7–3 trampling of the Cards.

Lou Gehrig ranks as one of the game's best long-ball sluggers. His 493 career mark ranks him twelfth on the all-time career homer list, while his four homers hit on June 3, 1932, make him the first player to perform the feat in the twentieth century. As was the case throughout the gentle giant's career, Gehrig didn't receive any banner headlines for that mighty effort. No, this time he wasn't topped by Babe Ruth. June 3 was the day Manager John McGraw picked to resign from the New York Giants after thirty years at the helm.

On July 4, 1939, in The Bronx, New York, an overflow crowd of 62,000 fans packed Yankee Stadium to honor the greatest Yankee captain, a man who knew he only had a short while to live. It was Lou Gehrig Day in New York City, and the lumbering first baseman, now twenty pounds lighter because of his illness, stepped up to the bank of microphones to address the crowd. Behind him, the great 1927 Yankees in their civilian clothes stood and listened.

"Fans, for the past two weeks you have been reading about a bad break I got. Yet today I consider myself the luckiest man on the face of the earth. I have been in ball parks and have never received anything but kindness and encouragement from you fans.

"Look at these grand men. Which of you wouldn't consider it the highlight of his career just to associate with them for even one day? Sure, I'm lucky. Who wouldn't consider it an honor to have known Jacob Ruppert, and also the builder of baseball's greatest empire, Ed Barrow; to have spent six years with that wonderful little fellow, Miller Huggins; then to have spent the next nine years with that outstanding leader, that smart student of psychology, the best manager in baseball today, Joe McCarthy.

"Who wouldn't feel honored to have roomed with such a good guy as Bill Dickey?

"Sure, I'm lucky. When the New York Giants, a team you would give your right arm to beat, and vice versa, sends you a gift, that's something. When everybody down to the groundskeepers and those boys in the white coats remember you with trophies, that's something.

"When you have a wonderful mother-in-law who takes sides with you in squabbles against her own daughter, that's something. When you have a father and mother who work all their lives so that you can have an education and build your body, it's a blessing. When you have a wife who has been a tower of strength and shows more courage than you knew existed, that's the finest I know.

"So I close in saying that I might have had a tough break, but I have an awful lot to live for."

Normally, after retirement from the major leagues, a ball player must wait at least five years before he can be considered as a candidate for the Hall of Fame. Lou Gehrig was not normal. The great Yankee captain was inducted a few months after his Yankee Stadium speech. He died two years later in the Riverdale section of The Bronx, not too far from the muffled roars of Yankee Stadium.

PITCHERS

William Arthur "Candy" Cummings is credited by baseball archivists as being the inventor of the curveball. In the following article, written when he was sixty years old, a reflective Cummings tells how it all came about. Cummings was a petite man: five feet nine inches tall and weighing only 130 pounds. Even so, he seems to have been a ball of fire on the mound. Records are scanty, but in 1872 he was 34–19 for the New York Mutuals and three seasons later went 34–11 while playing for Hartford.

Cummings died in 1924 and was posthumously selected to baseball's Hall of Fame in 1939. This article first appeared in *The Baseball Magazine* in 1908.

How I Pitched the First Curve
by William Arthur Cummings

EDITOR'S NOTE: To William Arthur Cummings of Athol, Mass., belongs the honor of having discovered—or invented— how to curve a ball. What thirty-eight years ago was considered a work of magic, is now a common practice. The curved ball has completely revolutionized baseball methods. This is the first authentic article ever published on the subject.

I have often been asked how I first got the idea of making a ball curve. I will now explain. It is such a simple matter, though, that there is not much explanation.

In the summer of 1863 a number of boys and myself were amusing ourselves by throwing clam shells (the hard shell variety) and watching them sail along through the air, turning now to the right, and now to the left. We became interested in the mechanics of it and experimented for an hour or more.

All of a sudden it came to me that it would be a good joke on the boys if I could make a baseball curve the same way. We had been playing "three-old-cat'" and town-ball, and I had been doing the pitching. The joke seemed so good that I made a firm decision that I would try to play it.

I set to work on my theory and practiced every spare moment that I had out of school. I had no one to help me and had to fight it out alone. Time after time I would throw the ball, doubling up into all manner of positions, for I thought my pose had something to do with it; and then I tried holding the ball in different shapes. Sometimes I thought I had it, and then maybe again in twenty-five tries I could not get the slightest curve. My visionary successes were just enough to tantalize me. Month after month I kept pegging away at my theory.

In 1864 I went to Fulton, New York, to a boarding school, and remained there for a year and a half. All the time I kept experimenting with my curved ball. My boy friends began to laugh at me, and to throw jokes at my theory of making a ball go sideways. I fear that some of them thought it was so preposterous that it was no joke and that I should be carefully watched over.

I don't know what made me stick at it. The great wonder to me now is that I did not give up in disgust, for I had not one single word of encouragement in all that time, while my attempts were a standing joke among my friends.

After graduating I went back to my home in Brooklyn, New York, and joined the "Star Juniors," an amateur team. We were very successful. I was solicited to join as a junior member the Excelsior club, I accepted the proposition.

In 1867 I, with the Excelsior club, went to Boston, where we played the Lowells, the Tri-Mountains, and Harvard clubs. During these games I kept trying to make the ball curve. It was during the Harvard game that I became fully convinced that I had succeeded in doing what all these years I had been striving to do. The batters were missing a lot of balls; I began to watch the flight of the ball through the air, and distinctly saw it curve.

A surge of joy flooded over me that I shall never forget. I felt like shouting out that I had made a ball curve; I wanted to tell everybody; it was too good to keep to myself.

But I said not a word, and saw many a batter at that game throw down his stick in disgust. Every time I was successful I could scarcely keep from dancing from pure joy. The secret was mine.

There was trouble though, for I could not make it curve when I wanted to. I would grasp it the same, but the ball seemed to do just as it pleased. It would curve all right, but it was very erratic in its choice of places to do so. But still it curved!

The baseball came to have a new meaning to me; it almost seemed to have life.

It took time and hard work for me to master it, but I kept on pegging away until I had fairly good control.

In those days the pitcher's box was six feet by four, and the ball could be thrown from any part of it; one foot could be at the forward edge of the box, while the other could be stretched back as far as the pitcher liked; but both feet had to be on the ground until the ball was delivered. It is surprising how much speed could be generated under those rules.

It was customary to swing the arm perpendicularly and to deliver the ball at the height of the knee. I still threw this way, but brought in wrist action.

I found that the wind had a whole lot to do with the ball curving. With a wind against me I could get all kinds of a curve, but the trouble lay in the fact that the ball was apt not to break until it was past the batter. This was a sore trouble; but I learned not to try to curve a ball very much when the wind was unfavorable.

I have often been asked to give my theory of why a ball curves. Here it is: I give the ball a sharp twist with the middle finger, which causes it to revolve with a swift rotary motion. The air also, for a limited space around it begins to revolve, making a great swirl, until there is enough pressure to force the ball out of true line. When I first began practising this new legerdemain, the pitchers were not the only ones who were fooled by the ball. The umpire also suffered. I would throw the ball straight at the batter; he would jump back, and then the umpire would call a ball. On this I lost, but when I started the spheroid toward the center of the plate he would call it a strike., When it got to the batter it was too far out, and the batter would not even swing. Then there would be a clash between the umpire and batter.

But my idlest dreams of what a curved ball would do, as I dreamed of them that afternoon while throwing clam shells, have been filled more than a hundred times. At that time I thought of it only as a good way to fool the boys, its real practical significance never entering my mind.

I get a great deal of pleasure now in my old age out of going to games and watching the curves, thinking that it was through my blind efforts that all this was made possible.

Rube Marquard: A Quiet Afternoon in Pikesville

At eighty-nine years of age he is currently the oldest living member of the Hall of Fame. His career stretches back to the time when the ball park was a little better than a pasture. When Rube Marquard first stepped into the Polo Grounds to pitch for the Giants on September 25, 1908, Cy Young was 21–11 with Boston, while Giant mainstay Christy Mathewson was in the ninth year of his eighteen-year reign in the majors. Big Six went 37–11 that season and took the young Marquard under his wing.

If Richard "Rube" Marquard, an avowed "speed pitcher," had been pitching under today's rules, he would have been officially credited with 20 consecutive victories in 1912, instead of his record-setting 19. In the disputed game that would have raised Marquard's record, the young Giant pitcher was sent in by manager John McGraw in the eighth inning of a game that the Giants were losing 3–2. Marquard held on and the Giants roared back in the ninth to win the game 4–3. The victory went to Charles Tesreau, the future Dartmouth College coach, who had pitched seven and one third innings, and all Marquard got was a little exercise. But still, Marquard's 19 consecutive victories almost seventy years ago has withstood the assaults of major-league pitching.

Marquard came to the Giants with much fanfare and ballyhoo. McGraw had bought his contract from Indianapolis in the American Association for the then astronomical sum of $11,000. Marquard was eighteen years old at the time and had a 28–19 season at Indianapolis to his credit.

His name at birth was Richard William Marquard, but even today his wife, Jane, calls him "Rube," a name he got because his pitching reminded enough people of the other great pitching star, Rube Waddell. The new name stuck when Marquard came to the Giants, but when he was easily tagged in the 1909 season, unhappy Giant fans called him an imposter and even worse, "the eleven-thousand-dollar lemon."

Marquard's second season went slightly better. He appeared in eleven games for the Giants and posted a 4–4 record. His glory years with the club were soon coming. From 1911 to 1913, the Giants won the National League and Marquard won a total of 73 games. Included in his career-best 1912 season when he went 26–11, were his 19 consecutive victories.

During the off-season, the handsome Cleveland native took good advantage of his proximity to New York's vaudeville and spent much time on the stage. The popular "Marquard Glide" was named for this Giant pitcher turned

Rube Marquard

hoofer. Marquard was one of the best-dressed men of his time and certainly broke the hearts of many women when he married actress Blossom Seeley and let her help him choose his wardrobe.

Rube Marquard won 201 games during his nineteen years in the Bigs. When he retired in 1925, after finishing up with Boston, he did some managing and scouting in the South for a few years. He finally settled into his "other" career as a pari-mutuel clerk at the Baltimore racetracks.

Today Rube Marquard walks in a slow, shuffling gait with the aid of a lightweight aluminum walker. His spirits are high and he likes to keep active. One evening in March 1979, he and his wife were going to their club's dinner-dance. Before he went to take a nap to rest up for the affair, we sat in the comfortable anteroom of his Pikesville, Maryland, apartment, and Marquard spoke of the early days of baseball. He gesticulated often with his left hand, the one that had powered 1,593 strikeout pitches. "Ring Lardner and I used to eat bags of peanuts out in the bullpen; anything that would happen with the team, I'd always tell Ring.

"I told my mother when I was six that I wanted to be a ball player and that one day I would show her what I could do on the field. She died the next year and never got to see me play. My dad was the chief engineer of the city of Cleveland, and he never liked baseball. When I told him that I wanted to be a ball player he just looked at me and said, 'So, you want to be a bum for the rest of your life.'

" 'If I'm going to be a bum,' I told him, 'then I'll be a good bum. If I'm bad I won't go that far.'

"My father wouldn't listen to me, so when I was sixteen I had to run away from home. I rode boxcars out to Iowa to find a team to play for. By leaving home my father got so mad that he never came out to a ball game. Never! Like my mother, he never saw me play ball either.

"One time my dad took me aside and said, 'Ball players are good today and bad tomorrow. In my business, I'm always good.' My dad always believed that I could learn his business much quicker than the time that it took to be a good pitcher.

"As a pitcher my whole ambition was to win as many games as I could. In 1912, when I was pitching so well for the Giants, my teammates hustled and bustled for me and really helped out. The players on the other teams were nice about it too. When they saw that I could set a record they'd shake my hand and wish me luck. Then I'd go out and beat 'em.

"More power to Ron Guidry [winner of thirteen consecutive games in 1978] and the other pitchers today. I had my time and had the best pitchers going against me and I'd still win—one to nothing, two to nothing. I got everything that I wanted out of baseball and gave everything that I could to the game.

"When I go to a ball game now, I especially watch the work between the pitcher and catcher. On the day of the game I was going to pitch, I'd get together with Chief Meyers, our catcher, and figure which batters we'd be facing and how we'd attack them. We never had a bit of trouble working together.

"One of the tricks that the Chief and I would use on tough batters was for me to shake off a certain pitch. The Chief would then ask the umpire to call time and he would come out to the mound for a conference. This would really shake up the batter. The Chief would go back, and then I'd throw him the original pitch that he had called for. Nine times out of ten the plan worked and we got the batter out.

"I idolized Christy Mathewson when I was young, and never thought that one day I'd get to meet him. The idea of playing with him was something I never thought would happen. Matty was the greatest in my book.

"Another good one was Scoops Carey of Pittsburgh. He was one of the fastest runners in baseball. Ever. I had to be careful when he got on base because I knew that he was going to try to steal the first chance that he got. I came up with a special "half balk" that I would love to use on him. Three or four times in a row I'd use it, and I can still picture him sliding back to first trying to beat my throw. He'd be so tired from sliding that I'd usually get him on the fifth try.

"When I came up against Rogers Hornsby, I'd just talk to him. 'So you're Hornsby the Great? Let's see how far you can hit it.'

"After that I would throw him a knuckleball.

"Hornsby would yell back, 'Don't you know how to throw a fastball?'

" 'Yes,' I'd tell him. 'Here it comes.'

"I'd then throw the ball right underneath his throat!

"Honus Wagner has to be the greatest player of all time. He could play any position that you put him in. Ty Cobb? He doesn't count. He played in the *other* league.

"I don't think there is any fun in baseball today. People used to come out to the park and see the players do different things on the field. Now, before you can get them to do anything, the first thing they will do is ask, 'How much do I get for doing it?' Years ago they really loved to play the game. You would come into a town and the people would all come down to the field and talk to you. Boston was one of the greatest baseball towns for this.

"I don't think that anything can be done to get back the enthusiasm that was once in big-league baseball. Every player is money mad. It's always 'How much?' before they will do anything.

"The question of money was always in baseball. At the end of the season when I was playing, they'd say, 'Rube, come on up to the office. I'd like to talk to you about your contract for next season.'

"I'd go up and sit down with the owner, and he'd start out by saying, 'What do you think you're worth, Rube?' Well, I knew this game, so right away I'd tell him, 'I'm worth an awful lot.' The owner would write down a figure and say that he thought I was worth that amount. There were no agents in those days, so I had to do my own bargaining. That's something that you don't see anymore.

"When I played, the fans talked about the heroes that they had. This doesn't happen anymore. Instead, they talk about the player who is getting the most money."

Walter Johnson: The Big Train

He originated fireball pitching—the kind you hear but never can see. They called him "the Big Train," Walter Johnson by birth, and for twenty-one seasons he toiled in the American League trying to keep the Washington Senators out of the cellar. Johnson threw a record 113 shutouts, won 416 games, and struck out 3,508 batters in this time. Johnson's fastball was his meal ticket, and its speed was legendary.

"I throw as hard as I can, when I think that I have to throw as hard as I can," said Johnson, one of the original five selectees to the Hall of Fame, when quizzed on his favorite pitch.

Johnson was playing in the hinterlands of Idaho when he was first spotted by a traveling liquor salesman who thought he knew something about baseball talent. He was certain he had a winner in Johnson and sent his rave reviews along to the Washington Senators. The Senators were skeptical about a nineteen-year-old busher, but they signed him anyway. Three years later, Johnson had a 13–25 season for the dead-last Senators, but the next year (1910) he went 25–17. This great season was only a preview of the nightmare coming for American League batters. In the next nine seasons, the rubber-armed Johnson won more than 20 games a season, going 32–12 in 1912 and 36–7 the following year! The 56 scoreless innings he pitched in 1913 is still the American League record.

Baseball experts tend to agree that Johnson might have been the game's most successful pitcher if he had had some defensive support from his fielders and some clout from their bats. On sixty-four separate occasions, Johnson was involved in 1–0 ball games. Twenty-six times he lost; and it wasn't until after eighteen long years with his team that he finally made it to the World Series—winning 4–3 from the Giants, thanks to 37-year-old Johnson's clutch pitching in a 12-inning final-game thriller.

Walter Johnson's record-setting came to an end in 1927, when he suffered a serious injury in spring training. He was close to forty years old, and it seems ironic that the legendary fireballer who never had any serious arm problems would be knocked out of the game by a broken leg.

Johnson managed the Senators from 1929 to 1932 and then retired completely from the game to raise cattle on his ranch in Maryland. He died of a brain tumor in 1946 at the age of sixty-nine.

Sandy Koufax: Strikeout King

Sandy Koufax's first love was basketball, and in 1954 the six-foot-two-inch guard went to the University of Cincinnati on a basketball scholarship. The following spring he tried out for the university's baseball team. Koufax had played a little back home, so he thought he'd give it a try at college. It was a way to get down South for the spring, too, since the team was going there for some games. Koufax fanned 34 batters in two games on the southern trip.

If success is measured by a professional contract, then Sandy Koufax was successful in his first real try in baseball. He was quickly offered a tidy amount to give up basketball, postpone his college education, and take $20,000 back home with him to Brooklyn and become a Dodger. After some period of indecision, Koufax relented, and in December 1955 he signed on the dotted line.

Koufax never went to the minor leagues, but he experienced all the same frustrations that minor-leaguers go through. He spent most of his early career in the Dodger bullpen. Statistics for his first six seasons show 40 losses in 76 games. Koufax had talent though, and most of all, he had speed. He struck out 41 batters in three consecutive games in 1959. This was a record for lefties. But his record for the year was 8–6, fairly uninspiring, as was his 4.06 earned run average. Being the low-ranking member of a World Series contender was not an ideal place for a player with Koufax's disposition. He was impatient and wanted to be in the starting rotation. Some thought that Koufax would have been better off with a weaker team. That way he would have been pitching regularly and not sulking in the bullpen. There was no way the Dodgers would part with Koufax.

In 1961, everything finally started to fall in place for the quiet left-handed speedballer. He won 18 games that year, but more important, he notched 269 strikeouts—and that was only a taste of what was to come. In the following five

Sandy Koufax

seasons, he left a trail of shattered regular-season and World Series pitching records that astounded those who had seen Walter Johnson, Bob Feller, and Warren Spahn at their best.

In 1963, Koufax threw 11 shutouts, the best ever for a left-hander. He had four no-hitters (1962, 1963, 1964, 1965) and one perfect game, September 5, 1965. For five seasons, 1962 to 1966, he led the National League in earned run average; his 1966 ERA of 1.73 was the lowest ever in his twelve-year career.

Then, before anyone realized it, it was all over. A shocked audience listened in disbelief when in November 1966 Sandy Koufax sadly announced his retirement from baseball. He was only thirty years old and at the height of a brilliant career, a career dramatically cut short by Sandy Koufax himself.

The young basketball player from Brooklyn who wanted to become an architect after college but ended up as one of baseball's best pitchers didn't want the chronic arthritis in his pitching elbow to cripple him for life.

"I don't regret the twelve seasons I've had in baseball," Koufax told reporters, "but I could regret one season too many."

Five years later, Sandy Koufax became the youngest man ever to be selected to the Hall of Fame.

AT THE PLATE

Key Dates in Batting

1846: Alexander J. Cartwright organized a committee and laid down the basic rules of baseball. Nine men per team, 90 feet between bases, and three outs per inning.

1858: Pitching distance is designated at 45 feet. Strikes are introduced to the game, and four strikes equal an out.

1862: The first player to die from batting is reported.

The remains of the late James P. Creighton, familiar in baseball and cricket circles as one of the best players in the Union, were yesterday conveyed to their last resting place, followed by large numbers of friends and relatives. The circumstances of his death are very touching. In the late match with the Unions (Tuesday last) the deceased sustained an internal injury occasioned by strain while batting. After suffering for a few days he expired on Saturday afternoon last at the residence of his father, 307 Henry Street. 21 years, 7 months, and 2 days.

—Brooklyn *Eagle*
October 20, 1862

1863: Balls and strikes are called during the games.

1870: Switch-hitting first used in a game. On June 14, Robert V. Ferguson, captain of the Atlantics of Brooklyn, first used this tactic. Normally a right-handed hitter, he switched to bat lefty so he could avoid hitting to George Wright, the Cincinnati Red Stockings shortstop. His lefty single brought in the winning run, and the Atlantics sent the Reds down to their first defeat in two seasons.

1871: A batter could call to the pitcher to throw either a high pitch or a low pitch.

1879: Eight called balls earned a free base.

1880: The square bat was introduced into play by Boston playing-manager Harry Wright. He later discarded it when the bat chipped after not being squarely hit.

1881: The pitcher's box was moved back to 50 feet.

1882: Seven balls equal a walk.

1883: Foul ball caught on the first bounce no longer equals an out.

1884: Pitchers are now allowed to throw overhand; six called balls equal a walk.

Ed Williams of the Chicago White Stockings became the first in baseball to hit three homers in one game. By the end of the season he had 27, only two of which were not hit over the short left-field fence in Chicago's ball park. The record 27 lasted until 1919, when Babe Ruth started to go on his rampage.

1887: Five balls earn a walk, and four strikes equal an out. The strike zone was fixed as being from the top of the batter's shoulders to the bottom of the knees.

1888: Three strikes and you're out.

1889: Four balls and you walk.

1894: Bobby Lowe, Boston second baseman, became the first to hit four home runs in one game.

1895: Due to a surveyor's error, the pitching distance set at 60'0″ was incorrectly read as 60'6″ and has remained so to this day.

1897: Wee Willie Keeler of the Baltimore Spiders hit safely in 44 consecutive games before being shut out on June 18. A lifetime .345 hitter, the five-feet-four-inch slugger coined the phrase "Keep your eyes clear and hit 'em where they ain't" when asked how he hit so well.

1901: A foul ball counts as a strike.

1902: He went for the fences. The final score was 51–3 in a June 15 Texas League game between Corsicana, the winner, and Texarkana. The Sunday "blue laws" prohibited playing in the designated home ball park, so the game was played in a small field in Ennis, Texas. Nig Clark of Corsicana took full advantage of the miniature dimensions and hit 8 home runs that day, personally knocking in 16 runs.

1908: Pitchers could not attempt to alter a new ball that was put into play.

1911: Frank "Home Run" Baker, Philadelphia A's third baseman, had two timely home runs in a World Series game against the New York Giants. Using his favorite 52-ounce bat, "Home Run" led the American League in hitting that season with a league-high 9 home runs. Baker was to hit 82 more four-baggers before retiring after the 1922 season.

1914: The shortest home run in pro baseball: At Washington P^rk in Brooklyn

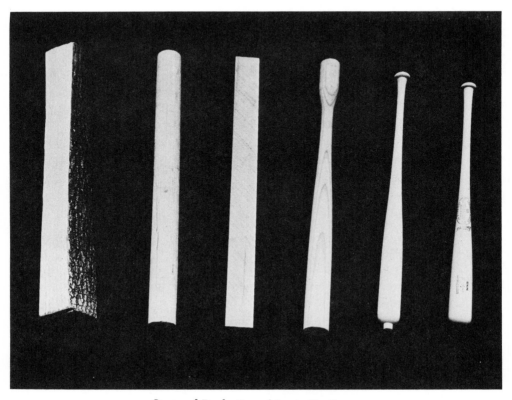

Stages of Production of Louisville Sluggers

a game took place between the Brooklyn Feds and the Chicago Whales, member of the renegade Federal League. Normally, two umpires would officiate at the games, one behind the plate, the other in the field; but because of illness, only one umpire, Bill Brennan, showed up to work the game. Brennan took the field and positioned himself behind the pitcher. From this vantage point he called balls and strikes and watched the action on the base paths. Everything was going well, considering the circumstances, until Brennan tired of having to walk to the dugout to get new balls for use in play. He decided to get around this by piling new balls in pyramid fashion about 70 feet from home plate, between the pitcher's mound and second base. In the fifth inning, Brooklyn catcher Grover Land came to bat. To Brennan's chagrin, Land did the unexpected. He lined a shot right into his neatly stacked baseballs. The balls scattered, the official game ball included, and the infielders scrambled madly for the ball they thought was the game ball. As Land rounded the bases he was tagged many times, eventually by the flustered catcher who also had a "game" ball ready. Ump Brennan was in a quandary, but he quickly resolved the problem. He did not allow any of the tags to count, and Land was given credit for a inside-the-park home run. At 70 feet, this was certainly the shortest homer in the history of baseball!

1919: Joe Wilhoit, who was playing for Seattle in the Pacific Coast League in 1919, was sent to Wichita because of his poor hitting. Wilhoit, either happy to be away or angry at being traded, went on a hitting spree that lasted for 69 consecutive games. From June 14 to August 19, Joe Wilhoit collected 151 hits for his 299 times at bat (505 average) before he was finally cooled off on August 20.

1922: It was August 24 in the Windy City, and the Phillies were in town to tangle with the Cubs. The Cubs led at the top of the ninth 26–23 (this *is* baseball we're talking about), but the Phils had bases loaded and were threatening to score. In came 215-pound rookie reliever Tiny Osborne to shut out the Phils, and he did just that. He struck out Bevo LeBouvreau and retired the sides. On that late summer day, the two teams scored more runs than any other two teams in modern baseball. Their record 51 hits in a nine-inning game has yet to be equaled.

1933: Joe DiMaggio, eighteen-year-old player for the San Francisco Seals, hit safely in 61 games from May 28 to July 25, going 104 for 257 at bat (.405 average). Later, with the New York Yankees in 1941, DiMaggio hit in 56 consecutive games, a major-league record that will be difficult for anyone to top.

1953: At the bottom of the seventh inning, the hometown Boston Red Sox sent 23 batters up, and they proceeded to rap three Detroit Tiger pitchers for a total of 14 hits. They were issued 6 walks and scored an amazing 17 runs in that inning. Outfielder Gene Stephens was credited with 3 hits and catcher Sammy White scored 3 runs, both setting major league records for their inning of play. Yes, for their efforts Boston won the game that day.

1965: On January 7, Tony Conigliaro, the Boston Red Sox hotshot, was no longer a teenager, but he left a record that future teenage major-leaguers may find hard to break. Conigliaro had hit 24 home runs by his twentieth birthday. He was the darling of the Sox and their hope for the future. Sadly, on February 24, 1972, it all came to an end. Conigliaro announced his retirement from baseball due to a serious eye problem stemming from an August 1967 beaning that left him almost blind in one eye. He ended his career with 164 homers.

1974: Hank Aaron, the Atlanta Braves star who broke Babe Ruth's career home run record when he hit No. 715 on April 28, 1974, seemed to like Dodger pitching. His record-breaker came off Al Downing of Los Angeles, but the most during his career came from Dodger hurler Don Drysdale. In the 14 seasons that he faced the burly pitcher, Aaron banged him for 17 of his round-trippers.

Since 1900, only eight major-leaguers have hit .400 or better. Ted Williams, who performed the feat in 1941 when he hit .406 for the season, was the last to break the barrier.

NATIONAL LEAGUE	AMERICAN LEAGUE
Rogers Hornsby (3 times), Saint Louis Browns	Ty Cobb (3 times), Detroit
1922: .401	1911: .420
1924: .424	1912: .410
1925: .403	1922: .401
George Sisler (2 times), Saint Louis Browns	Harry Heilmann, Detroit
1920: .407	1923: .403
1922: .420	Joe Jackson, Cleveland
Bill Terry, New York Giants	1908: .408
1930: .401	Nap Lajoie, Philadelphia
	1901: .422
	Ted Williams, Boston
	1941: .406

Bats

Some players believe that a bat contains a certain number of hits, and they discard it immediately when they reach that quota. And certain players will use only one model, while others are known to switch continually, looking for the right combination of wood and balance that will boost their batting average, maintain their sanity, and keep them in the big leagues.

The bat has always been a ballplayer's meal ticket. Thus, much lore and legend has sprung up about this finely sculpted wooden club. For more than twenty-five seasons, Eddie Collins always used a bat of half-red and half-white timber. This was his trademark, and his .333 lifetime batting average became his Hall of Fame statistic. Red Sox star Ted Williams was so finicky about his bats that he would travel annually to the Hillerich and Bradsby Company in Louisville, Kentucky, and spend hours going through the lumber stacks looking for pieces of wood with the narrowest grain. Only from the wood that Williams personally selected would the bats be made. With a lifetime average of .344, and the last one in the major leagues to hit over .400 for a season, Williams must have learned something about the special attraction of horsehide to wood that no player since has been able to understand.

Al "Bucketfoot" Simmons, Most Valuable Player of the American League in 1922, was a lifetime .334 hitter who would also go to Louisville for his bats. Unlike Williams, Simmons would go through the lumberyard looking for wood with the widest grain. Hugh Duffy, a .330 lifer and a .438 slugger in 1894, was perhaps the most difficult batter to make happy in Louisville. The workers at Bud Hillerich's company would first have to bounce the wood off the concrete floor. If had a certain ring to it, Duffy would allow it to be used for his bats.

From Wee Willie Keeler's special 30½-inch bat to Babe Ruth and his preference for bats with small pin knots in the barrel, the Hillerich and Bradsby Company of Louisville, Kentucky, the maker of the world-famous Louisville Sluggers, has been meeting the needs of organized baseball for almost a century. But things might have turned out differently if Bud Hillerich's father had had his way. He wanted his son to make more salable and practical items instead of wasting his time with baseball. This was probably due in part to his Old World German heritage.

When J. Frederich Hillerich was eight years old, he emigrated from Germany to America with his parents. Hillerich quickly adapted to American ways, and as a teenager growing up in Louisville, Kentucky, he found work as an apprentice to a woodturner. By 1859, he was a twenty-five-year-old shop owner who ran his own wood-turning business right in the family house. Increasing de-

Bat-turning and Bat-branding Then and Now

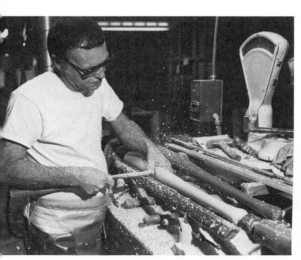

mands for his quality work forced him to find a larger building to house his company, and so he ended up in a shop near the Ohio River.

Fourteen-year-old Bud Hillerich was just out of grade school when he joined his father's company as an apprentice. He learned how to make bowling balls and pins, bedposts, handrails, and outdoor ornamental trappings that helped dress up the stately Louisville mansions.

Louisville was like other American cities of the era; it had its own baseball team in the American Association, the major leagues of early baseball. With hard-hitting Pete "The Gladiator" Browning in the lineup, Louisville was one of the powers in the league, and local interest was very high.

One day during the 1884 season, Bud Hillerich was at a game in which Browning snapped his favorite bat. Instilled with the idea of helping the local star, Hillerich cornered Browning after the game and personally offered to make a new bat for him at his father's shop.

Browning was surprised by the offer, but he was desperately in need of a bat for the following day's game and went along with the eighteen-year-old craftsman. He was panic-stricken at the thought of having broken his best bat. These were not the days when you just called over to the batboy to bring out a new bat. In baseball's early times, bats were precious objects; each bat was hand-crafted, often by the individual player, and they were therefore highly valued.

Hillerich selected a piece of timber, and, with Browning watching closely, stating now and then his personal preferences on the dimensions, Hillerich proceeded to turn out his first bat. The following day, Browning swung the custom-made bat and, according to legend, went 3 for 3.

Hillerich senior, of course, was not infused with his son's new-found zeal in turning the family company into a bat-making concern. He didn't feel that making bats for players of a "mere game" was a serious endeavor. After all, there were swinging churns (those simple wooden devices that took the back-breaking pain out of churning butter) to be turned out. Even though his father was to win out, Bud Hillerich continued to fill orders for bats from the local players, taking mental notes on their preferences with regard to weight, length, and styling.

By 1894, Hillerich reached his first plateau. The name "Louisville Slugger" was trademarked that year and branded on all bat barrels Hillerich produced. This was in addition to the player's signature, which Hillerich always included. Up until this time, players could identify their bats only by their carved initials on the bat knob or barrel, and this often led not only to confusion over ownership but also to fights.

The Louisville Slugger ended all this trouble. Now, in addition to offering a quality custom bat, each player could know which bat was his.

Such stars of the day as Pete Browning, Wee Willie Keeler, John McGraw, Honus Wagner, and Cap Anson started to use Hillerich's bats exclusively. Wagner, who was one of baseball's foremost shortstops, played for Louisville in 1897 and came to know Hillerich very well. They kept up their friendship even when Wagner went on to star for Pittsburgh from 1900 to 1917. In 1905, Wagner signed a contract with his friend granting permission to use his autograph on Louisville Slugger bats that were sold in sporting-goods stores around the country. By doing so, Wagner became the first in the now long line of pro athletes to cash in on his name and popularity through endorsement advertising.

Four future Hall-of-Famers soon followed suit: Nap Lajoie (Cleveland), 1905; Ty Cobb (Detroit), 1908; Eddie Collins (Philadelphia), 1910; and Frank "Home Run" Baker (Philadelphia), 1911.

At the turn of the century, as baseball started to grow and gain in popularity, so did Bud Hillerich's company. Bats became big business, and the entire process of making a bat—from taking the wood from the forest, making it into a bat, and putting it into the player's hands in the ball park—was carefully mapped out by Hillerich. Since hickory and Cuban timber was favored by early batters because of its denseness (heavy bats were in vogue), tree scouts were sent to look for that wood exclusively. Later, when lighter bats became more popular, the scouts were sent to the northern regions, especially to Pennsylvania and the Adirondack Mountains of New York, to look for white ash, a wood known for its light weight, moisture content, and strength.

Today, as in the past, after a section of forest has been selected for cutting, the trees are felled, the trunks cut, and the wood taken to the sawmill. At the mill they are cut into bolts 40 inches long, and after being split and graded according to durability and straightness of grain, they are shipped to Hillerich and Bradsby's Slugger Park timber yards in Jeffersonville, Indiana, just across the river from Louisville. After being air cured for at least eight months, the wood is ready to be made into a potential home-run club.

Bud Hillerich died in 1946 at the age of eighty, but the company that bears his name still carries on his fine tradition of serving the sluggers of baseball. Over five thousand different autograph bats are currently in use in organized baseball, and in the tradition of Browning, Wagner, and Cobb, today's hitters use their Louisville Sluggers and aim for the farthest fences.

Balls

You can't play without them.

The ball must not weigh less than 5¼ ounces avoirdupois. It must measure not less than nine nor more than 9¼ inches in circumference. It must be composed of india-rubber and yarn and covered with leather. The quantity of rubber used in the composition of the ball shall be one ounce.
—November 30, 1870, *Guidelines of*
The National Association of Baseball Players

Mostly Oddball Facts . . .

1876: A. G. Spalding Company became the official supplier of baseballs to the National League. Prior to this, many pitchers made their own baseballs for use in the game.

1900: A. G. Spalding became the official supplier of balls to the American League (under the A. J. Reach label).

1906: ALLENTOWN, PA.

A sad fatality occurred at Catasauqua, not far from this city, on August 21, in a game of semi-professional ball. Casper Musselman, aged 19, catcher of the Lehigh University team, was [batting] for Catasauqua in a contest with the All-Phillipsburg Club, when a curved ball struck him in the left breast over the heart. He immediately started off towards first base on a run, and when within a few feet of the base faltered and then-fell. Within half an hour he had died from the effect of the blow. Kane, the Phillipsburg pitcher who delivered the ball, is suffering a nervous collapse and will probably never touch a baseball again. *Sporting Life*, Sept. 8, 1906

SHAMOKIN, PA.

Reuben Walt, aged thirty years, was killed in a ball game at Herndon today by a thrown ball accidentally crushing his skull, as he was running to first base. *Sporting Life*, June 23, 1906

1908: Listed among the baseball casualties for the 1908 season by *Sporting Life* was Christopher Bergaman of Cincinnati, who was killed when a baseball exploded.

1920: On August 17, Roy Chapman, the popular Cleveland Indian shortstop and perpetual plate-crowder, was struck in the head by a ball pitched by Yankee hurler Carl Mays. No one is certain whether the taciturn Mays threw intentionally at Chapman in order to move him from the plate or

Seasoning Bats

Billets in Seasoning Sheds

whether the ball was scuffed and accidentally "sailed." From the sound of the ball's impact, Mays first thought the ball had hit Chapman's bat, so he ran in for the ball and threw it to first base to get the out; but Chapman's skull had been fractured. He died later in a hospital, the only active major-league player to be killed from a baseball-related injury. Mays, often accused of throwing at batters in the past, received several death threats after Chapman's death. A movement was started to have him barred from baseball, but it soon fizzled out. Batting helmets did not become mandatory in the majors until 1958!

1928: Pitchers have been known to throw the ball intentionally at the opposing batter, either out of revenge or on instruction from the manager. These pitchers have been called headhunters, barbers, or just "crazy s.o.b.'s" Most pitchers would never admit to throwing at a batter, saying instead that the ball "sailed" or "got out of control."

One man whose pitches certainly got out of control was Boston Braves reliever Ray "Lefty" Boggs. Boggs stayed in the majors for only one season, appearing in four games. His appearance for the Braves on September 27 was his adieu. Entering the game in the ninth inning against the Chicago Cubs, Ray Boggs hit the first three batters he faced, thus tying the major-league record for the most hit batters in one inning. He was mercifully yanked before he could break the record. A case of nerves? Poor pitching form? No one knows for sure. Ray Boggs never pitched again in the major leagues, and the batters breathed a collective sigh of relief.

Four other pitchers, most recently Wilbur Wood (September 10, 1977), have equaled Boggs's dubious distinction for inaccuracy. It is hoped that no one will try to top the mark.

1942: A shy twenty-one-year-old rookie from Buffalo, New York, showed up at manager Casey Stengel's Boston Braves spring training camp. The six-footer worked hard under Stengel, but the "Ole Perfesser" was not too impressed. What spelled the young hopeful's immediate disfavor was an incident in an exhibition game with the Brooklyn Dodgers. The young man was on the mound for the Braves and received direct orders from Stengel that he was to brush back Pee Wee Reese, the Dodgers' shortstop, who was crowding the plate. Three times the pitcher refused to throw at Reese. Finally Stengel could stand it no longer. He rushed out to the mound and yanked his pitcher out of the game. "You've got no guts," he growled at him.

Casey was a bit off on his judgment that day and would live long enough to see his "gutless" pitcher inducted into the Hall of Fame three

Official American League Baseball

Spalding Baseball Advertisement

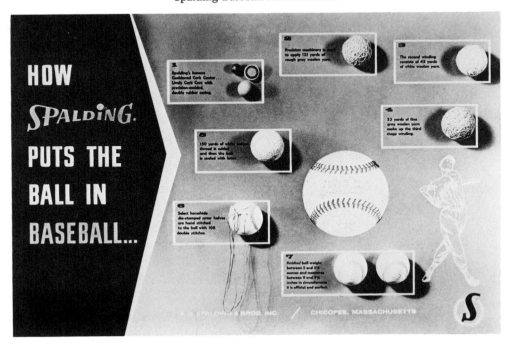

decades later in 1973. The young man's name was Warren Spahn, and he notched 100 or more strikeouts for 17 consecutive seasons in the National League. Along with his 2,583 career strikeout total are two no-hitters and 363 lifetime wins. Warren Spahn remains one of the best pitchers in the history of the game. "You can't say I don't miss 'em when I miss 'em," said a humble Casey Stengel.

1971: Ron Hunt, Montreal Expo second baseman, broke the long-standing and unwanted (for obvious reasons) record of Hugh Jennings by being hit by a pitched ball 50 times in one season. Hunt, who even got hit by the pitching machine in practice, leads all major leaguers in the unenviable category of "hit by pitch." His twelve seasons, 1963 to 1974, were marked by bruises, scrapes, pain, and hospital visits, and he was awarded 243 trips to first base by getting there the hard way—being hit by a pitch.

The Rawlings Sporting Goods Company of Saint Louis, a company bought by A. G. Spalding in 1955 and divested by government order thirteen years later, began manufacturing major league balls with the Reach label on them.

1974: Spalding caused a stir in the major leagues when they substituted cowhide covers on baseballs for the original horsehide. The company claimed the cowhide was as durable and less expensive; major-leaguers complained that some of the covers fell off when they were hit solidly with a bat.

1976: Spalding was dropped by both leagues as the official supplier of baseballs, due to a rejection of a "modest" price increase on the company's baseballs. Over 250,000 baseballs had been used annually at a cost of $2 per ball.

1977: Rawlings Sporting Goods Company became the official supplier of baseballs after Spalding was dropped. The ball, now made of American parts, is assembled by hand in Haiti, where each of the 108 stitches is sewn by workers paid $1.50 an hour.

The Specifications of an American League Baseball

1. Cushion cork center consisting of composition cork sphere surrounded by one black layer and one red layer of rubber ⅞ ounce.
2. Approximately 121 yards of 4/11 blue-gray woolen yard to make the circumference 7¾ inches and the weight 2⅞ ounces.
3. Approximately 45 yards of 3/11 white woolen yarn to make the circumference 8 3/16 inches and weight approximately 3 11/16 ounces.

4. Approximately 53 yards of 3/11 blue-gray woolen yarn to make the circumference 8¾ inches and weight approximately 4¼ ounces.

5. Approximately 150 yards 20/2-ply fine cotton yarn to make the circumference 8⅞ inches and the weight 4½ to 4⅝ ounces.

6. Yarn used, with the exception of cotton finishing yarn, to be 99 percent wool, 1 percent other fibers; of the wool, 75 percent to be virgin wool, and 24 percent reprocessed.

7. Coating of special rubber cement.

8. Special alum-tanned leather is sewn with a double stitch of 10/5 red thread. Weight of the cover is to be ½ to 9/16 ounces. Thickness can be .045 to .055 inches; the whole to make the size 9 to 9¼ inches and weight 5 to 5¼ ounces. The size of the ball shall be measured by a steel tape in gradations of one tenth of an inch, with two pounds tension applied to the tape, measuring twice over two seams and once over four seams, and thereafter averaging three measurements, which shall establish the size of the ball.

9. When tested on an indoor driving machine (machine to be approved by the president of the American League) to determine and measure the resiliency of baseballs through the coefficient of restitution with an initial velocity of 85 feet per second, the rebound of velocity shall be 54.6 percent of the initial velocity, with a tolerance of 3.2 percent plus or minus of said initial velocity. NOTE: Eighty-five feet per second is determined to be approximately equal to the velocity of a baseball which after being hit by a bat would carry 400 feet.

OUTFIELDERS

Dead Men Never Lie

The 1925 World Series between the National League pennant winners, the Pittsburgh Pirates, and the Washington Senators, the victors of the 1924 Series, was one in which the playing of two men was particularly outstanding. One player, Max "Scoops" Carey, was to earn baseball immortality in his lifetime for his Series work. The second man, Sam Rice, was badgered throughout his life by a certain play he made in the 1925 Series; he was vindicated only after his death, forty-nine years after the game.

Pittsburgh outfielder Scoops Carey was known for his clever baserunning and his incredible ability to steal at will. Although his .295 lifetime batting average is more than respectable, his .458 batting (11 for 24) for Pittsburgh in the 1925 Series was spectacular.

Carey had four hits in the seventh and final game, tagging the aging Walter Johnson for three doubles and a single. Had they given a game ball to the best player, it should have gone to Carey, the man with two broken ribs who led his team to a 9–7 victory over the Senators in the last game and a 4–3 sweep of the Series. Max Carey's performance is considered exemplary in World Series play. He overcame great physical pain and adversity, rose to meet the ultimate baseball challenge, and conquered.

Edgar Charles "Sam" Rice, the Senators' outfielder, also rose to meet the challenge. This was Rice's second Series (he played in the Senators' 1924 victory and would also play in 1933), but even though he would hit .302 in fifteen Series games, his one disputed play in the 1925 Series stands out and perhaps tints everything else he was to do in baseball. Did he catch the ball in the third game of the Series or didn't he? That's what everybody wanted to know, and that's what Sam Rice refused to talk about.

The day was October 10. The games were split evenly at one apiece, and the Senators were in their home park for the first time to play the third game. By the top of the eighth inning, they held a slim lead over the challenging Pirates. Firpo Mayberry was on the mound for the Senators. Mayberry was a bit weak-armed that season on the mound with Washington, but despite his record he was pitching confidently and he retired the first two batters.

Catcher Earl "Oil" Smith was the next man up for Pittsburgh. This temperamental slugger from Hot Springs, Arkansas, would break the jaw of Boston Braves manager Dave Bancroft two years later. Smith had a successful season in 1925, hitting .313. If the Bucs could count on anyone to break the deadlock it was the hard-hitting Smith.

The Pirates were not disappointed when Oil lashed into Mayberry's pitch and sent it on its way arching toward the temporary bleachers set up in right field. As the infielders turned and watched, they saw that Sam Rice was the last Senator who stood between the ball and what was sure to be a home run.

Rice took off in a sprint toward the bleachers, took one desperate lunge at the ball, and then cartwheeled over into the stands, disappearing from view. Charles Rigler, the umpire who followed the entire play, called Smith out, but the disbelieving Pirates stormed from the dugout, protesting his decision. They claimed that partisan Senator spectators had put the ball in Rice's glove or that Rice had picked the ball up himself when he was in the stands. Rice remained mute on the subject except to say, "The ump called it an out."

The controversy surrounding the disputed catch by Rice raged throughout the Series, stoked both by Pirate players and by their supporters, who didn't want to see Rice's disputed catch cause the Pirates to lose the Series. Thanks to Scoops Carey's heroic efforts in the final game, the Pirates were able to hold on and win in a thriller. Sam Rice was still not to be forgotten, however.

Did he or didn't he catch the ball? Rice, who had a 31-game consecutive hitting streak in 1924 and who currently holds the American League record he set in 1925 for most singles in a season (182), retired from baseball in 1934 after nineteen years in the major leagues. He still refused to say any more than "the ump called it an out."

In 1963, Rice was elected to the Hall of Fame. A couple of years later, while on a visit to baseball's shrine in Cooperstown, friends persuaded him to settle the matter of the disputed catch once and for all. Rice finally agreed. He sat down and wrote a letter telling exactly what happened. His letter was then sealed in an envelope, and it was agreed that it would not be opened until after his death. When Sam Rice, a lifetime .322 hitter, died on October 13, 1974, at the age of eighty-four, the long-awaited truth would finally be revealed. Dead men carry no secrets.

Monday, July 26, 1965

It was a cold and windy day. The right-field bleachers were crowded with people in overcoats and wrapped in blankets. The ball was a line drive headed for the bleachers toward right center. I turned slightly to my right and had the ball in view all the way. Going at top speed, and about fifteen feet from the bleachers, I jumped as high as I could and backhanded, and the ball hit the center of the pocket in the glove (I had a death grip on it). I hit the ground about five feet from a barrier about four feet high in front of the bleachers with all the brakes on. I couldn't stop, so I tried to jump it to land in the crowd, but my feet hit the barrier about a foot from the top and I toppled over on my stomach into the first row of bleachers. I hit my adam's apple on something which sort of knocked me out for a few seconds, but McNeely arrived about that time and grabbed me by the shirt and pulled me out. I remember trotting back toward the infield still carrying the ball for about halfway and then tossed it toward the pitcher's mound. (How I have wished many times I had kept it.)

At no time did I lose possession of the ball.

"Sam" Rice

P.S. After this was announced at the dinner last night I approached Bill McKechnie (one of the finest men that I have ever known in baseball) and I said, "Bill, you were the manager of Pittsburgh at that time. What do you think will be in the letter?" His answer was, "Sam, there was never any doubt in my mind that you caught the ball."

I thanked him as much to say, you were right.

S. Rice

During the week that Tyrus Raymond Cobb first broke into the major leagues, his mother blasted his father's head off with a fusillade of shotgun pellets. Young Cobb was never the same again.

Cold, calculating, incredible, amazing, compulsive, crazy. Cobb was the first player elected to the Hall of Fame, falling only four votes shy of a unanimous selection.

Dedicated, determined, mean, combative. No one will ever approach his lifetime mark of 4,191 hits.

Battling, pugnacious, psychotic, hotheaded, crazy, cruel. Although he didn't have many friends on the team, in 1912 his Detroit Tiger teammates went out on strike when Cobb was "unjustly" suspended for attacking a spectator in the stands in New York. Cobb claimed the man was calling him names.

Selfish, egotistical, hateful, hated. Ty Cobb would take the postage stamps from prestamped and addressed letters that admiring autograph-seeking fans had sent. Cobb would use the stamps for his own correspondence.

Crafty, quick, clever, fiery. He led the American League five times in runs scored, and hit over .400 three separate times, winning twelve batting titles during his career.

Hot-tempered, fanatical, possessed, intimidating, feared, disliked, despised. Cobb ruled the American League for twenty-two seasons while with Detroit and for two more with Philadelphia. Today he still remains the all-time leader with a lifetime batting average of .367. In each season, except one, he batted over .300.

Bad loser, unsportsmanlike, brutal, savage, short-tempered, unkind, incomparable, unequaled, peerless, one-of-a-kind, the best: Ty Cobb.

Ty Cobb's Wild Ten-Month Fight to Live
by Al Stump

Ever since sundown the Nevada inter-mountain radio had been crackling warnings: "Route 50 now highly dangerous. Motorists stay off. Repeat: *Avoid Route 50.*"

By 1 in the morning the 21-mile, steep-pitched passage from Lake Tahoe's 7,000 feet into Carson City, a snaky grade most of the way, was snow-struck, ice-sheeted, thick with rock slides and declared unfit for all transport vehicles by the State Highway Patrol.

Such news was right down Ty Cobb's alley. Anything that smacked of the impossible brought an unholy gleam to his eye. The gleam had been there in 1959 when a series of lawyers advised Cobb that he stood no chance against the sovereign State of California in a dispute over income taxes, whereupon he bellowed defiance and sued the commonwealth for $60,000 and damages. It had been there more recently when doctors warned that liquor would kill him. From a pint of whiskey per day he upped his consumption to a quart and more.

Sticking out his chin, he told me, "I think we'll take a little run into town tonight."

A blizzard rattled the windows of Cobb's luxurious hunting lodge on the crest of Lake Tahoe, but to forbid him anything—even at the age of seventy-three—was to tell an ancient tiger not to snarl. Cobb was both the greatest of all ballplayers and a multimillionaire whose monthly income from stock dividends, rents and interest ran to $12,000. And he was a man contemptuous, all his life, of any law other than his own.

"We'll drive in," he announced, "and shoot some craps, see a show and say hello to Joe DiMaggio; he's in Reno at the Riverside Hotel."

I looked at him and felt a chill. Cobb, sitting there haggard and unshaven in his pajamas and a fuzzy old green bathrobe at 1 o'clock in the morning, wasn't fooling.

"Let's not," I said. "You shouldn't be anywhere tonight but in bed."

"Don't argue with me!" he barked. "There are fee-simple sonsofbitches all over the country who've tried it and wish they hadn't." He glared at me, flaring the whites of his eyes the way he'd done for twenty-four years to quaking pitchers, basemen, umpires and fans.

"If you and I are going to get along," he went on ominously, *"don't increase my tension."*

We were alone in his isolated ten-room $75,000 lodge, having arrived six days earlier, loaded with a large smoked ham, a 20-pound turkey, a case of Scotch and another of champagne, for purposes of collaborating on Ty's book-length autobiography—a book which he'd refused to write for thirty years, but then suddenly decided to place on record before he died. In almost a week's time we hadn't accomplished thirty minutes of work.

The reason: Cobb didn't need a risky auto trip into Reno, but immediate hospitalization, and by the emergency-door entrance. He was desperately ill and had been even before we'd left California.

We had traveled 250 miles to Tahoe in Cobb's black Imperial limousine, carrying with us a virtual drugstore of medicines. These included Digoxin (for his leaky heart), Darvon (for his aching back), Tace (for a recently-operated-upon malignancy of the pelvic area), Fleet's compound (for his infected bowels), Librium (for his "tension," that is, his violent rages), codeine (for his pain) and an insulin needle-and-syringe kit (for his diabetes), among a dozen other panaceas which he'd substituted for doctors. Cobb despised the medical profession.

At the same time, his sense of balance was almost gone. He tottered about the lodge, moving from place to place by grasping the furniture. On any public street, he couldn't navigate 20 feet without clutching my shoulder, leaning most of his 208 pounds upon me and shuffling along at a spraddle-legged gait. His bowels wouldn't work: they impacted, repeatedly, an almost total stoppage which brought moans of agony from Cobb when he sought relief. He was feverish, with no one at his Tahoe hideaway but the two of us to treat this dangerous condition.

Everything that hurts had caught up with his big, gaunt body at once and he stuffed himself with pink, green, orange, yellow and purple pills—guessing at the amounts, often, since labels had peeled off many of the bottles. But he wouldn't hear of hospitalizing himself.

"The hacksaw artists have taken $50,000 from me," he said, "and they'll get no more." He spoke of "a quack" who'd treated him a few years earlier. "The joker got funny and said he found urine in my whiskey. I fired him."

Ty Cobb

His diabetes required a precise food-insulin balance. Cobb's needle wouldn't work. He'd misplaced the directions for the needed daily insulin dosage and his hands shook uncontrollably when he went to plunge the needle into a stomach vein. He spilled more of the stuff than he injected.

He'd been warned by experts from Johns Hopkins to California's Scripps Clinic that liquor was deadly. Tyrus snorted and began each day with several gin-and-orange-juices, then switched to Old Rarity Scotch, which held him until the night hours, when sleep was impossible, and he tossed down cognac, champagne or "Cobb Cocktails"—Southern Comfort stirred into hot water and honey.

A careful diet was essential. Cobb wouldn't eat. The lodge was without a cook or manservant—since, in the previous six months, he had fired two cooks, a male nurse and a handyman in fits of anger—and any food I prepared for him he pushed away. As of the night of the blizzard, the failing, splenetic old king of ballplayers hadn't touched food in three days, existing solely on quarts of booze and booze mixtures.

My reluctance to prepare the car for the Reno trip burned him up. He beat his fists on the arms of his easy chair. "I'll go alone," he threatened.

It was certain he'd try it. The storm had worsened, but once Cobb set his mind on an idea, nothing could change it. Beyond that I'd already found that to oppose or annoy him was to risk a violent explosion. An event of a week earlier had proved *that* point. It was then I discovered that he carried a loaded Luger wherever he went and looked for opportunities to use it.

En route to Lake Tahoe, we'd stopped overnight at a motel near Hangtown, California. During the night a party of drunks made a loud commotion in the parking lot. In my room next to Cobb's, I heard him cursing and then his voice, booming out the window.

"Get out of here, you ———heads!"

The drunks replied in kind. Then everyone in the motel had his teeth jolted.

Groping his way to the door, Tyrus the Terrible fired three shots into the dark that resounded like cannon claps. There were screams and yells. Reaching my door, I saw the drunks climbing each other's backs in their rush to flee. The frightened motel manager, and others, arrived. Before anyone could think of calling the police, the manager was cut down by the most caustic tongue ever heard in a baseball clubhouse.

"What kind of a pest house is this?" roared Cobb. "Who gave you a license, you mugwump? Get the hell out of here and see that I'm not disturbed! I'm a sick man and I want it quiet!"

"B-b-beg your pardon, Mr. Cobb," the manager said feebly. He apparently felt so honored to have baseball's greatest figure as a customer that no police were called. When we drove away the next morning, a crowd gathered and stood gawking with open mouths.

Down the highway, with me driving, Cobb checked the Luger and re-loaded its nine-shell clip. "Two of those shots were in the air," he remarked. "The *third* kicked up gravel. I've got permits for this gun from governors of three states. I'm an honorary deputy sheriff of California and a Texas Ranger. So we won't be getting any complaints."

He saw nothing strange in his behavior. Ty Cobb's rest had been dis-turbed—therefore he had every right to shoot up the neighborhood.

About then I began to develop a twitch of the nerves, which grew worse with time. In past years, I'd heard reports of Cobb's weird and violent ways, without giving them much credence. But until 1960 my own experience with the legendary Georgian had been slight, amounting only to meetings in Scotts-dale, Arizona, and New York to discuss book-writing arrangements and to sign the contract.

Locker-room stories of Ty's eccentricities, wild temper, ego and miserli-ness sounded like the usual scandalmongering you get in sports. I'd heard that Cobb had flattened a heckler in San Francisco's Domino Club with one punch; he'd been sued by Elbie Felts, an ex-Coast League player, after assaulting Felts; that he boobytrapped his Spanish villa at Atherton, California, with high-voltage wires; that he'd walloped one of his ex-wives; that he'd been jailed in Placerville, California, at the age of sixty-eight for speeding, abusing a traffic cop and then inviting the judge to return to law school at his, Cobb's expense.

I passed these things off. The one and only Ty Cobb was to write his memoirs and I felt highly honored to be named his collaborator.

As the poet Cowper reflected, "The innocents are gay." I was eager to start. Then—a few weeks before book work began—I was taken aside and tipped off by an in-law of Cobb's and one of Cobb's former teammates with the Detroit Tigers that I hadn't heard the half of it. "Back out of this book deal," they urged. "You'll never finish it and you might get hurt."

They went on: "Nobody can live with Ty. Nobody ever has. That includes two wives who left him, butlers, housekeepers, chauffeurs, nurses and a few mis-tresses. He drove off all his friends long ago. Max Fleischmann, the yeast-cake heir, was a pal of Ty's until the night a house guest of Fleischmann's made a re-mark about Cobb spiking other players when he ran the bases. The man only asked if it was true. Cobb knocked the guy into a fish pond and after that Max never spoke to him again. Another time, a member of Cobb's family crossed him—a woman, mind you. He broke her nose with a ball bat.

"Do you know about the butcher? Ty didn't like some meat he bought. In the fight, he broke up the butcher shop. Had to settle $1,500 on the butcher out of court."

"But I'm dealing with him strictly on business," I said.

"So was the butcher," replied my informants. "In baseball, a few of us who really knew him well realized that he was wrong in the head—unbalanced. He played like a demon and had everybody hating him because he *was* a demon. That's how he set all those records that nobody has come close to since 1928. It's why he was always in a brawl, on the field, in the clubhouse, behind the stands and in the stands. The public's never known it, but Cobb's always been off the beam where other people are concerned. Sure, he made millions in the stock market—but that's only cold business. He carried a gun in the big league and scared hell out of us. He's mean, tricky and dangerous. Look out he doesn't blow up some night and clip you with a bottle. He specializes in throwing bottles.

"Now that he's sick he's worse than ever. And you've signed up to stay with him for months. You poor sap."

Taken aback, but still skeptical, I launched the job—with my first task to drive Cobb to his Lake Tahoe retreat, where, he declared, we could work uninterrupted.

As indicated, nothing went right from the start. The Hangtown gunplay incident was an eye-opener. Next came a series of events, such as Cobb's determination to set forth in a blizzard to Reno, which were too strange to explain away. Everything had to suit his pleasure or he had a tantrum. He prowled about the lodge at night, suspecting trespassers, with the Luger in hand. I slept with one eye open ready to move fast if necessary.

At 1 o'clock of the morning of the storm, full of pain and 90-proof, he took out the Luger, letting it casually rest between his knees. I had continued to object to a Reno excursion in such weather.

He looked at me with tight fury and said, biting out the words: "In 1912—and you can write this down—I killed a man in Detroit. He and two other hoodlums jumped me on the street early one morning with a knife. I was carrying something that came in handy in my early days—a Belgian-made pistol with a heavy raised sight at the barrel end.

"Well, the damned gun wouldn't fire and they cut me up the back."

Making notes as fast as he talked, I asked, "Where in the back?"

"Well, dammit all to hell, if you don't believe me, come and look!" Cobb flared, jerking up his shirt. When I protested that I believed him implicitly, only wanted a story detail, he picked up a half-full whiskey glass and smashed it against the brick fireplace. So I gingerly took a look. A faint whitish scar ran about five inches up the lower left back.

"Satisfied?" jeered Cobb.

He described how, after a battle, the men fled before his fists.

"What with you wounded and the odds three to one," I said, "that must have been a relief."

"Relief? Do you think they could pull that on *me*? *I went after them!*"

Where anyone else would have felt lucky to be out of it, Cobb chased one of the mugs into a dead-end alley. "I used that gunsight to rip and slash and tear him for about ten minutes until he had no face left," related Ty, with relish. "Left him there, not breathing, in his own rotten blood."

"What was the situation—where were you going when it happened?"

"To catch a train to a ball game."

"You saw a doctor, instead?"

"*I did nothing of the sort, dammit! I played the next day and got two hits in three times up!*"

Records I later inspected bore out every word of it: on June 3, 1912, in a blood-soaked, makeshift bandage, Ty Cobb hit a double and triple for Detroit, and only then was treated for the knife wound. He was that kind of ball player through a record 3,033 games. No other player burned with Cobb's flame. Boze Bulger, a great old-time baseball critic, said, "He was possessed by the Furies."

Finishing his tale, Cobb looked me straight in the eye.

"*You're driving with me into Reno tonight,*" he said softly. The Luger was in his hand.

Even before I opened my mouth, Cobb knew he'd won. He had a sixth sense about the emotions he produced in others: in this case, fear. As far as I could see (lacking expert diagnosis and as a layman understands the symptoms), he wasn't merely erratic and trigger-tempered, but suffering from megalomania, or acute self-worship; delusions of persecution; and more than a touch of dipsomania.

Although I'm not proud of it, he scared hell out of me most of the time I was around him.

And now he gave me the first smile of our association. "As long as you don't aggravate my tension," he said, "we'll get along."

Before describing the Reno expedition, I would like to say in this frank view of a mighty man that the greatest, and strangest, of all American sport figures had his good side, which he tried to conceal. During the final ten months of his life I was his one constant companion. Eventually, I put him to bed, prepared his insulin, picked him up when he fell down, warded off irate taxi drivers, bartenders, waiters, clerks and private citizens whom Cobb was inclined to punch, cooked what food he could digest, drew his bath, got drunk with him and knelt with him in prayer on black nights when he knew death was near. I ducked a few bottles he threw, too.

I think, because he forced upon me a confession of his most private thoughts, that I knew the answer to the central, overriding secret of his life: was Ty Cobb psychotic throughout his baseball career?

Kids, dogs and sick people flocked to him and he returned their instinctive liking. Money was his idol, but from his $4-million fortune he assigned large sums to create the Cobb Educational Foundation, which financed hundreds of needy youngsters through college. He built and endowed a first-class hospital for the poor of his backwater home town, Royston, Georgia. When Ty's spinster sister, Florence, was crippled, he tenderly cared for her until her last days. The widow of a onetime American League batting champion would have lived in want but for Ty's steady money support. A Hall of Fame member, beaned by a pitched ball and enfeebled, came under Cobb's wing for years. Regularly he mailed dozens of anonymous checks to indigent old ballplayers (relayed by a third party)—a rare act among retired tycoons in other lines of business.

If you believe such acts didn't come hard for Cobb, guess again: he was the world's champion pinchpenny.

Some 150 fan letters reached him each month, requesting his autograph. Many letters enclosed return-mail stamps. Cobb used the stamps for his own outgoing mail. The fan letters he burned.

"Saves on firewood," he'd mutter.

In December of 1960, Ty hired a one-armed "gentleman's gentleman" named Brownie. Although constantly criticized, poor Brownie worked hard as cook and butler. But when he mixed up the grocery order one day, he was fired with a check for a week's pay—$45—and sent packing.

Came the middle of that night and Cobb awakened me.

"We're driving into town *right now*," he stated, "to stop payment on Brownie's check. The bastard talked back to me when I discharged him. He'll get no more of my money."

All remonstrations were futile. There was no phone, so we had to drive the 20 miles from Cobb's Tahoe lodge into Carson City, where he woke up the president of the First National Bank of Nevada and arranged for a stop-pay on the piddling check. The president tried to conceal his anger—Cobb was a big depositor in his bank.

"Yes, sir, Ty," he said, "I'll take care of it first thing in the morning."

"You goddamn well better," snorted Cobb. And then we drove through the 3 A.M. darkness back to the lake.

But this trip was a light workout compared to that Reno trip.

Two cars were available at the lodge. Cobb's 1956 Imperial had no tire chains, but the other car did.

"We'll need both for this operation," he ordered. "One car might get stuck or break down. I'll drive mine and you take the one with chains. You go first. I'll follow your chain marks."

For Cobb to tackle precipitous Route 50 was unthinkable in every way. The Tahoe road, with 200-foot drop-offs, has killed a recorded eighty motorists. Along with his illness, his drunkenness, and no chains, he had bad eyes and was without a driver's license. California had turned him down at his last test; he hadn't bothered to apply in Nevada.

Urging him to ride with me was a waste of breath.

A howling wind hit my car a solid blow as we shoved off. Sleet stuck to the windshield faster than the wipers could work. For the first three miles, snowplows had been active and at 15 mph, in second gear, I managed to hold the road. But then came Spooner's Summit, 7,000 feet high, and then a steep descent of nine miles. Behind me, headlamps blinking, Cobb honked his horn, demanding more speed. Chainless, he wasn't getting any traction. *The hell with him,* I thought. Slowing to first gear, fighting to hold a roadbed I couldn't see even with my head stuck out the window, I skidded along. No other traffic moved as we did our crazy tandem around icy curves, at times brushing the guardrails. Cobb was blaring his horn steadily now.

And then here came Cobb.

Tiring of my creeping pace, he gunned the Imperial around me in one big skid. I caught a glimpse of an angry face under a big Stetson hat and a waving fist. He was doing a good 30 mph when he'd gained 25 yards on me, fishtailing right and left, but straightening as he slid out of sight in the thick sleet.

I let him go. Suicide wasn't in my contract.

The next six miles was a matter of feeling my way and praying. Near a curve, I saw tail-lights to the left. Pulling up, I found Ty swung sideways and buried, nose down, in a snowbank, his hind wheels two feet in the air. Twenty yards away was a sheer drop-off into a canyon.

"You hurt?" I asked.

"Bumped my ——— head," he muttered. He lit a cigar and gave four-letter regards to the Highway Department for not illuminating the "danger" spot. His forehead was bruised and he'd broken his glasses.

In my car, we groped our way down-mountain, a nightmare ride, with Cobb alternately taking in Scotch from a thermos jug and telling me to step on it. At 3 A.M. in Carson City, an all-night garageman used a broom to clean the car of snow and agreed to pick up the Imperial—"when the road's passable."

With dawn breaking, we reached Reno. All I wanted was a bed and all Cobb wanted was a craps table.

He was rolling now, pretending he wasn't ill, and with the Scotch bracing him, Ty was able to walk into the Riverside Hotel casino with a hand on my shoulder and without staggering so obviously as usual. Everybody present wanted to meet him. Starlets from a film unit on location in Reno flocked around and comedian Joe E. Lewis had the band play "Sweet Georgia Brown"—Ty's favorite tune.

"Hope your dice are still honest," he told Riverside co-owner Bill Miller. "Last time I was here I won $12,000 in three hours."

"How I remember, Ty," said Miller. "How I remember."

A scientific craps player who'd won and lost huge sums in Nevada in the past, Cobb bet $100 chips, his eyes alert, not missing a play around the board. He soon decided that the table was "cold" and we moved to another casino, then a third. At this last stop, Cobb's legs began to grow shaky. Holding himself up by leaning on the table edge with his forearms, he dropped $300, then had a hot streak in which he won over $800. His voice was a croak as he told the other players, "Watch 'em and weep."

But then suddenly his voice came back. When the stickman raked the dice his way, Cobb loudly said, "You touched the dice with your hand."

"No, sir," said the stickman. "I did *not*."

"I don't lie," snarled Cobb.

"I don't lie either," insisted the stickman.

"Nobody touches my dice!" Cobb, swaying on his feet, eyes blazing, worked his way around the table toward the croupier. It was a weird tableau. In his crumpled Stetson and expensive camel's-hair coat, stained and charred with cigarette burns, a three-day beard grizzling his face, the gaunt old giant of baseball towered over the dapper gambler.

"You fouled the dice, I saw you," growled Cobb, and then he swung.

The blow missed, as the stickman dodged, but, cursing and almost falling, Cobb seized the wooden rake and smashed it over the table. I jumped in and caught him under the arms as he sagged.

And then, as quickly as possible, we were put into the street by two large uniformed guards. "Sorry, Mr. Cobb," they said, unhappily, "but we can't have this."

A crowd had gathered and as we started down the street, Cobb swearing and stumbling and clinging to me, I couldn't have felt more conspicuous if I'd been strung naked from the neon arch across Reno's main drag, Virginia Street. At the street corner, Ty was struck by an attack of breathlessness. "Got to stop," he gasped. Feeling him going limp on me, I turned his six-foot body against a lamppost, braced my legs and with an underarm grip held him there until he caught his breath. He panted and gulped for air.

His face gray, he murmured, "Reach into my left-hand coat pocket." Thinking he wanted his bottle of heart pills, I did, but instead pulled out a six-inch-thick wad of currency, secured by a rubber band. "Couple of thousand there," he said weakly. "Don't let it out of sight."

At the nearest motel, where I hired a single, twin-bed room, he collapsed on the bed in his coat and hat and slept. After finding myself some breakfast, I turned in. Hours later I heard him stirring. "What's this place?" he muttered.

I told him the name of the motel—Travelodge.

"Where's the bankroll?"

"In your coat. You're wearing it."

Then he was quiet.

After a night's sleep, Cobb felt well enough to resume his gambling. In the next few days, he won more than $3,000 at the tables, and then we went sightseeing in historic Virginia City. There as in all places, he stopped traffic. And had the usual altercation. This one was at the Bucket of Blood, where Cobb accused the bartender of serving watered Scotch. The bartender denied it. Crash! Another drink went flying.

Back at the lodge a week later, looking like the wrath of John Barleycorn and having refused medical aid in Reno, he began to suffer new and excruciating pains—in his hips and lower back. But between groans he forced himself to work an hour a day on his autobiography. He told inside baseball tales never published:

". . . Frank Navin, who owned the Detroit club for years, faked his turnstile count to cheat the visiting team and Uncle Sam. So did Big Bill Devery and Frank Farrell, who owned the New York Highlanders—later called the Yankees.

". . . Walter Johnson, the Big Train, tried to kill himself when his wife died.

". . . Grover Cleveland Alexander wasn't drunk out there on the mound, the way people thought—he was an epileptic. Old Pete would fall down with a seizure between innings, then go back and pitch another shutout.

". . . John McGraw hated me because I tweaked his nose in broad daylight in the lobby of the Oriental Hotel, in Dallas, after earlier beating the hell out of his second baseman, Buck Herzog, upstairs in my room."

But before we were well started, Cobb suddenly announced we'd go riding in his 23-foot Chris-Craft speedboat, tied up in a boathouse below the lodge. When I went down to warm it up, I found the boat sunk to the bottom of Lake Tahoe in 15 feet of water.

My host broke all records for blowing his stack when he heard the news.

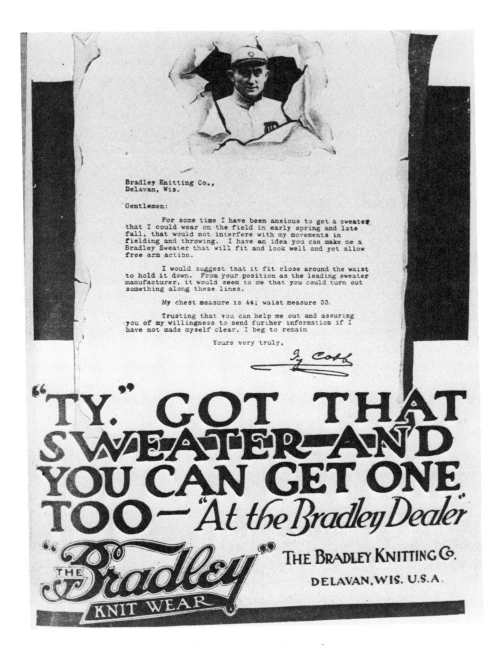

Ty Cobb Bradley Knit Wear Advertisement

He saw in this a sinister plot. "I told you I've got enemies all around here! It's sabotage as sure as I'm alive."

A sheriff's investigation turned up no clues. Cobb sat up all night for three nights with his Luger. "I'll salivate the first dirty skunk who steps foot around here after dark," he swore.

Parenthetically, Cobb had a vocabulary all his own. To "salivate" something meant to destroy it. Anything easy was "soft-boiled," to outsmart someone was to "slip him the oskafagus," and all doctors were "truss-fixers." People who displeased him—and this included almost everyone he met—were "fee-simple sonsofbitches," "mugwumps" or (if female) "lousy slits."

Lake Tahoe friends of Cobb's had stopped visiting him long before, but one morning an attractive blonde of about fifty came calling. She was an old chum—in a romantic way, I was given to understand, of bygone years—but Ty greeted her coldly. "Lost my sexual powers when I was sixty-nine," he said, when she was out of the room. "What the hell use to me is a woman?"

The lady had brought along a three-section electric vibrator bed, which she claimed would relieve Ty's back pains. We helped him mount it. He took a twenty-minute treatment. Attempting to dismount, he lost balance, fell backward, the contraption jackknifed and Cobb was pinned, yelling and swearing, under a pile of machinery.

When I freed him and helped him to a chair, he told the lady—in the choicest gutter language—where she could put her bed. She left, sobbing.

"That's no way to talk to an old friend, Ty," I said. "She was trying to do you a favor."

"And you're a hell of a poor guest around here, too!" he thundered. "You can leave any old time!" He quickly grabbed a bottle and heaved it in my direction.

"Thought you could throw straighter than that!" I yelled back.

Fed up with him, I started to pack my bags. Before I'd finished, Cobb broke out a bottle of vintage Scotch, said I was "damned sensitive," half apologized, and the matter was forgotten.

While working one morning on an outside observation deck, I heard a thud inside. On his bedroom floor, sprawled on his back, lay Ty. He was unconscious, his eyes rolled back, breathing shallowly. I thought he was dying.

There was no telephone. "Eavesdroppers on the line," Cobb had told me. "I had it cut off." I ran down the road to a neighboring lodge and phoned a Carson City doctor, who promised to come immediately.

Back at the lodge, Ty remained stiff and stark on the floor, little bubbles escaping his lips. His face was bluish-white. With much straining, I lifted him halfway to the bed and by shifting holds finally rolled him onto it, and covered him with a blanket. Twenty minutes passed. No doctor.

Ten minutes later, I was at the front door, watching for the doctor's car, when I heard a sound. There stood Ty, swaying on his feet. "You want to do some work on the book?" he said.

His recovery didn't seem possible. "But you were just out cold a minute ago," I said.

"Just a dizzy spell. Have 'em all the time. Must have hit my head on the bedpost when I fell."

The doctor, arriving, found Cobb's blood pressure standing at a grim 210 on the gauge. His temperature was 101 degrees and from gross neglect of his diabetes, he was in a state of insulin shock, often fatal if not quickly treated. "I'll have to hospitalize you, Mr. Cobb," said the doctor.

Weaving his way to a chair, Cobb angrily waved him away. "Just send me your bill," he grunted. "I'm going home."

"Home" was the multimillionaire's main residence at Atherton, California, on the San Francisco Peninsula, 250 miles away, and it was there he headed later that night. With some hot soup and insulin in him, Cobb recovered with the same unbelievable speed he'd shown in baseball. In his heyday, trainers often sewed up deep spike cuts in his knees, shins and thighs, on a clubhouse bench, without anesthetic, and he didn't lose an inning. Grantland Rice one 1920 day sat beside a bedridden, feverish Cobb, whose thighs, from sliding, were a mass of raw flesh. Sixteen hours later, he hit a triple, double, three singles and stole two bases to beat the Yankees. On the Atherton ride, he yelled insults at several motorists who moved too slowly to suit him. Reaching Atherton, Ty said he felt ready for another drink.

My latest surprise was Cobb's eighteen-room, two-story richly landscaped Spanish-California villa at 48 Spencer Lane, an exclusive neighborhood. You could have held a ball game on the grounds.

But the $90,000 mansion had no lights, no heat, no hot water.

"I'm suing the Pacific Gas & Electric Company," he explained, "for overcharging me on the service. Those rinky-dinks tacked an extra $16 on my bill. Bunch of crooks. When I wouldn't pay, they cut off my utilities. Okay—I'll see them in court."

For months previously, Ty Cobb had lived in a totally dark house. The only illumination was candlelight. The only cooking facility was a portable Coleman stove, such as campers use. Bathing was impossible, unless you could take it cold. The electric refrigerator, stove, deepfreeze, radio and television, of course, didn't work. Cobb had vowed to "hold the fort" until his trial of the P.G.&E. was settled. Simultaneously, he had filed a $60,000 suit in San Francisco Superior Court against the State of California to recover state income taxes already collected—on the argument that he wasn't a permanent resident of California, but of Nevada, Georgia, Arizona and other way-points. State's attorneys claimed he spent at least six months per year in Atherton, thus had no case.

"I'm gone so much from here," he claimed, "that I'll win hands down." All legal opinion, I later learned, held just the opposite view, but Cobb ignored their advice.

Next morning, I arranged with Ty's gardener, Hank, to turn on the lawn sprinklers. In the outdoor sunshine, a cold-water shower was easier to take. From then on, the back yard became my regular washroom.

The problem of lighting a desk so that we could work on the book was solved by stringing 200 feet of cord, plugged into an outlet of a neighboring house, through hedges and flower gardens and into the window of Cobb's study, where a single naked bulb hung over the chandelier provided illumination.

The flickering shadows cast by the single light made the vast old house seem haunted. No ghost writer ever had more ironical surroundings.

At various points around the premises, Ty showed me where he'd once installed high-voltage wires to stop trespassers. "Curiosity seekers?" I asked. "Hell, no," he said. "Detectives broke in here once looking for evidence against me in a divorce suit. After a couple of them got burned, they stopped coming."

To reach our bedrooms, Cobb and I groped our way down long, black corridors. Twice he fell in the dark. And then, collapsing completely, he became so ill that he was forced to check in at Stanford Hospital in nearby Palo Alto. Here another shock was in store.

One of the physicians treating Ty's case, a Dr. E. R. Brown, said, "Do you mean to say that this man has traveled 700 miles in the last month without medical care?"

"Doctor," I said, "I've hauled him in and out of saloons, motels, gambling joints, steam baths and snowbanks. There's no holding him."

"It's a miracle he's alive. He has almost every major ailment I know about."

Dr. Brown didn't reveal to me Ty's main ailment, which news Cobb, himself, broke late one night from his hospital bed. "It's cancer," he said, bluntly. "Almost a year ago I had most of my prostate gland removed when they found it was malignant. Now it's spread up into the back bones. These pill-peddlers here won't admit it, but I haven't got a chance."

Cobb made me swear I'd never divulge the fact before he died. "If it gets in the papers, the sob sisters will have a field day. I don't want sympathy from anybody."

At Stanford, where he absorbed seven massive doses of cobalt radiation, the ultimate cancer treatment, he didn't act like a man on his last legs. Even before his strength returned, he was in the usual form.

"They won't let me have a drink," he said indignantly. "I want you to get me a bottle. Smuggle it in in your tape-recorder case."

I tried, telling myself that no man with terminal cancer deserves to be dried up, but sharp-eyed nurses and orderlies were watching. They searched Ty's closet, found the bottle and over his roars of protest appropriated it.

"We'll have to slip them the oskafagus," said Ty.

Thereafter, a drink of Scotch-and-water sat in plain view in his room, on his bedside table, under the very noses of his physicians—and nobody suspected a thing. The whiskey was in an ordinary water glass, and in the liquid reposed Ty's false teeth.

There were no dull moments while Cobb was in the hospital. He was critical of everything. He told one doctor that he was not even qualified to be an intern, and told the hospital dietician—at the top of his voice—that she and the kitchen workers were in a conspiracy to poison him with their "foul" dishes. To a nurse he snapped, "If Florence Nightingale knew about you, she'd spin in her grave."

(Stanford Hospital, incidentally, is one of the largest and top-rated medical plants in the United States.)

But between blasts he did manage to buckle down to work on the book, dictating long into the night into a microphone suspended over his bed. Slowly the stormy details of his professional life came out. He spoke often of having "forgiven" his many baseball enemies, then lashed out at them with such passionate phrases that it was clear he'd done no such thing. High on his "hate" list were McGraw; New York sportswriters; Hub Leonard, a pitcher who in 1926 accused Cobb and Tris Speaker of "fixing" a Detroit-Cleveland game; American League president Ban Johnson; onetime Detroit owner Frank Navin; former Baseball Commissioner Kenesaw Mountain Landis; and all those who intimated that Cobb ever used his spikes on another player without justification.

After a night when he slipped out of the hospital, against all orders, and we drove to a San Francisco Giants–Cincinnati Reds game at Candlestick Park, 30 miles away, Stanford Hospital decided it couldn't help Tyrus R. Cobb, and he was discharged. For extensive treatment his bill ran to more than $1,200.

"That's a nice racket you boys have here," he told the discharging doctors. "You clip the customers and then every time you pass an undertaker, you wink at him."

"Good-bye, *Mr.* Cobb," snapped the medical men.

Soon after this Ty caught a plane to his native Georgia and I went along.

"I want to see some of the old places again before I die," he said.

It now was Christmas Eve of 1960 and I'd been with him for three months and completed but four chapters. The project had begun to look hopeless. In Royston, a village of 1,200, Cobb headed for the town cemetery. I drove him there, we parked, and I helped him climb a windswept hill through the growing dusk. Light snow fell. Faintly, Yule chimes could be heard.

Among the many headstones, Ty looked for the plot he'd reserved for himself while in California and couldn't locate it. His temper began to boil. "Dammit, I ordered the biggest damn mausoleum in the graveyard! I know it's around here somewhere." On the next hill, we found it: a large marble, walk-in-size structure with "Cobb" engraved over the entrance.

"You want to pray with me?" he said gruffly. We knelt and tears came to his eyes.

Within the tomb, he pointed to crypts occupied by the bodies of his father, Professor William Herschel Cobb, his mother, Amanda (Chitwood) Cobb, and his sister Florence, whom he'd had disinterred and placed here. "My father," he said reverently, "was the greatest man I ever knew. He was a scholar, state senator, editor and philosopher. I worshiped him. So did all the people around here. He was the only man who ever made me do his bidding."

Arising painfully, Ty braced himself against the marble crypt that soon would hold his body. There was an eerie silence in the tomb. He said deliberately: "My father had his head blown off with a shotgun when I was eighteen years old—*by a member of my own family.* I didn't get over that. I've never gotten over it."

We went back down the hill to the car. I asked no questions that day.

Later, from family sources and old Georgia friends of the baseball idol, I learned about the killing. One night in August of 1905, they related, Professor Cobb announced that he was driving from Royston to a neighboring village and left home by buggy. But, later that night, he doubled back and crept into his wife's bedroom by way of the window. "He suspected her of being unfaithful to him," said these sources. "He thought he'd catch her in the act. But Amanda Cobb was a good woman. She was all alone when she saw a menacing figure climb through her window and approach her bed. In the dark, she assumed it to be a robber. She kept a shotgun handy by her bed and she used it. Everybody around here knew the story, but it was hushed up when Ty became famous."

News of the killing reached Ty in Augusta, where he was playing minor-league ball, on August 9. A few days later he was told that he'd been purchased by the Detroit Tigers, and was to report immediately. "In my grief," Cobb says in the book, "it didn't matter much. . . ."

Came March of 1961 and I remained stuck to the Georgia Peach like court plaster. He'd decided that we were born pals, meant for each other, that we'd complete a baseball book beating anything ever published. He had astonished doctors by rallying from the spreading cancer and, between bouts of transmitting his life and times to a tape recorder, was raising more whoopee than he had at Lake Tahoe and Reno.

Spring-training time for the big leagues had arrived and we were ensconced in a $30-a-day suite at the Ramada Inn at Scottsdale, Arizona, close by the practice parks of the Red Sox, Indians, Giants and Cubs. Here, each year, Cobb held court. He didn't go to see anybody; Ford Frick, Joe Cronin, Ted Williams, and other diamond notables came to him. While explaining to sportswriters why modern stars couldn't compare to the Wagners, Lajoies, Speakers, Jacksons, Mathewsons and Planks of his day, Ty did other things.

For one, he commissioned a noted Arizona artist to paint him in oils. He was emaciated, having dropped from 208 to 176. The preliminary sketches showed up his sagging cheeks and thin neck.

"I wouldn't let you calcimine my toilet," ripped out Ty, and fired the artist.

But at analyzing the Dow-Jones averages and playing the stock market, he was anything but eccentric. Twice a week he phoned experts around the country, determined good buys and bought in blocks of 500 to 1,500 shares. He made money consistently, even when bedridden, with a mind that read behind the fluctuations of a dozen different issues. "The State of Georgia," Ty remarked, "will realize about one million dollars from inheritance taxes when I'm dead. But there isn't a man alive who knows what I'm worth." According to the *Sporting News*, there was evidence upon Cobb's death that his worth approximated $12 million. Whatever the true figure, he did not confide the amount to me—or, most probably, to anyone except attorneys who drafted his last will and testament. And Cobb fought off making his will until the last moment.

His fortune began in 1908, when he bought into United (later General) Motors; as of 1961, he was "Mr. Coca-Cola," holding more than 20,000 shares of that stock, valued at $85 per share. Wherever we traveled, he carried with him, stuffed into an old brown bag, more than $1 million in stock certificates and negotiable government bonds. The bag never was locked up. Cobb assumed nobody would dare rob him. He tossed the bag into any handy corner of a room, inviting theft. And in Scottsdale it turned up missing.

Playing Sherlock, he narrowed the suspects to a room maid and a man he'd hired to cook meals. When questioned, the maid broke into tears and the cook quit (fired, said Cobb). Hours later, I discovered the bag under a pile of dirty laundry.

Major-league owners and league officials hated to see him coming, for he thought their product was putrid and said so, incessantly. "Today they hit for ridiculous averages, can't bunt, can't steal, can't hit-and-run, can't place-hit to the opposite field and you can't call them ballplayers." He told sportswriters, "I blame Frick, Cronin, Bill Harridge, Horace Stoneham, Dan Topping and others for wrecking baseball's traditional league lines. These days, any tax-dodging mugwump with a bankroll can buy a franchise, field some semipros and get away with it. Where's our integrity? Where's *baseball?*"

No one could quiet Cobb. Who else had a lifetime average of .367, made 4,191 hits, scored 2,244 runs, won 12 batting titles, stole 892 bases, repeatedly beat whole teams singlehandedly? Who was first into the Hall of Fame? Not Babe Ruth—but Cobb, by a landslide vote.

By early April, he could barely make it up the ramp of the Scottsdale Stadium, even hanging onto me. He had to stop, gasping for breath, every few steps. But he kept coming to games—loving the sounds of the ball park. His courage was tremendous. "Always be ready to catch me if I start to fall," he said. "I'd hate to go down in front of the fans."

People of all ages were overcome with emotion upon meeting him; no sports figure I've known produced such an effect upon the public.

We went to buy a cane. At a surgical supply house, Cobb inspected a dozen $25 malacca sticks, bought the cheapest, $4, white-ash cane they had. "I'm a plain man," he informed the clerk, the $7,500 diamond ring on his finger glittering.

But pride kept the old tiger from ever using the cane, any more than he'd wear the $600 hearing aid built into the bow of his glasses.

One day a Mexican taxi driver aggravated Cobb with his driving. Throwing the fare on the ground, he waited until the cabby had bent to retrieve it, then tried to punt him like a football.

"What's your sideline," he inquired, "selling opium?"

It was all I could do to keep the driver from swinging on him. Later, a lawyer called on Cobb, threatening a damage suit. "Get in line, there's five hundred ahead of you," said Tyrus, waving him away.

Every day was a new adventure. He was fighting back against the pain that engulfed him again—cobalt treatments no longer helped—and I could count on trouble anywhere we went. He threw a saltshaker at a Phoenix waiter, narrowly missing. One of his most treasured friendships—with Ted Williams— came to an end.

From the early 1940s, Williams had sat at Ty Cobb's feet. They often met, exchanged long letters on the art of batting. At Scottsdale one day, Williams dropped by Ty's rooms. He hugged Ty, fondly rumpled his hair and accepted a drink. Presently the two greatest hitters of past and present fell into an argument over what players should comprise the all-time, All-Star team. Williams declared, "I want DiMaggio and Hornsby on my team over anybody you can mention."

Cobb's face grew dark. "Don't give me that! Hornsby couldn't go back for a pop fly and he lacked smartness. DiMaggio couldn't hit with Speaker or Joe Jackson."

"The hell you say!" came back Williams jauntily. "Hornsby outhit *you* a couple of years."

Almost leaping from his chair, Cobb shook a fist. He'd been given the insult supreme—for Cobb always resented, and finally hated, Rogers Hornsby. Not until Cobb was in his sixteenth season did Hornsby top him in the batting averages. "Get . . . away from me!" choked Cobb. "Don't come back!"

Williams left with a quizzical expression, not sure how much Cobb meant it. The old man meant it all the way. He never invited Williams back, nor talked to him, nor spoke his name again. "I cross him off," he told me.

We left Arizona shortly thereafter for my home in Santa Barbara, California. Now failing fast, Tyrus had accepted my invitation to be my guest. Two doctors inspected him at my beach house by the Pacific and gave their opinions: he had a few months of life left, no more. The cancer had invaded the bones of his skull. His pain was intense, unrelenting—requiring heavy sedation—yet with teeth bared and sweat pouring down his face, he fought off medical science. "They'll never get me on their damned hypnotics," he swore. "I'll never die an addict . . . an idiot. . . ."

He shouted, "Where's anybody who cares about me? Where are they? The world's lousy . . . no good."

One night later, on May 1, Cobb sat propped up in bed, overlooking a starlit ocean. He had a habit, each night, of rolling up his trousers and placing them under his pillow—an early-century ballplayer's trick, dating from the time when Ty slept in strange places and might be robbed. I knew that his ever-present Luger was tucked into that pants roll.

I'd never seen him so sunk in despair. At last the fire was going out. "Do we die a little at a time, or all at once?" he wondered aloud. "I think Max had the right idea."

The reference was to his onetime friend, multimillionaire Max Fleischmann, who'd cheated lingering death by cancer some years earlier by putting a bullet through his brain. Ty spoke of Babe Ruth, another cancer victim. "If Babe had been told what he had in time, he could've got it over with."

Had I left Ty that night, I believe he would have pulled the trigger. His three living children (two were dead) had withdrawn from him. In the wide world that had sung his fame, he had not one intimate friend remaining.

But we talked, and prayed, until dawn, and then sleep came; in the morning, aided by friends, I put him into a car and drove him home, to the big, gloomy house in Atherton. He spoke only twice during the six-hour drive.

"Have you got enough to finish the book?" he asked.

"More than enough."

"Give 'em the word then. I had to fight all my life to survive. They were against me . . . tried every dirty trick to cut me down. But I beat the bastards and left them in the ditch. Make sure the book says that. . . ."

I was leaving him now, permanently, and I had to ask one question I'd never put to him before.

"Why did you fight so hard in baseball, Ty?"

He'd never looked fiercer than then, when he answered, "I did it for my father, who was an exalted man. They killed him when he was still young. They blew his head off the same week I became a major leaguer. He never got to see me play. But I knew he was watching me and I never let him down."

You can make what you want of that. Keep in mind what Casey Stengel said, later: "I never saw anyone like Cobb. No one even close to him. When he wiggled those wild eyes at a pitcher, you knew you were looking at the one bird nobody could beat. It was like he was superhuman."

To me it seems that the violent death of a father whom a sensitive, highly talented boy loved deeply, and feared, engendered, through some strangely supreme desire to vindicate that father, the most violent, successful, thoroughly maladjusted personality ever to pass across American sports. The shock tipped the eighteen-year-old mind, making him capable of incredible feats.

Off the field, he was still at war with the world. For the emotionally disturbed individual, in most cases, does not change his pattern. To reinforce that pattern, he was viciously hazed by Detroit Tiger veterans when he was a rookie. He was bullied, ostracized and beaten up—in one instance, a 210-pound catcher named Charlie Schmidt broke the 165-pound Ty Cobb's nose. It was persecution immediately heaped upon the deepest desolation a young man can experience.

Yes, Ty Cobb was a badly disturbed personality. It is not hard to understand why he spent his entire life in deep conflict. Nor why a member of his family, in the winter of 1960, told me, "I've spent a lot of time terrified of him . . . I think he was psychotic from the time that he left Georgia to play in the big league."

"Psychotic" is not a word I'd care to use. I believe that he was far more than the fiercest of all competitors. He was a vindicator who believed that "Father was watching" and who could not put that father's terrible fate out of his mind. The memory of it threatened his sanity.

The fact that he recognized and feared this is revealed in a tape recording he made, in which he describes his own view of himself: "I was like a steel spring with a growing and dangerous flaw in it. If it is wound too tight or has the slightest weak point, the spring will fly apart and then it is done for...."

The last time I saw him, he was sitting in his armchair in the Atherton mansion. The place still was without lights or heat. I shook his hand in farewell, and he held it a moment longer.

"What about it. Do you think they'll remember me?" He tried to say it as if it didn't matter.

"They'll always remember you," I said.

On July 8, I received in the mail a photograph of Ty's mausoleum on the hillside in the Royston cemetery with the words scribbled on the back: "*Any time now.*" Nine days later he died in an Atlanta hospital. Before going, he opened the brown bag, piled $1 million in negotiable securities beside his bed and placed the Luger atop them.

From all of major-league baseball, three men and three only appeared for his funeral.

Joe DiMaggio: All-star 11 times, a lifetime .325 hitter. Had 2,214 hits for 6,281 times at bat. Played 1736 games in his fabled career with the New York Yankees. Hit 361 home runs. Held 9 World Series titles. Most Valuable Player in the American League in 1939, 1941, and 1947. His record 56-consecutive-game hitting streak stands as a baseball legend.

"People don't change that much," said author Gay Talese recently when asked about Joe DiMaggio. Although his close-up portrait of the elusive DiMaggio first appeared more than a decade ago, it has not been at all affected by the passage of time. In reality, Talese's subject is not DiMaggio, but Everyman.

The Silent Season of a Hero

by Gay Talese

"I would like to take the great DiMaggio fishing," the old man said. "They say his father was a fisherman. Maybe he was as poor as we are and would understand."

—Ernest Hemingway, *The Old Man and the Sea*

It was not quite spring, the silent season before the search for salmon, and the old fishermen of San Francisco were either painting their boats or repairing their nets along the pier or sitting in the sun talking quietly among themselves, watching the tourists come and go, and smiling, now, as a pretty girl paused to take their picture. She was about twenty-five, healthy and blue-eyed and wearing a red turtle-neck sweater, and she had long, flowing blonde hair that she brushed back a few times before clicking her camera. The fishermen, looking at her, made admiring comments but she did not understand because they spoke a Sicilian dialect; nor did she notice the tall grey-haired man in a dark suit who stood watching her from behind a big bay window on the second floor of Di-Maggio's Restaurant that overlooks the pier.

He watched until she left, lost in the crowd of newly arrived tourists that had just come down the hill by cable car. Then he sat down again at the table in the restaurant, finishing his tea and lighting another cigarette, his fifth in the last half hour. It was eleven-thirty in the morning. None of the other tables was occupied, and the only sounds came from the bar where a liquor salesman was laughing at something the headwaiter had said. But then the salesman, his brief-case under his arm, headed for the door, stopping briefly to peek into the dining room and call out, "See you later, Joe." Joe DiMaggio turned and waved at the salesman. Then the room was quiet again.

At fifty-one, DiMaggio was a most distinguished-looking man, aging as gracefully as he had played on the ball field, impeccable in his tailoring, his nails manicured, his six-foot two-inch body seeming as lean and capable as when he posed for the portrait that hangs in the restaurant and shows him in Yankee Stadium swinging from the heels at a pitch thrown twenty years ago. His grey hair was thinning at the crown, but just barely, and his face was lined in the right places, and his expression, once as sad and haunted as a matador's, was more in repose these days, though, as now, tension had returned and he chain-smoked and occasionally paced the floor and looked out the window at the people below. In the crowd was a man he did not wish to see.

The man had met DiMaggio in New York. This week he had come to San Francisco and had telephoned several times but none of the calls had been returned because DiMaggio suspected that the man, who had said he was doing research on some vague sociological project, really wanted to delve into DiMaggio's private life and that of DiMaggio's former wife, Marilyn Monroe. DiMaggio would never tolerate this. The memory of her death is still very painful to him, and yet, because he keeps it to himself, some people are not sensitive to it. One night in a supper club a woman who had been drinking approached his table, and when he did not ask her to join him, she snapped:

"All right, I guess I'm *not* Marilyn Monroe."

He ignored her remark, but when she repeated it, he replied, barely controlling his anger, "No—I wish you were, but you're not."

The tone of his voice softened her, and she asked, "Am I saying something wrong?"

"You already have," he said. "Now will you please leave me alone?"

His friends on the wharf, understanding him as they do, are very careful when discussing him with strangers, knowing that should they inadvertently betray a confidence he will not denounce them but rather will never speak to them again; this comes from a sense of propriety not inconsistent in the man who also, after Marilyn Monroe's death, directed that fresh flowers be placed on her grave "forever."

Some of the older fishermen who have known DiMaggio all his life remember him as a small boy who helped clean his father's boat, and as a young man who sneaked away and used a broken oar as a bat on the sandlots nearby. His father, a small mustachioed man known as Zio Pepe, would become infuriated and call him *lagnuso,* lazy, *meschino,* good-for-nothing, but in 1936 Zio Pepe was among those who cheered when Joe DiMaggio returned to San Francisco after his first season with the New York Yankees and was carried along the wharf on the shoulders of the fishermen.

The fishermen also remember how, after his retirement in 1951, DiMaggio brought his second wife, Marilyn, to live near the wharf, and sometimes they would be seen early in the morning fishing off DiMaggio's boat, the *Yankee Clipper,* now docked quietly in the marina, and in the evening they would be sitting and talking on the pier. They had arguments, too, the fishermen knew, and one night Marilyn was seen running hysterically, crying as she ran, along the road away from the pier, with Joe following. But the fishermen pretended they did not see this; it was none of their affair. They knew that Joe wanted her to stay in San Francisco and avoid the sharks in Hollywood, but she was confused and torn then—"She was a child," they said—and even today DiMaggio loathes Los Angeles and many of the people in it. He no longer speaks to his onetime friend, Frank Sinatra, who had befriended Marilyn in her final years, and he also is cool to Dean Martin and Peter Lawford and Lawford's former wife, Pat, who once gave a party at which she introduced Marilyn Monroe to Robert Kennedy, and the two of them danced often that night, Joe heard, and he did not take it well. He was very possessive of her that year, his close friends say, because Marilyn and he had planned to remarry; but before they could she was dead, and DiMaggio banned the Lawfords and Sinatra and many Hollywood people from her funeral. When Marilyn Monroe's attorney complained that DiMaggio was keeping her friends away, DiMaggio answered coldly, "If it weren't for those friends persuading her to stay in Hollywood she would still be alive."

Joe DiMaggio now spends most of the year in San Francisco, and each day tourists, noticing the name on the restaurant, ask the men on the wharf if they ever see him. Oh yes, the men say, they see him nearly every day; they have not seen him yet this morning, they add, but he should be arriving shortly. So the tourists continue to walk along the piers past the crab vendors, under the circling sea gulls, past the fish 'n' chips stands, sometimes stopping to watch a large vessel steaming toward the Golden Gate Bridge which, to their dismay, is painted red. Then they visit the Wax Museum, where there is a life-size figure of DiMaggio in uniform, and walk across the street and spend a quarter to peer through the silver telescopes focused on the island of Alcatraz, which is no longer a Federal prison. Then they return to ask the men if DiMaggio has been seen. Not yet, the men say, although they notice his blue Impala parked in the lot next to the restaurant. Sometimes tourists will walk into the restaurant and have lunch and will see him sitting calmly in a corner signing autographs and being extemely gracious with everyone. At other times, as on this particular morning when the man from New York chose to visit, DiMaggio was tense and suspicious.

When the man entered the restaurant from the side steps leading to the dining room he saw DiMaggio standing near the window talking with an elderly maître d' named Charles Friscia. Not wanting to walk in and risk intrusion, the man asked one of DiMaggio's nephews to inform Joe of his presence. When DiMaggio got the message he quickly turned and left Friscia and disappeared through an exit leading down to the kitchen.

Astonished and confused, the visitor stood in the hall. A moment later Friscia appeared and the man asked, "Did Joe leave?"

"Joe who?" Friscia replied.

"Joe DiMaggio!"

"Haven't seen him," Friscia said.

"You haven't *seen* him! He was standing right next to you a second ago!"

"It wasn't me," Friscia said.

"You were standing next to him. I saw you. In the dining room."

"You must be mistaken," Friscia said, softly, seriously. "It wasn't me."

"You *must* be kidding," the man said, angrily, turning and leaving the restaurant. Before he could get to his car, however, DiMaggio's nephew came running after him and said, "Joe wants to see you."

He returned expecting to see DiMaggio waiting for him. Instead he was handed a telephone. The voice was powerful and deep and so tense that the quick sentences ran together.

"*You are invading my rights, I did not ask you to come, I assume you have a lawyer, you must have a lawyer, get your lawyer!*"

"I came as a friend," the man interrupted.

"That's beside the point," DiMaggio said. "I have my privacy, I do not want it violated, you'd better get a lawyer. . . ." Then, pausing, DiMaggio asked, "Is my nephew there?"

He was not.

"Then wait where you are."

A moment later DiMaggio appeared, tall and red-faced, erect and beautifully dressed in his dark suit and white shirt with the grey silk tie and the gleaming silver cuff links. He moved with big steps toward the man and handed him an airmail envelope, unopened, that the man had written from New York.

"Here," DiMaggio said. "This is yours."

Then DiMaggio sat down on a small table. He said nothing, just lit a cigarette and waited, legs crossed, his head held high and back so as to reveal the intricate construction of his nose, a fine sharp tip above the big nostrils and tiny bones built out from the bridge, a great nose.

"Look," DiMaggio said, more calmly. "I do not interfere with other people's lives. And I do not expect them to interfere with mine. There are things about my life, personal things, that I refuse to talk about. And even if you asked my brothers they would be unable to tell you about them because they do not know. There are things about me, so many things, that they simply do not know. . . ."

"I don't want to cause trouble," the man said. "I think you're a great man, and . . ."

"I'm not great," DiMaggio cut in. "I'm not great," he repeated, softly. "I'm just a man trying to get along."

Then DiMaggio, as if realizing that he was intruding upon his own privacy, abruptly stood up. He looked at his watch.

"I'm late," he said, very formal again. "I'm ten minutes late. *You're* making me late."

The man left the restaurant. He crossed the street and wandered over to the pier, briefly watching the fishermen hauling their nets and talking in the sun, seeming very calm and contented. Then, after he had turned and was headed back toward the parking lot, a blue Impala stopped in front of him and Joe DiMaggio leaned out the window and asked, "Do you have a car?" His voice was very gentle.

Joe DiMaggio

"Yes," the man said.

"Oh," DiMaggio said. "I would have given you a ride."

Joe DiMaggio was not born in San Francisco but in Martinez, a small fishing village twenty-five miles northeast of the Golden Gate. Zio Pepe had settled there after leaving Isola delle Femmine, an islet off Palermo where the DiMaggios had been fishermen for generations. But in 1915, hearing of the luckier waters off San Francisco's wharf, Zio Pepe left Martinez, packing his boat with furniture and family, including Joe who was one year old.

San Francisco was placid and picturesque when the DiMaggios arrived, but there was a competitive undercurrent and struggle for power along the pier. At dawn the boats would sail out to where the bay meets the ocean and the sea is rough, and later the men would race back with their hauls, hoping to beat their fellow fishermen to shore and sell it while they could. Twenty or thirty boats would sometimes be trying to gain the channel shoreward at the same time, and a fisherman had to know every rock in the water, and later know every bargaining trick along the shore, because the dealers and restaurateurs would play one fisherman off against the other, keeping the prices down. Later the fishermen became wiser and organized, predetermining the maximum amount each fisherman would catch, but there were always some men who, like the fish, never learned, and so heads would sometimes be broken, nets slashed, gasoline poured onto their fish, flowers of warning placed outside their doors.

But these days were ending when Zio Pepe arrived, and he expected his five sons to succeed him as fishermen, and the first two, Tom and Michael, did; but a third, Vincent, wanted to sing. He sang with such magnificent power as a young man that he came to the attention of the great banker, A. P. Giannini, and there were plans to send him to Italy for tutoring and the opera. But there was hesitation around the DiMaggio household and Vince never went; instead he played ball with the San Francisco Seals and sportswriters misspelled his name.

It was *De*Maggio until Joe, at Vince's recommendation, joined the team and became a sensation, being followed later by the youngest brother, Dominic, who was also outstanding. All three later played in the big leagues and some writers like to say that Joe was the best hitter, Dom the best fielder, Vince the best singer, and Casey Stengel once said: "Vince is the only player I ever saw who could strike out three times in one game and not be embarrassed. He'd walk into the clubhouse whistling. Everybody would be feeling sorry for him, but Vince always thought he was doing good."

After he retired from baseball Vince became a bartender, then a milkman, now a carpenter. He lives forty miles north of San Francisco in a house he partly built, has been happily married for thirty-four years, has four grandchildren, has in the closet one of Joe's tailor-made suits that he has never had altered to fit, and when people ask if he envies Joe he always says, "No, maybe Joe would like to have what I have. He won't admit it, but he just might like to have what I have." The brother Vince most admired was Michael, "a big earthy man, a dreamer, a fisherman who wanted things but didn't want to take from Joe, or to work in the restaurant. He wanted a bigger boat, but wanted to earn it on his own. He never got it." In 1953, at the age of forty-four, Michael fell from his boat and drowned.

Since Zio Pepe's death in 1949, Tom, at sixty-two the oldest brother—two of his four sisters are older—has become nominal head of the family and manages the restaurant that was opened in 1937 as Joe DiMaggio's Grotto. Later Joe sold out his share and now Tom is the co-owner of it with Dominic. Of all the brothers, Dominic, who was known as the "Little Professor" when he played with the Boston Red Sox, is the most successful in business. He lives in a fashionable Boston suburb with his wife and three children and is president of a firm that manufactures fiber-cushion materials and grossed more than $3,500,000 last year.

Joe DiMaggio lives with his widowed sister, Marie, in a tan stone house on a quiet residential street not far from Fisherman's Wharf. He bought the house almost thirty years ago for his parents, and after their death he lived there with Marilyn Monroe; now it is cared for by Marie, a slim and handsome dark-eyed woman who has an apartment on the second floor, Joe on the third. There are some baseball trophies and plaques in the small room off DiMaggio's bedroom, and on his dresser are photographs of Marilyn Monroe, and in the living room downstairs is a small painting of her that DiMaggio likes very much: it reveals only her face and shoulders and she is wearing a very wide-brimmed sun hat, and there is a soft sweet smile on her lips, an innocent curiosity about her that is the way he saw her and the way he wanted her to be seen by others—a simple girl, "a warm bighearted girl," he once described her, "that everybody took advantage of."

The publicity photographs emphasizing her sex appeal often offended him, and a memorable moment for Billy Wilder, who directed her in *The Seven Year Itch,* occurred when he spotted DiMaggio in a large crowd of people gathered on Lexington Avenue in New York to watch a scene in which Marilyn, standing over a subway grating to cool herself, had her skirts blown high by a sudden wind below. "What the hell is going on here?" DiMaggio was overheard to have said in the crowd, and Wilder recalled, "I shall never forget the look of death on Joe's face."

He was then thirty-nine, she was twenty-seven. They had been married in

January of that year, 1954, despite disharmony in temperament and time: he was tired of publicity, she was thriving on it; he was intolerant of tardiness, she was always late. During their honeymoon in Tokyo an American general had introduced himself and asked if, as a patriotic gesture, she would visit the troops in Korea. She looked at Joe. "It's your honeymoon," he said, shrugging, "go ahead if you want to."

She appeared on ten occasions before 100,000 servicemen, and when she returned she said, "It was so wonderful, Joe. You never heard such cheering."

"Yes I have," he said.

Across from her portrait in the living room, on a coffee table in front of a sofa, is a sterling-silver humidor that was presented to him by his Yankee teammates at a time when he was the most talked about man in America, and when Les Brown's band had recorded a hit that was heard day and night on the radio:

> *. . . From Coast to Coast, that's all you hear*
> *Of Joe the One-Man Show*
> *He's glorified the horsehide sphere,*
> *Jolting Joe DiMaggio . . .*
> *Joe . . . Joe . . . DiMaggio . . . we*
> *want you on our side. . . .*

The year was 1941, and it began for DiMaggio in the middle of May after the Yankees had lost four games in a row, seven of their last nine, and were in fourth place, five-and-a-half games behind the leading Cleveland Indians. On May 15th, DiMaggio hit only a first-inning single in a game that New York lost to Chicago, 13–1; he was barely hitting .300, and had greatly disappointed the crowds that had seen him finish with a .352 average the year before and a .381 in 1939.

He got a hit in the next game, and the next, and the next. On May 24th, with the Yankees losing 6–5 to Boston, DiMaggio came up with runners on second and third and singled them home, winning the game, extending his streak to ten games. But it went largely unnoticed. Even DiMaggio was not conscious of it until it had reached twenty-nine games in mid-June. Then the newspapers began to dramatize it, the public became aroused, they sent him good-luck charms of every description, and DiMaggio kept hitting, and radio announcers would interrupt programs to announce the news, and then the song again: "*Joe . . . Joe . . . DiMaggio . . . we want you on our side . . .*"

Sometimes DiMaggio would be hitless his first three times up, the tension would build, it would appear that the game would end without his getting another chance—but he always would, and then he would hit the ball against the left-field wall, or through the pitcher's legs, or between two leaping infielders. In the forty-first game, the first of a double-header in Washington, DiMaggio tied an American League record that George Sisler had set in 1922. But before the second game began a spectator sneaked onto the field and into the Yankees' dugout and stole DiMaggio's favorite bat. In the second game, using another of his bats, DiMaggio lined out twice and flied out. But in the seventh inning, borrowing one of his old bats that a teammate was using, he singled and broke Sisler's record, and he was only three games away from surpassing the major-league record of forty-four set in 1897 by Willie Keeler while playing for Baltimore when it was a National League franchise.

An appeal for the missing bat was made through the newspapers. A man from Newark admitted the crime and returned it with regrets. And on July 2, at Yankee Stadium, DiMaggio hit a home run into the left-field stands. The record was broken.

He also got hits in the next eleven games, but on July 17th in Cleveland, at a night game attended by 67,468, he failed against two pitchers, Al Smith and Jim Bagby, Jr., although Cleveland's hero was really its third baseman, Ken Keltner, who in the first inning lunged to his right to make a spectacular backhanded stop of a drive and, from the foul line behind third base, he threw DiMaggio out. DiMaggio received a walk in the fourth inning. But in the seventh he again hit a hard shot at Keltner, who again stopped it and threw him out. DiMaggio hit sharply toward the shortstop in the eighth inning, the ball taking a bad hop, but Lou Boudreau speared it off his shoulder and threw to the second baseman to start a double play and DiMaggio's streak was stopped at fifty-six games. But the New York Yankees were on their way to winning the pennant by seventeen games, and the World Series too, and so in August, in a hotel suite in Washington, the players threw a surprise party for DiMaggio and toasted him with champagne and presented him with this Tiffany silver humidor that is now in San Francisco in his living room. . . .

Marie was in the kitchen making toast and tea when DiMaggio came down for breakfast; his grey hair was uncombed but, since he wears it short, it was not untidy. He said good morning to Marie, sat down and yawned. He lit a cigarette. He wore a blue wool bathrobe over his pajamas. It was eight A.M. He had many things to do today and he seemed cheerful. He had a conference with the president of Continental Television, Inc., a large retail chain in California of which he is a partner and vice-president; later he had a golf date, and then a big banquet to attend, and, if that did not go on too long and he were not too tired afterward, he might have a date.

Picking up the morning paper, not rushing to the sports page, DiMaggio read the front-page news, the people-problems of '66: Kwame Nkrumah was overthrown in Ghana, students were burning their draft cards (DiMaggio shook his head), the flu epidemic was spreading through the whole state of California. Then he flipped inside through the gossip columns, thankful they did not have him in there today—they had printed an item about his dating "an electrifying airline hostess" not long ago, and they also spotted him at dinner with Dori Lane, "the frantic frugger" in Whiskey à Go Go's glass cage—and then he turned to the sports page and read a story about how the injured Mickey Mantle may never regain his form.

It had all happened so quickly, the passing of Mantle, or so it seemed; he had succeeded DiMaggio as DiMaggio had succeeded Ruth, but now there was no great young power hitter coming up and the Yankee management, almost desperate, had talked Mantle out of retirement; and on September 18, 1965, they gave him a "day" in New York during which he received several thousand dollars' worth of gifts—an automobile, two quarter horses, free vacation trips to Rome, Nassau, Puerto Rico—and DiMaggio had flown to New York to make the introduction before 50,000: it had been a dramatic day, an almost holy day for the believers who had jammed the grandstands early to witness the canonization of a new stadium saint. Cardinal Spellman was on the committee, President Johnson sent a telegram, the day was officially proclaimed by the Mayor of New York, an orchestra assembled in center field in front of the trinity of monuments to Ruth, Gehrig, Huggins; and high in the grandstands, billowing in the breeze of early autumn, were white banners that read: "Don't Quit Mick," "We Love the Mick."

The banners had been held by hundreds of young boys whose dreams had been fulfilled so often by Mantle, but also seated in the grandstands were older men, paunchy and balding, in whose middle-aged minds DiMaggio was still vivid and invincible, and some of them remembered how one month before, during a pre-game exhibition at Old-timer's Day in Yankee Stadium, DiMaggio had hit a pitch into the left-field seats, and suddenly thousands of people had jumped wildly to their feet, joyously screaming—the great DiMaggio had returned, they were young again, it was yesterday.

But on this sunny September day at the Stadium, the feast day of Mickey Mantle, DiMaggio was not wearing No. 5 on his back nor a black cap to cover his greying hair; he was wearing a black suit and white shirt and blue tie, and he stood in one corner of the Yankees' dugout waiting to be introduced by Red Barber, who was standing near home plate behind a silver microphone. In the outfield Guy Lombardo's Royal Canadians were playing soothing soft music; and moving slowly back and forth over the sprawling green grass between the left-field bullpen and the infield were two carts driven by groundskeepers and

containing dozens of large gifts for Mantle—a six-foot, one-hundred-pound He-
brew National salami, a Winchester rifle, a mink coat for Mrs. Mantle, a set of
Wilson golf clubs, a Mercury 95-horsepower outboard motor, a Necchi portable,
a year's supply of Chunky Candy. DiMaggio smoked a cigarette, but cupped it
in his hands as if not wanting to be caught in the act by teen-aged boys near
enough to peek down into the dugout. Then, edging forward a step, DiMaggio
poked his head out and looked up. He could see nothing above except the
packed towering green grandstands that seemed a mile high and moving, and
he could see no clouds or blue sky, only a sky of faces. Then the announcer
called out his name—"*Joe DiMaggio!*"—and suddenly there was a blast of
cheering that grew louder and louder, echoing and reechoing within the big
steel canyon, and DiMaggio stomped out his cigarette and climbed up the dugout steps and onto the soft green grass, the noise resounding in his ears. He could
almost feel the breeze, the breath of 50,000 lungs upon him, 100,000 eyes
watching his every move and for the briefest instant as he walked he closed his
eyes.

Then in his path he saw Mickey Mantle's mother, a smiling elderly woman wearing an orchid, and he gently reached out for her elbow, holding it as he
led her toward the microphone next to the other dignitaries lined up on the infield. Then he stood, very erect and without expression, as the cheers softened
and the Stadium settled down.

Mantle was still in the dugout, in uniform, standing with one leg on the
top step, and lined on both sides of him were the other Yankees who, when the
ceremony was over, would play the Detroit Tigers. Then into the dugout, smiling, came Senator Robert Kennedy, accompanied by two tall curly-haired young
assistants with blue eyes, Fordham freckles. Jim Farley was the first on the field
to notice the Senator, and Farley muttered, loud enough for others to hear,
"Who the hell invited *him*?"

Toots Shor and some of the other committeemen standing near Farley
looked into the dugout, and so did DiMaggio, his glance seeming cold, but he remaining silent. Kennedy walked up and down within the dugout shaking hands
with the Yankees, but he did not walk onto the field.

"Senator," said the Yankees' manager, Johnny Keane, "why don't you sit
down?" Kennedy quickly shook his head, smiled. He remained standing, and
then one Yankee came over and asked about getting relatives out of Cuba, and
Kennedy called over one of the aides to take down the details in a notebook.

On the infield the ceremony went on, Mantle's gifts continued to pile
up—a Mobilette motor bike, a Sooner Schooner wagon barbecue, a year's supply
of Chock Full O'Nuts coffee, a year's supply of Topps Chewing Gum—and the
Yankee players watched, and Maris seemed glum.

"Hey, Rog," yelled a man with a tape recorder, Murray Olderman, "I want to do a thirty-second tape with you."

Maris swore angrily, shook his head.

"It'll only take a second," Olderman said.

"Why don't you ask Richardson? He's a better talker than me."

"Yes, but the fact that it comes from you . . ."

Maris swore again. But finally he went over and said in an interview that Mantle was the finest player of his era, a great competitor, a great hitter.

Fifteen minutes later, standing behind the microphone at home plate, DiMaggio was telling the crowd, "I'm proud to introduce the man who succeeded me in center field in 1951," and from every corner of the Stadium the cheering, whistling, clapping came down. Mantle stepped forward. He stood with his wife and children, posed for the photographers kneeling in front. Then he thanked the crowd in a short speech, and, turning, shook hands with the dignitaries standing nearby. Among them now was Senator Kennedy, who had been spotted in the dugout five minutes before by Red Barber, and been called out and introduced. Kennedy posed with Mantle for a photographer, then shook hands with the Mantle children, and with Toots Shor and James Farley and others. DiMaggio saw him coming down the line and at the last second he backed away, casually, hardly anybody noticing it, and Kennedy seemed not to notice it either, just swept past shaking more hands . . . .

Finishing his tea, putting aside the newspaper, DiMaggio went upstairs to dress, and soon he was waving good-bye to Marie and driving toward his business appointment in downtown San Francisco with his partners in the retail television business. DiMaggio, while not a millionaire, has invested wisely and has always had, since his retirement from baseball, executive positions with big companies that have paid him well. He also was among the organizers of the Fisherman's National Bank of San Francisco last year, and, though it never came about, he demonstrated an acuteness that impressed those businessmen who had thought of him only in terms of baseball. He has had offers to manage big-league baseball teams but always has rejected them, saying, "I have enough trouble taking care of my own problems without taking on the responsibilities of twenty-five ballplayers."

So his only contact with baseball these days, excluding public appearances, is his unsalaried job as a batting coach each spring in Florida with the New York Yankees, a trip he would make once again on the following Sunday, three days away, if he could accomplish what for him is always the dreaded responsibility of packing, a task made no easier by the fact that he lately has fallen into the habit of keeping his clothes in two places—some hang in his closet at home, some hang in the back room of a saloon called Reno's.

Reno's is a dimly-lit bar in the center of San Francisco. A portrait of Di-Maggio swinging a bat hangs on the wall, in addition to portraits of other star athletes, and the clientele consists mainly of the sporting crowd and newspapermen, people who know DiMaggio quite well and around whom he speaks freely on a number of subjects and relaxes as he can in few other places. The owner of the bar is Reno Barsocchini, a broad-shouldered and handsome man of fifty-one with greying wavy hair who began as a fiddler in Dago Mary's tavern thirty-five years ago. He later became a bartender there and elsewhere, including Di-Maggio's Restaurant, and now he is probably DiMaggio's closest friend. He was the best man at the DiMaggio-Monroe wedding in 1954, and when they separated nine months later in Los Angeles, Reno rushed down to help DiMaggio with the packing and drive him back to San Francisco. Reno will never forget the day.

Hundreds of people were gathered around the Beverly Hills home that DiMaggio and Marilyn had rented, and photographers were perched in the trees watching the windows, and others stood on the lawn and behind the rose bushes waiting to snap pictures of anybody who walked out of the house. The newspapers that day played all the puns—"Joe Fanned on Jealousy"; "Marilyn and Joe—Out at Home"—and the Hollywood columnists, to whom DiMaggio was never an idol, never a gracious host, recounted instances of incompatibility, and Oscar Levant said it all proved that no man could be a success in two national pastimes. When Reno Barsocchini arrived he had to push his way through the mob, then bang on the door for several minutes before being admitted. Marilyn Monroe was upstairs in bed, Joe DiMaggio was downstairs with his suitcases, tense and pale, his eyes bloodshot.

Reno took the suitcases and golf clubs out to DiMaggio's car, and then Di-Maggio came out of the house, the reporters moving toward him, the lights flashing.

"Where are you going?" they yelled. "I'm driving to San Francisco." he said, walking quickly.

"Is that going to be your home?"

"That *is* my home and always has been."

"Are you coming back?"

DiMaggio turned for a moment, looking up at the house.

"No," he said, "I'll never be back."

Reno Barsocchini, except for a brief falling out over something he will not discuss, has been DiMaggio's trusted companion ever since, joining him whenever he can on the golf course or on the town, otherwise waiting for him in the bar with other middle-aged men. They may wait for hours sometimes, waiting

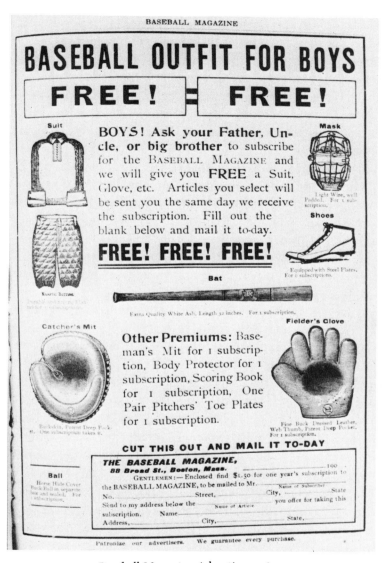

Baseball Magazine Advertisement

and knowing that when he arrives he may wish to be alone; but it does not seem to matter, they are endlessly awed by him, moved by the mystique, he is a kind of male Garbo. They know that he can be warm and loyal if they are sensitive to his wishes, but they must never be late for an appointment to meet him. One man, unable to find a parking place, arrived a half-hour late once and DiMaggio did not talk to him again for three months. They know, too, when dining at night with DiMaggio, that he generally prefers male companions and occasionally one or two young women, but never wives; wives gossip, wives complain, wives are trouble, and men wishing to remain close to DiMaggio must keep their wives at home.

When DiMaggio strolls into Reno's bar the men wave and call out his name, and Reno Barsocchini smiles and announces, "Here's the Clipper!" the "Yankee Clipper" being a nickname from his baseball days.

"Hey, Clipper, Clipper," Reno had said two nights before, "where you been, Clipper? . . . Clipper, how 'bout a belt?"

DiMaggio refused the offer of a drink, ordering instead a pot of tea, which he prefers to all other beverages except before a date, when he will switch to vodka.

"Hey, Joe," a sportswriter asked, a man researching a magazine piece on golf, "Why is it that a golfer, when he starts getting older, loses his putting touch first? Like Snead and Hogan, they can still hit a ball well off the tee, but on the greens they lose the strokes . . ."

"It's the pressure of age," DiMaggio said, turning around on his bar stool. "With age you get jittery. It's true of golfers, it's true of any man when he gets into his fifties. He doesn't take chances like he used to. The younger golfer, on the greens, he'll stroke his putts better. The older man, he becomes hesitant. A little uncertain. Shaky. When it comes to taking chances the younger man, even when driving a car, will take chances that the older man won't."

"Speaking of chances," another man said, one of the group that had gathered around DiMaggio, "did you see that guy on crutches in here last night?"

"Yeah, had his leg in a cast," a third said. "Skiing."

"I would never ski," DiMaggio said. "Men who ski must be doing it to impress a broad. You see these men, some of them forty, fifty, getting onto skis. And later you see them all bandaged up, broken legs . . ."

"But skiing's a very sexy sport, Joe. All the clothes, the tight pants, the fireplace in the ski lodge, the bear rug—Christ, nobody goes to ski. They just go out there to get it cold so they can warm it up . . ."

"Maybe you're right," DiMaggio said. "I might be persuaded."

"Want a belt, Clipper?" Reno asked.

DiMaggio thought for a second, then said, "All right—first belt tonight."

Now it was noon, a warm sunny day. DiMaggio's business meeting with the television retailers had gone well; he had made a strong appeal to George Shahood, president of Continental Television, Inc., which has eight retail outlets in Northern California, to cut prices on color television sets and increase the sales volume, and Shahood had conceded it was worth a try. Then DiMaggio called Reno's bar to see if there were any messages, and now he was in Lefty O'Doul's car being driven along Fisherman's Wharf toward the Golden Gate Bridge en route to a golf course thirty miles upstate. Lefty O'Doul was one of the great hitters in the National League in the early Thirties, and later he managed the San Francisco Seals when DiMaggio was the shining star. Though O'Doul is now sixty-nine, eighteen years older than DiMaggio, he nevertheless possesses great energy and spirit, is a hard-drinking, boisterous man with a big belly and a roving eye; and when DiMaggio, as they drove along the highway toward the golf club, noticed a lovely blonde at the wheel of a car nearby and exclaimed, "Look at *that* tomato!" O'Doul's head suddenly spun around, he took his eyes off the road, and yelled, "Where, *where?*" O'Doul's golf game is less than what it was—he used to have a two-handicap—but he still shoots in the 80's, as does DiMaggio.

DiMaggio's drives range between 250 and 280 yards when he doesn't sky them, and his putting is good, but he is distracted by a bad back that both pains him and hinders the fullness of his swing. On the first hole, waiting to tee off, DiMaggio sat back watching a foursome of college boys ahead swinging with such freedom. "Oh," he said with a sigh, "to have *their* backs."

DiMaggio and O'Doul were accompanied around the golf course by Ernie Nevers, the former football star, and two brothers who are in the hotel and movie-distribution business. They moved quickly up and down the green hills in electric golf carts, and DiMaggio's game was exceptionally good for the first nine holes. But then he seemed distracted, perhaps tired, perhaps even reacting to a conversation of a few minutes before. One of the movie men was praising the film *Boeing, Boeing*, starring Tony Curtis and Jerry Lewis, and the man asked DiMaggio if he had seen it.

"No," DiMaggio said. Then he added, swiftly, "I haven't seen a film in eight years."

DiMaggio hooked a few shots, was in the woods. He took a No. 9 iron and tried to chip out. But O'Doul interrupted DiMaggio's concentration to remind him to keep the face of the club closed. DiMaggio hit the ball. It caromed off the side of his club, went skipping like a rabbit through the high grass down toward a pond. DiMaggio rarely displays any emotion on a golf course, but now, without saying a word, he took his No. 9 iron and flung it into the air. The club landed in a tree and stayed up there.

"Well," O'Doul said, casually, "there goes *that* set of clubs."

DiMaggio walked to the tree. Fortunately the club had slipped to the lower branch and DiMaggio could stretch up on the cart and get it back."

"Every time I get advice," DiMaggio muttered to himself, shaking his head slowly and walking toward the pond, "I shank it."

Later, showered and dressed, DiMaggio and the others drove to a banquet about ten miles from the golf course. Somebody had said it was going to be an elegant dinner, but when they arrived they could see it was more like a county fair; farmers were gathered outside a big barnlike building, a candidate for sheriff was distributing leaflets at the front door, and a chorus of homely ladies were inside singing "You Are My Sunshine."

"How did we get sucked into this?" DiMaggio asked, talking out of the side of his mouth, as they approached the building.

"O'Doul," one of the men said. "It's his fault. Damned O'Doul can't turn *anything* down."

"Go to hell," O'Doul said.

Soon DiMaggio and O'Doul and Ernie Nevers were surrounded by the crowd, and the woman who had been leading the chorus came rushing over and said, "Oh, Mr. DiMaggio, it certainly is a pleasure having you."

"It's a pleasure being here, ma'am," he said, forcing a smile.

"It's too bad you didn't arrive a moment sooner, you'd have heard our singing."

"Oh, I heard it," he said, "and I enjoyed it very much."

"Good, good," she said. "And how are your brothers Dom and Vic?"

"Fine. Dom lives near Boston. Vince is in Pittsburgh."

"Why, *hello* there, Joe," interrupted a man with wine on his breath, patting DiMaggio on the back, feeling his arm. "Who's gonna take it this year, Joe."

"Well, I have no idea," DiMaggio said."

"What about the Giants?"

"Your guess is as good as mine."

"Well, you can't count the Dodgers out," the man said.

"You sure can't," DiMaggio said.

"Not with all that pitching."

"Pitching is certainly important," DiMaggio said.

Everywhere he goes the questions seem the same, as if he has some special vision into the future of new heroes, and everywhere he goes, too, older men grab his hand and feel his arm and predict that he could still go out there and hit one, and the smile on DiMaggio's face is genuine. He tries hard to remain as he was—he diets, he takes steam baths, he is careful; and flabby men in the locker rooms of golf clubs sometimes steal peeks at him when he steps out of the shower, observing the tight muscles across his chest, the flat stomach, the long sinewy legs. He has a young man's body, very pale and little hair; his face is dark and lined, however, parched by the sun of several seasons. Still he is always an impressive figure at banquets such as this—an *immortal*, sportswriters called him, and that is how they have written about him and others like him, rarely suggesting that such heroes might ever be prone to the ills of mortal men, carousing, drinking, scheming; to suggest this would destroy the myth, would disillusion small boys, would infuriate rich men who own ball clubs and to whom baseball is a business dedicated to profit and in pursuit of which they trade mediocre players' flesh as casually as boys trade players' pictures on bubble-gum cards. And so the baseball hero must always act the part, must preserve the myth, and none does it better than DiMaggio, none is more patient when drunken old men grab an arm and ask, "Who's gonna take it this year, Joe?"

Two hours later, dinner and the speeches over, DiMaggio is slumped in O'Doul's car headed back to San Francisco. He edged himself up, however, when O'Doul pulled into a gas station in which a pretty red-haired girl sat on a stool, legs crossed, filing her fingernails. She was about twenty-two, wore a tight black skirt and tighter white blouse.

"Look at *that*," DiMaggio said.

"Yeah," O'Doul said.

O'Doul turned away when a young man approached, opened the gas tank, began wiping the windshield. The young man wore a greasy white uniform on the front of which was printed the name "Burt." DiMaggio kept looking at the girl, but she was not distracted from her fingernails. Then he looked at Burt, who did not recognize him. When the tank was full, O'Doul paid and drove off. Burt returned to his girl; DiMaggio slumped down in the front seat and did not open his eyes again until they'd arrived in San Francisco.

"Let's go see Reno," DiMaggio said.

"No, I gotta go see my old lady," O'Doul said. So he dropped DiMaggio off in front of the bar, and a moment later Reno's voice was announcing in the smoky room, "Hey, here's the Clipper!" The men waved and offered to buy him a drink. DiMaggio ordered a vodka and sat for an hour at the bar talking to a half dozen men around him. Then a blonde girl who had been with friends at the other end of the bar came over, and somebody introduced her to DiMaggio. He bought her a drink, offered her a cigarette. Then he struck a match and held it. His hand was unsteady.

"Is that me that's shaking?" he asked.

"It must be," said the blonde. "I'm calm."

Two nights later, having collected his clothes out of Reno's back room, Di-Maggio boarded a jet; he slept crossways on three seats, then came down the steps as the sun began to rise in Miami. He claimed his luggage and golf clubs, put them into the trunk of a waiting automobile, and less than an hour later he was being driven into Fort Lauderdale, past palm-lined streets, toward the Yankee Clipper Hotel.

"All my life it seems I've been on the road traveling," he said, squinting through the windshield into the sun. "I never get a sense of being in any one place."

Arriving at the Yankee Clipper Hotel, DiMaggio checked into the largest suite. People rushed through the lobby to shake hands with him, to ask for his autograph, to say, "Joe, you look great." And early the next morning, and for the next thirty mornings, DiMaggio arrived punctually at the baseball park and wore his uniform with the famous No. 5, and the tourists seated in the sunny grandstands clapped when he first appeared on the field each time, and then they watched with nostalgia as he picked up a bat and played "pepper" with the younger Yankees, some of whom were not even born when, twenty-five years ago this summer, he hit in fifty-six straight games and became the most celebrated man in America.

But the younger spectators in the Fort Lauderdale park, and the sportswriters, too, were more interested in Mantle and Maris, and nearly every day there were news dispatches reporting how Mantle and Maris felt, what they did, what they said, even though they said and did very little except walk around the field frowning when photographers asked for another picture and when sportswriters asked how they felt.

After seven days of this, the big day arrived—Mantle and Maris would swing a bat—and a dozen sportswriters were gathered around the big batting cage that was situated beyond the left-field fence; it was completely enclosed in wire, meaning that no baseball could travel more than thirty or forty feet before being trapped in rope; still Mantle and Maris would be swinging, and this, in spring, makes news.

Mantle stepped in first. He wore black gloves to help prevent blisters. He hit right-handed against the pitching of a coach named Vern Benson, and soon Mantle was swinging hard, smashing line drives against the nets, going *ahhh*, *ahhh* as he followed through with his mouth open.

Then Mantle, not wanting to overdo it on his first day, dropped his bat in the dirt and walked out of the batting cage. Roger Maris stepped in. He picked up Mantle's bat.

"This damn thing must be thirty-eight ounces," Maris said. He threw the bat down into the dirt, left the cage and walked toward the dugout on the other side of the field to get a lighter bat.

DiMaggio stood among the sportswriters behind the cage, then turned when Vern Benson, inside the cage, yelled, "Joe, wanna hit some?"

"No chance," DiMaggio said.

"Com'on, Joe," Benson said.

The reporters waited silently. Then DiMaggio walked slowly into the cage and picked up Mantle's bat. He took his position at the plate but obviously it was not the classic DiMaggio stance; he was holding the bat about two inches from the knob, his feet were not so far apart, and, when DiMaggio took a cut at Benson's first pitch, fouling it, there was none of that ferocious follow through, the blurred bat did not come whipping all the way around, the No. 5 was not stretched full across his broad back.

DiMaggio fouled Benson's second pitch, then he connected solidly with the third, the fourth, the fifth. He was just meeting the ball easily, however, not smashing it, and Benson called out, "I didn't know you were a choke hitter, Joe."

"I am now," DiMaggio said, getting ready for another pitch.

He hit three more squarely enough, and then he swung again and there was a hollow sound.

"Ohhh," DiMaggio yelled, dropping the bat, his fingers stung, "I was waiting for that one." He left the batting cage rubbing his hands together. The reporters watched him. Nobody said anything. Then DiMaggio said to one of them, not in anger nor in sadness, but merely as a simply stated fact, "There was a time when you couldn't get me out of there."

You would think that a well-conditioned baseball player with eye and hand reflexes that are the best developed of all professional sportspeople would be able to hit a baseball at least every four tries out of ten. Ted Williams was the last major-leaguer to accomplish that feat, an even more amazing achievement when you realize that it happened almost forty baseball seasons ago.

Ted Williams was the American League leader in hitting nine times; six times he had the highest batting average, and on four separate occasions he was the home-run king. His hitting power was so feared that from 1955 to 1957 he was the league leader in intentional walks.

Williams was a hero to all youngsters, but he remained an anomaly to his older fans. In 1957, he was fined $5,000 by baseball commissioner Ford Frick for spitting at his Boston rooters in Boston.

He was, as journalist Ed Linn points out, "a struggle of two opposing forces, almost two different persons."

Williams retired from the Red Sox after the 1960 season, leaving a team that he had been with for nineteen memorable and controversial seasons. He was a flamboyant, abrasive, rude, and at the same time gentle man; a player who wanted only to be remembered as the greatest hitter who ever lived. Ted Williams was elected to the Hall of Fame in 1966. They did not forget at Cooperstown.

The Kid's Last Game

by Ed Linn

Wednesday, September 26 [1960] was a cold and dreary day in Boston, a curious bit of staging on the part of those gods who always set the scene most carefully for Ted Williams. It was to be the last game Ted would ever play in Boston. Not until the game was over would Williams let it be known that it was the last game he would play anywhere.

Ted came into the locker room at 10:50, very early for him. He was dressed in dark brown slacks, a yellow sport shirt and a light tan pullover sweater, tastily brocaded in the same color. Ted went immediately to his locker, pulled off the sweater, then strolled into the trainer's room.

Despite all the triumphs and honors, it had been a difficult year for him. As trainer Jack Fadden put it: "It hasn't been a labor of love for Ted this year; it's just been labor." On two separate occasions, he had come very close to giving it all up.

The spring training torture had been made no easier for Ted by manager Billy Jurges. Jurges believed that the only way for a man Ted's age to stay in condition was to reach a peak at the beginning of the season and hold it by playing just as often as possible. "The most we can expect from Williams," Jurges had said, at the time of Ted's signing, "is 100 games. The least is pinch-hitting." Ted played in 113 games.

Throughout the training season, however, Ted seemed to be having trouble with his timing. Recalling his .254 average of the previous season, the experts wrote him off for perhaps the 15th time in his career. But on his first time at bat in the opening game, Ted hit a 500-foot home run, possibly the longest of his career, off Camilo Pascual, probably the best pitcher in the league. The next day, in the Fenway Park opener, he hit a second homer, this one off Jim Coates. Ted pulled a leg muscle running out that homer, though, and when a man's muscles go while he is doing nothing more than jogging around the bases, the end is clearly in sight.

It took him almost a month to get back into condition, but the mysterious virus infection that hits him annually, a holdover from his service in Korea, laid him low again almost immediately. Since the doctors have never been able to diagnose this chronic illness, the only way they can treat him is to shoot a variety of drugs and antibiotics into him, in the hope that one of them takes hold. Ted, miserable and drugged when he finally got back in uniform, failed in a couple of pinch-hitting attempts and was just about ready to quit. Against the Yankees, Ralph Terry struck him out two straight times. The third time up, the count went to 3-2 when Williams unloaded on a waist-high fastball and sent it into the bullpen in right-center, 400 feet away.

The blast triggered the greatest home-run spurt of Ted's career. Seven days later, he hit his 500th home run. He had started only 15 1960 games and he had hit eight 1960 homers. When he hit his 506th (and 11th of the year), he had homered once in every 6.67 times at bat.

Cold weather always bothered Ted, even in his early years, and so when he strained his shoulder late in August, he was just about ready to announce his retirement again. He had found it difficult to loosen up even in fairly warm weather, and to complicate matters he had found it necessary—back in the middle of 1959—to cut out the calisthenics routine he had always gone through in the clubhouse. The exercising had left him almost too weary to play ball.

Ted started almost every game so stiff that he was forced to exaggerate an old passion for swinging at balls, only in the strike zone. In his first time at bat, he would look for an inside pitch between the waist and knees, the only pitch he could swing at naturally. In the main, however, Ted was more than willing to take the base on balls his first time up.

He stayed on for two reasons. Mike Higgins, who had replaced Jurges as Sox Manager, told him bluntly, "You're paid to play ball, so go out and play." The strength behind those words rested in the fact that both Williams and Higgins knew very well that owner Tom Yawkey would continue to pay Ted whether he played or not.

In addition, the Red Sox had two series remaining with the Yankees and Orioles, who were still locked together in the pennant race. Ted did not think it fair to eliminate himself as a factor in the two-team battle. He announced his retirement just after the Yankees clinched the pennant.

Four days earlier, Ted had been called to a special meeting with Yawkey, Higgins, Dick O'Connell (who was soon to be named business manager) and publicity director Jack Malaney. This was to offer Ted the job of general manager, a position that had been discussed occasionally in the past.

Ted refused to accept the title until he proved he could do the job. He agreed, however, to work in the front office in 1961, assisting Higgins with player personnel, and O'Connell with business matters.

The coverage of Ted's last game was at a minimum. It was thought for a while that *Life* magazine wanted to send a crew down to cover the game, but it developed that they only wanted to arrange for Ted to represent them at the World Series. Dave Garroway's "Today" program tried to set up a telephone interview the morning of the game, but they couldn't get in touch with Ted. The Red Sox, alone among big-league clubs, have offered little help to anyone on the public relations front—and never any help at all where Ted Williams was concerned. Ted didn't live at the Kenmore Hotel with the rest of the unattached players. He lived about 100 yards down Commonwealth Avenue, at the Somerset. All calls and messages for him were diverted to the manager's office.

The ceremonies that were to mark his departure were rather limited, too. The Boston Chamber of Commerce had arranged to present him with a silver bowl, and the mayor's office and governor's office had quickly muscled into the picture. By Wednesday morning, however, the governor's office—which had apparently anticipated something more spectacular—begged off. The governor's spokesman suggested the presentation of a scroll at Ted's hotel, a suggestion which Ted simply ignored.

The only civilian in the clubhouse when Ted entered was the man from *Sport*, and he was talking to Del Baker, who was about to retire, too, after 50 years in the game. Ted looked over, scowled, seemed about to say something but changed his mind.

Our man was well aware what Ted was about to say. The Red Sox have a long-standing rule—also unique in baseball—that no reporter may enter the dressing room before the game, or the first 15 minutes after the game. It was a point of honor with Ted to pick out any civilian who wasn't specifically with a ballplayer and to tell him, as loudly as possible: "You're not supposed to be in here, you know."

Sure enough, when our man started toward Ted's locker in the far corner of the room, Ted pointed a finger at him and shouted: "You're not supposed to be in here, you know."

"The same warm, glad cry of greeting I always get from you," our man said. "It's your last day. Why don't you live a little?"

Ted started toward the trainer's room again, but wheeled around and came back. "You've got a nerve coming here to interview me after the last one you wrote about me!"

Our man wanted to know what was the matter with the last one.

"You called me 'unbearable,' that's what's the matter."

The full quote, it was pointed out, was that he "was sometimes unbearable but never dull," which holds a different connotation entirely.

"You've been after me for 12 years, that flogging magazine," he said, in his typically well-modulated shout. "Twelve years. I missed an appointment for some kind of luncheon. I forgot what happened . . . it doesn't matter anyway . . . but I forgot some appointment 12 years ago and *Sport* Magazine hasn't let up on me since."

Our man, lamentably eager to disassociate himself from this little magazine, made it clear that while he had done most of *Sport*'s Williams' articles in the past few years, he was not a member of the staff. "And," our man pointed out, "I have been accused of turning you into a combination of Paul Bunyan and Santa Claus."

"Well, when you get back there, tell them what . . . (he searched for the appropriate word, the *mot juste* as they say in the dugouts) . . . "what *flog-heads* they are. Tell them that for me."

Our man sought to check the correct spelling of the adjectives with him but got back only a scowl. Ted turned around to fish something out of a cloth bag at the side of his locker. "Why don't you just write your story without me?" he said. "What do you have to talk to me for?" And then, in a suddenly weary voice: "What can I tell you now that I haven't told you before?"

"Why don't you let me tell you what the story is supposed to be?" our man said. "Then you can say yes or no." It was an unfortunate way to put the question since it invited the answer it brought.

"I can tell you before you tell me," Ted shouted. "No! No, no, no."

Our man had the impression Williams was trying to tell him something. He was right. "Look," Williams said. "If I tell you I don't want to talk to you, why don't you just take my word for it?"

The clubhouse boy had come over with a glossy photo to be signed, and Ted sat down on his stool, turned his back and signed it.

Although we are reluctant to bring *Sport* into the context of the story itself, Ted's abiding hatred toward us tells much about him and his even longer feud with Boston sportswriters. Twelve years ago, just as Ted said, an article appeared to which he took violent exception. (The fact that he is so well aware that it *was* 12 years ago suggests that he still has the magazine around somewhere, so that he can fan the flames whenever he feels them dying.) What Ted objected to in that article was an interview with his mother in San Diego. Ted objects to any peering into his private life. When he holes himself up in his hotel, when he sets a barrier around the clubhouse, when he disappears into the Florida Keys at the end of the season, he is deliberately removing himself from a world he takes to be dangerous and hostile. His constant fighting with the

Ted Williams

newspapermen who cover him most closely is a part of the same pattern. What do newspapermen represent except the people who are supposed to pierce personal barriers? Who investigate, who pry, *who find out?*

Ted's mother has been a Salvation Army worker in San Diego all her life. She is a local character, known—not without affection—as "Salvation Mary." Ted himself was dedicated to the Salvation Army when he was a baby. His generosity, his unfailing instinct to come to the aid of any underdog, is in direct line with the teachings of the Army, which is quite probably the purest charitable organization in the world. Even as a boy, Ted regularly gave his 30-cent luncheon allowance to classmates he considered more needy than himself, a considerable sacrifice since the Williams family had to struggle to make ends meet.

When Ted signed with San Diego at the age of 17, he was a tall, skinny kid (6-3, 146 pounds). He gave most of his $150-a-month salary toward keeping up the family house and he tried to build up his weight by gorging himself on the road where the club picked up the check. One day, Ted was coming into the clubhouse when Bill Lane, the owner of the Padres, motioned him over. In his deep, foghorn voice, Lane said: "Well, kid, you're leading the list. You've got the others beat."

Ted, pleased that his ability was being noted so promptly, smiled and asked: "Yeah, what list?"

"The dining room list," Lane said. "Hasn't anyone told you that your meal allowance is supposed to be five dollars a day?"

Nobody had. "Okay, Bill," Ted said, finally. "Take anything over five dollars off my salary."

Bill did, too.

Even before *Sport* went into details about his background, the Boston press had discovered his weak point and hit him hard and—it must be added—most unfairly. During Ted's second season with the Sox, one reporter had the ill grace to comment, in regard to a purely personal dispute: "But what can you expect of a youth so abnormal that he didn't go home in the off-season to see his own mother?"

When Williams' World War II draft status was changed from 1A to 3A after he claimed his mother as a dependent, one Boston paper sent a private investigator to San Diego to check on her standard of living; another paper sent reporters out onto the street to ask casual passers-by to pass judgment on Ted's patriotism.

Reporters were sent galloping out into the street to conduct a public-opinion poll once again when Williams was caught fishing in the Everglades while his wife was giving birth to a premature baby.

A press association later sent a story out of San Diego that Ted had sold the furniture out from under his mother—although a simple phone call could have established that it wasn't true. Ted had bought the house and the furniture for his mother. His brother—who had been in frequent trouble with the law— had sold it. The Boston papers picked up that story and gave it a big play, despite the fact that every sports editor in the city had enough background material on Ted's family to know—even without checking—that it couldn't possibly be true. It was, Ted's friends believed, their way of punishing him for not being "co-operative."

Ted had become so accustomed to looking upon any reference to his family as an unfriendly act that when *Sport* wrote about his mother, he bristled— even though her final quote was: "Don't say anything about Teddy except the highest and the best. He's a wonderful son." And when he searched for some reason why the magazine would do such a thing to him, he pounced upon that broken appointment, which everybody except himself had long forgotten.

After Ted had signed the photograph the day of his last game, he sat on his stool, his right knee jumping nervously, his right hand alternately buttoning and unbuttoning the top button of his sport shirt.

When he stripped down to his shorts, there was no doubt he was 42. The man once called The Splendid Splinter—certainly one of the most atrocious nicknames ever committed upon an immortal—was thick around the middle. A soft roll of loose fat, drooping around the waist, brought on a vivid picture of Archie Moore.

Williams is a tall, handsome man. If they ever make that movie of his life that keeps being rumored around, the guy who plays Bret Maverick would be perfect for the part. But ballplayers age quickly. Twenty years under the sun had baked Ted's face and left it lined and leathery. Sitting there, Ted Williams had the appearance of an old Marine sergeant who had been to the battles and back.

Sal Maglie, who had the end locker on the other side of the shower-room door, suddenly caught Ted's attention. "You're a National Leaguer, Sal," Ted said, projecting his voice to the room at large. "I got a hundred dollars that the Yankees win the World Series. The Yankees will win it in four or five games."

"I'm an American Leaguer now," Sal said, quietly.

"A hundred dollars," Ted said. "A friendly bet."

"You want a friendly bet? I'll bet you a friendly dollar."

"Fifty dollars," Ted said.

"All right," Sal said. "Fifty dollars." And then, projecting his own voice, he said: "I like the Pirates, anyway."

Williams went back to his mail, as the others dressed and went out onto the field.

At length, Ted picked up his spikes, wandered into the trainer's room again, and lifting himself onto the table, carefully began to put a shine on them. A photographer gave him a ball to sign.

Ted gazed at it with distaste, then looked up at the photographer with loathing. "Are you crazy?" he snapped.

The photographer backed away, pocketed the ball and began to adjust his camera sights on Ted. "You don't belong in here," Ted shouted. And turning to the clubhouse boy, he barked: "Get him out of here."

The locker room had emptied before Ted began to dress. For Ted did not go out to take batting practice or fielding practice. He made every entrance onto the field a dramatic event. He did not leave the locker room for the dugout until 12:55, only 35 minutes before the game was scheduled to start. By then, most of the writers had already gone up to Tom Yawkey's office to hear Jackie Jensen announce that he was returning to baseball.

As Ted came quickly up the stairs and into the dugout, he almost bumped into his close friend and fishing companion, Bud Leavitt, sports editor of the Bangor *Daily News*. "Hi, Bud," Ted said, as if he were surprised Leavitt was there. "You drive up?"

A semi-circle of cameramen closed in on Williams, like a bear trap, on the playing field just up above. Ted hurled a few choice oaths at them, and as an oath-hurler Ted never bats below .400. He guided Leavitt against the side of the dugout, just above the steps, so that he could continue the conversation without providing a shooting angle for the photographers. The photographers continued to shoot him in profile, though, until Ted took Leavitt by the elbow and walked him the length of the dugout. "Let's sit down," he said, as he left, "so we won't be bothered by all these blasted cameramen."

If there had been any doubt back in the locker room that Ted had decided to bow out with typical hardness, it had been completely dispelled by those first few minutes in the dugout. On his last day in Fenway Park, Ted Williams seemed resolved to remain true to his own image of himself, to permit no sentimentality or hint of sentimentality to crack that mirror through which he looks at the world and allows the world to look upon him.

And yet, in watching this strange and troubled man—the most remarkable and colorful and full-blooded human being to come upon the athletic scene since Babe Ruth—you had the feeling that he was overplaying his role, that he had struggled through the night against the impulse to make his peace, to express his gratitude, to accept the great affection that the city had been showering upon him for years. In watching him, you had the clear impression that in resisting this desire he was overreacting and becoming more profane, more impossible and—yes—more unbearable than ever.

Inside Ted Williams, there has always been a struggle of two opposing forces, almost two different persons. (We are fighting the use of the word schizophrenia.) The point we are making is best illustrated through Williams' long refusal to tip his hat in acknowledgment of the cheering crowds. It has always been his contention that the people who cheered him when he hit a home run were the same people who booed him when he struck out—which, incidentally, is probably not true at all. More to our point, Ted has always insisted that although he would rather be cheered than booed, he really didn't care what the fans thought of him, one way or the other.

Obviously, though, if he really didn't care he wouldn't have bothered to make such a show of not caring. He simply would have touched his finger to his cap in that automatic, thoughtless gesture of most players and forgot about it. Ted, in short, has always had it both ways. He gets the cheers and he pretends they mean nothing to him. He is like a rich man's nephew who treats his uncle with disrespect to prove he is not interested in his money, while all the time he is secretly dreaming that the uncle will reward such independence by leaving him most of the fortune.

Ted has it even better than that. The fans of Boston have always wooed him ardently. They always cheered him all the louder in the hope that he would reward them, at last, with that essentially meaningless tip of the hat.

This clash within Williams came to the surface as he sat and talked with Leavitt, alone and undisturbed. For, within a matter of minutes, the lack of attention began to oppress him; his voice began to rise, to pull everybody's attention back to him. The cameramen, getting the message, drifted toward him again, not in a tight pack this time but in a loose and straggling line.

With Ted talking so loudly, it was apparent that he and Leavitt were discussing how to get together, after the World Series, for their annual post-season fishing expedition. The assignment to cover the Series for *Life* had apparently upset their schedule.

"After New York," Ted said, "I'll be going right to Pittsburgh." He expressed his hope that the Yankees would wrap it all up in Yankee Stadium, so that he could join Leavitt in Bangor at the beginning of the following week. "But, dammit," he said, "if the Series goes more than five games, I'll have to go back to Pittsburgh again."

Leavitt reminded Ted of an appearance he had apparently agreed to make in Bangor. "All right," Ted said. "But no speeches or anything."

A young, redheaded woman, in her late twenties, leaned over from her box seat alongside the dugout and asked Ted if he would autograph her scorecard.

"I can't sign it, dear," Ted said. "League rules. Where are you going to be after the game?"

"You told me that once before," she said unhappily.

"Well, where are you going to be?" Ted shouted, in the impatient way one would shout at an irritating child.

"Right here," she said.

"All right."

"But I waited before and you never came."

He ignored her.

Joe Cronin, president of the American League, came down the dugout aisle, followed by his assistant, Joe McKenney. Through Cronin's office, the local 9:00 newsfeature program which follows the "Today" program in Boston had scheduled a filmed interview with Ted. The camera had already been set up on the home-plate side of the dugout, just in front of the box seats. Cronin talked to Ted briefly and went back to reassure the announcer that Ted would be right there. McKenney remained behind to make sure Ted didn't forget. At last, Ted jumped up and shouted: "Where is it, Joe, dammit?"

When Ted followed McKenney out, it was the first time he had stuck his head onto the field all day. There were still not too many fans in the stands, although far more than would have been there on any other day to watch a seventh-place team on a cold and threatening Wednesday afternooon. At this first sight of Ted Williams, they let out a mighty roar.

As he waited alongside interviewer Jack Chase, Ted bit his lower lip, and looked blankly into space, both characteristic mannerisms. At a signal from the cameraman, Chase asked Ted how he felt about entering "the last lap."

All at once, Ted was smiling. "I want to tell you, Jack, I honestly feel good about it," he said, speaking in that quick charming way of his. "You can't get blood out of a turnip, you know. I've gone as far as I can and I'm sure I wouldn't want to try it any more."

"Have we gone as far as we can with the Jimmy Fund?" he was asked.

Ted was smiling more broadly. "Oh, no. We could never go far enough with the Jimmy Fund."

Chase reminded Ted that he was scheduled to become a batting coach.

"Can you take a .250 hitter and make a .300 hitter out of him?"

"There has always been a saying in baseball that you can't make a hitter," Ted answered. "But I think that you can *improve* a hitter. More than you can improve a fielder. More mistakes are made in hitting than in any other part of the game."

At this point, Williams was literally encircled by photographers, amateur and pro. The pros were taking pictures from the front and from the sides. Behind them, in the stands, dozens of fans had their cameras trained on Ted, too, although they could hardly have been getting anything except the No. 9 on his back.

Ted was asked if he were going to travel around the Red Sox farm system in 1961 to instruct the young hitters.

"All I know is that I'm going to spring training," he said. "Other than that, I don't know anything."

The interview closed with the usual fulsome praise of Williams, the inevitable apotheosis that leaves him with a hangdog, embarrassed look upon his features. "I appreciate the kind words," he said. "It's all been fun. Everything I've done in New England from playing left field and getting booed, to the Jimmy Fund."

The Jimmy Fund is the money-raising arm of the Children's Cancer Hospital in Boston, which has become the world center for research into cancer and for the treatment of its young victims. Ted has been deeply involved with the hospital since its inception in 1947, serving the last four years as general chairman of the fund committee. He is an active chairman, not an honorary one. Scarcely a day goes by, when Ted is in Boston, that he doesn't make one or two stops for the Jimmy Fund somewhere in New England. He went out on the missions even days when he was too sick to play ball. (This is the same man, let us emphasize, who refuses to attend functions at which he himself is to be honored.) He has personally raised something close to $4,000,000 and has helped to build a modern, model hospital not far from Fenway Park.

But he has done far more than that. From the first, Williams took upon himself the agonizing task of trying to bring some cheer into the lives of these dying children and, perhaps even more difficult, of comforting their parents. He has, in those years, permitted himself to become attached to thousands of these children, knowing full well that they were going to die, one by one. He has become so attached to some of them that he has chartered special planes to bring him to their deathbeds.

Whenever one of these children asks to see him, whatever the time, he comes. His only stipulation is that there must be no publicity, no reporters, no cameramen.

We once suggested to Ted that he must get some basic return from all this work he puts into the Jimmy Fund. Ted considered the matter very carefully before he answered: "Look," he said, finally, "it embarrasses me to be praised for anything like this. The embarrassing thing is that I don't feel I've done anything compared to the people at the hospital who are doing the important work.

It makes me happy to think I've done a little good; I suppose that's what I get out of it.

"Anyway," he added, thoughtfully, "it's only a freak of fate, isn't it, that one of those kids isn't going to grow up to be an athlete and I wasn't the one who had the cancer."

At the finish of the filmed interview he had to push his way through the cameramen between him and the dugout. "Oh————," he said.

But when one of them asked him to pose with Cronin, Ted switched personalities again and asked, with complete amiability, "Where is he?"

Cronin was in the dugout. Ted met Joe at the bottom of the steps and threw an arm around him. They grinned at each other while the pictures were being taken, talking softly and unintelligibly. After a minute, Ted reached over to the hook just behind him and grabbed his glove. The cameramen were still yelling for another shot as he started up the dugout steps. Joe, grinning broadly, grabbed him by the shoulder and yanked him back down. While Cronin was wrestling Ted around and whacking him on the back, the cameras clicked. "I got to warm up, dammit," Ted was saying. He made a pawing gesture at the cameramen, as if to say, "I'd like to belt you buzzards." This, from all evidence, was the picture that went around the country that night, because strangely enough, it looked as if he were waving a kind of sad goodbye.

When he finally broke away and raced up the field, he called back over his shoulder, "See you later, Joe." The cheers arose from the stands once again.

The Orioles were taking infield practice by then, and the Red Sox were warming up along the sideline. Ted began to play catch with Pumpsie Green. As he did—sure enough—the cameramen lined up just inside the foul line for some more shots, none of which will ever be used. "Why don't you cockroaches get off my back?" Ted said, giving them his No. 1 sneer. "Let me breathe, will you?"

The bell rang before he had a chance to throw two dozen balls. Almost all the players went back to the locker room. Remaining on the bench were only Ted Williams, buttoned up in his jacket, and Vic Wertz. One of the members of the ground crew came with a picture of Williams. He asked Ted if he would autograph it. "Sure," Ted said. "For you guys, anything."

Vic Wertz was having his picture taken with another crew member. Wertz had his arm around the guy and both of them were laughing.

"How about you, Ted?" the cameraman asked. "One with the crewmen?"

Ted posed willingly with the man he had just signed for, with the result that the whole herd of cameramen came charging over again. Ted leaped to his feet. "Twenty-two years of this bull————," he cried.

The redhead was leaning over the low barrier again, but now three other young women were alongside her. One of them seemed to be crying, apparently at the prospect of Ted's retirement. An old photographer, in a long, weather-beaten coat, asked Ted for a special pose. "Get lost," Ted said. "I've seen enough of you, you old goat."

Curt Gowdy, the Red Sox broadcaster, had come into the dugout to pass on some information about the pre-game ceremonies. Ted shouted, "The devil with all you miserable cameramen." The women continued to stare, in fascination, held either by the thrill of having this last long look at Ted Williams or by the opportunity to learn a few new words.

A Baltimore writer came into the dugout, and Ted settled down beside him. He wanted to know whether the writer could check on the "King of Swat" crown that had been presented to him in his last visit to Baltimore. Ted wasn't sure whether he had taken it back to Boston with him or whether the organization still had it.

"You know," he told the writer, "Brown's a better pitcher now than he's ever been. Oh, he's a great pitcher. Never get a fat pitch from him. When he does, it comes in with something extra on it. Every time a little different. He knows what he's doing."

Ted is a student of such things. He is supposed to be a natural hitter, blessed with a superhuman pair of eyes. We are not about to dispute this. What we want to say is that when Ted first came to the majors the book on him was that he would chase bad balls. "All young sluggers do," according to Del Baker, who was managing Detroit when Ted came up. "Ted developed a strike zone of his own, though, by the second year."

When Ted took his physical for the Naval Reserve in World War II, his eyes tested at 20/10 and were so exceptional in every regard that while he was attending air gunnery school he broke all previous Marine records for hitting the target sleeve. But Ted has a point of his own here: "My eyesight," he says, "is now 20/15. Half the major leaguers have eyes as good as that. It isn't eyesight that makes a hitter; it's practice. *Con-sci-en-tious* practice. I say that Williams has hit more balls than any guy living, except maybe Ty Cobb. I don't say it to brag; I just state it as a fact. From the time I was 11 years old, I've taken every possible opportunity to swing at a ball. I've swung and I've swung and I've swung."

Ted always studied every little movement a pitcher made. He always remained on the bench before the game to watch them warming up. From his first day to his last, he hustled around to get all possible information on a new pitcher.

It has always been his theory that we are all creatures of habit, himself included. Pitchers, he believes, fall into observable patterns. A certain set of movements foretells a certain pitch. In a particular situation, or on a particular count, they go to a particular pitch. There were certain pitchers, Ted discovered, who would inevitably go to their big pitch, the pitch they wanted him to swing at, on the 2–2 count.

And so Ted would frequently ask a teammate, "What was the pitch he struck you out on?" or "What did he throw you on the 2–2 pitch?"

When a young player confessed he didn't know what the pitch had been, Ted would grow incredulous. "You don't know the pitch he struck you out on? I'm not talking about last week or last month. I'm not even talking about yesterday. Today! Just now! I'm talking about the pitch he struck you out on just now!"

Returning to his seat on the bench, he'd slump back in disgust and mutter: "What a rockhead. The guy's taking the bread and butter out of his mouth and he don't even care how."

In a very short time, the player would have an answer ready for Williams. Ted always got the young hitters thinking about their craft. He always tried to instruct them, to build up their confidence. "When you want to know who the best hitter in the league is," he'd tell the rookies, "just look into the mirror."

Among opposing players, Williams was always immensely popular. Yes, even among opposing pitchers. All pitchers love to say: "Nobody digs in against *me*." Only Ted Williams was given the right to dig in without getting flipped. Around the American League, there seemed to be a general understanding that Williams had too much class to be knocked down.

Waiting in the dugout for the ceremonies to get underway, Ted picked up a bat and wandered up and down the aisle taking vicious practice swings.

The photographers immediately swooped in on him. One nice guy was taking cameras from the people in the stands and getting shots of Ted for them.

As Ted put the bat down, one of them said: "One more shot, Teddy, as a favor."

"I'm all done doing any favors for you guys," Williams said. "I don't have to put up with you any more, and you don't have to put up with me."

An old woman, leaning over the box seats, was wailing: "Don't leave us, Ted. Don't leave us."

"Oh hell," Ted said, turning away in disgust.

The redhead asked him plaintively: "Why don't you act nice?"

Ted strolled slowly toward her, grinning broadly. "Come on, dear," he drawled, "with that High Street accent you got there."

Turning back, he stopped in front of the man from *Sport*, pointed over his shoulder at the cameramen and asked: "You getting it all? You getting what you came for?"

"If you can't make it as a batting coach," our man said, "I understand you're going to try it as a cameraman."

"What does *Sport* Magazine think I'm going to do?" Ted asked. "That's what I want to know. What does *Sport* Magazine think I'm going to be?"

Speaking for himself, our man told him, he had not the slightest doubt that Ted was going to be the new general manager.

"*Sport* Magazine," Ted said, making the name sound like an oath. "Always honest. Never prejudiced."

At this point, he was called onto the field. Taking off his jacket, he strode out of the dugout. The cheers that greeted him came from 10,454 throats.

Curt Gowdy, handling the introductions, began: "As we all know, this is the final home game for—in my opinion and most of yours—the greatest hitter who ever lived. Ted Williams."

There was tremendous applause.

"Twenty years ago," Gowdy continued, "a skinny kid from San Diego came to the Red Sox camp . . ."

Ted first came to the Red Sox training camp at Sarasota in the spring of 1938. General manager Eddie Collins, having heard that Ted was a creature of wild and wayward impulse, had instructed second-baseman Bobby Doerr to pick him up and deliver him, shining and undamaged.

It was unthinkable, of course, that Ted Williams would make a routine entrance. Just before Doerr was set to leave home, the worst flood of the decade hit California and washed out all the roads and telephone lines. When Williams and Doerr finally arrived in Sarasota, ten days late, there was a fine, almost imperceptible drizzle. Williams, still practically waterlogged from the California floods, held out a palm, looked skyward, shivered and said in a voice that flushed the flamingoes from their nests: "So this is Florida, is it? Do they always keep this state under a foot of water?"

Williams suited up for a morning workout in the field, jawed good-naturedly with the fans and got an unexpected chance to hit when a newsreel company moved in to take some batting-cage shots.

The magic of Ted Williams in a batter's box manifested itself that first day in camp. The tall, thin rookie stepped into the box, set himself in his wide stance, let his bat drop across the far corner of the plate, wiggled his hips and shoulders and jiggled up and down as if he were trying to tamp himself into the box. He moved his bat back and forth a few times, then brought it back into position and twisted his hands in opposite directions as if he were wringing the neck of the bat. He was set for the pitch.

And somehow, as if by some common impulse, all sideline activity stopped that day in 1938. Everybody was watching Ted Williams.

"Controversial, sure," Gowdy said, in bringing his remarks about Ted to a close, "but colorful."

The chairman of the Boston Chamber of Commerce presented Ted a shining, silver Paul Revere Bowl "on behalf of the business community of Boston." Ted seemed to force his smile as he accepted it.

A representative of the sports committee of the Chamber of Commerce then presented him with a plaque "on behalf of visits to kids' and veterans' hospitals."

Mayor John Collins, from his wheelchair, announced that "on behalf of all citizens" he was proclaiming this day "Ted Williams Day." The mayor didn't know how right he was.

As Mayor Collins spoke of Ted's virtues ("Nature's best, nature's nobleman"), the muscle in Ted's upper left jaw was jumping, constantly and rhythmically. The mayor's contribution to Ted Williams Day was a $1,000 donation to the Jimmy Fund from some special city fund.

Gowdy brought the proceedings to a close by proclaiming: "Pride is what made him great. He's a champion, a thoroughbred, a champion of sports." Curt then asked for a "round of applause, an ovation for No. 9 on his last game in his Boston." Needless to say, he got it.

Ted waited, pawed at the ground with one foot. Smiling, he thanked the mayor for the money. "Despite the fact of the disagreeable things that have been said of me—and I can't help thinking about it—by the Knights of the Keyboard out there (he jerked his head toward the press box), baseball has been the most wonderful thing in my life. If I were starting over again and someone asked me where is the one place I would like to play, I would want it to be in Boston, with the greatest owner in baseball and the greatest fans in America. Thank you."

He walked across the infield to the dugout, where the players were standing, applauding along with the fans. Ted winked and went on in.

In the press box, some of the writers were upset by the gratuitous rap at them. "I think it was bush," one of them said. "Whatever he thinks, this wasn't the time to say it."

Others made a joke of it. "Now that he's knighted me," one of them was saying, "I wonder if he's going to address me as Sir."

In the last half of the first inning, Williams stepped in against Steve Barber with Tasby on first and one out. When Barber was born—February 22, 1939—Ted had already taken the American Association apart, as it has never been taken apart since, by batting .366, hitting 43 home runs and knocking in 142 runs.

Against a lefthander, Williams was standing almost flush along the inside line of the batter's box, his feet wide, his stance slightly closed. He took a curve inside, then a fastball, low. The fans began to boo. The third pitch was also low. With a 3–0 count, Ted jumped in front of the plate with the pitch, like a high-school kid looking for a walk. It was ball four, high.

He got to third the easy way. Jim Pagliaroni was hit by a pitch, and everybody moved up on a wild pitch. When Frank Malzone walked, Jack Fisher came in to replace Barber. Lou Clinton greeted Jack with a rising liner to dead center. Jackie Brandt started in, slipped as he tried to reverse himself, but recovered in time to scramble back and make the catch. His throw to the plate was beautiful to behold, a low one-bouncer that came to Gus Triandos chest high. But Ted, sliding hard, was in under the ball easily.

Leading off the third inning against the righthanded Fisher, Ted moved back just a little in the box. Fisher is even younger than Barber, a week younger. When Fisher was being born—March 4, 1939—Ted was reporting to Sarasota again, widely proclaimed as the super-player of the future, the Red Sox' answer to Joe DiMaggio.

He hit Fisher's 1–1 pitch straightaway, high and deep. Brandt had plenty of room to go back and make the catch, but still, as Williams returned to the bench, he got another tremendous hand.

Up in the press box, publicity man Jack Malaney was announcing that uniform No. 9 was being retired "after today's game." This brought on some snide remarks about Ted wearing his undershirt at Yankee Stadium for the final three games of the season. Like Mayor Collins, Malaney was righter than he knew. The uniform was indeed going to be retired after the game.

Williams came to bat again in the fifth inning, with two out and the Sox trailing, 3–2. And this time he unloaded a tremendous drive to right center. As the ball jumped off the bat, the cry, "He did it!" arose from the stands. Right-fielder Al Pilarcik ran back as far as he could, pressed his back against the bull-pen fence, well out from the 380-foot sign, and stood there, motionless, his hands at his sides.

Although it was a heavy day there was absolutely no wind. The flag hung limply from the pole, stirring very occasionally and very faintly.

At the last minute, Pilarcik brought up his hands and caught the ball chest high, close to 400 feet from the plate. A moan of disappointment settled over the field, followed by a rising hum of excited conversation and then, as Ted came back toward the first-base line to get his glove from Pumpsie Green, a standing ovation.

"Damn," Ted said, when he returned to the bench at the end of the inning. "I hit the living hell out of that one. I really stung it. If that one didn't go out nothing is going out today!"

In the top of the eighth, with the Sox behind 4–2, Mike Fornieles came to the mound for the 70th time of the season, breaking the league record set by another Red Sox relief star, Ellis Kinder. Kinder set his mark in 1953, the year Williams returned from Korea.

As Fornieles was warming up, three teen-agers jumped out of the grandstand and ran toward Ted. They paused only briefly, however, and continued into the waiting arms of the park police.

Ted was scheduled to bat second in the last of the eighth, undoubtedly his last time at bat. The cheering began as soon as Willie Tasby came out of the dugout and strode to the plate, as if he was anxious to get out of there and make way for the main event. Ted, coming out almost directly behind Tasby, went to the on-deck circle. He was down on one knee and just beginning to swing the heavy, lead-filled practice bat as Tasby hit the first pitch to short for an easy out.

The cheering seemed to come to its peak as Ted stepped into the box and took his stance. Everybody in the park had come to his feet to give Ted a standing ovation.

Umpire Eddie Hurley called time. Fisher stepped off the rubber and Triandos stood erect. Ted remained in the box, waiting, as if he were oblivious to it all. The standing ovation lasted at least two minutes, and even then Fisher threw into the continuing applause. Only as the ball approached the plate did the cheering stop. It came in low, ball one. The spectators remained on their feet, but very suddenly the park had gone very quiet.

If there was pressure on Ted, there was pressure on Fisher, too. The Orioles were practically tied for second place, so he couldn't afford to be charitable. He might have been able to get Ted to go after a bad pitch, and yet he hardly wanted to go down in history as the fresh kid who had walked Ted Williams on his last time at bat in Boston.

The second pitch was neck high, a slider with, it seemed, just a little off it. Ted gave it a tremendous swing, but he was just a little out in front of the ball. The swing itself brought a roar from the fans, though, since it was such a clear announcement that Ted was going for the home run or nothing.

With a 1–1 count, Fisher wanted to throw a fastball, low and away. He got it up too much and in too much, a fastball waist high on the outside corner. From the moment Ted swung, there was not the slightest doubt about it. The ball cut through the heavy air, a high line drive heading straightaway to center field toward the corner of the special bullpen the Red Sox built for Williams back in 1941.

Jackie Brandt went back almost to the barrier, then turned and watched the ball bounce off the canopy above the bullpen bench, skip up against the wire fence which rises in front of the bleachers and bounce back into the bullpen.

It did not seem possible that 10,000 people could make that much noise.

Ted raced around the bases at a pretty good clip. Triandos had started toward the mound with the new ball, and Fisher had come down to meet him. As Ted neared home plate, Triandos turned to face him, a big smile on his face. Ted grinned back.

Ted didn't exactly offer his hand to Pagliaroni after he crossed the plate, but the young catcher reached out anyway and made a grab for it. He seemed to catch Ted around the wrist. Williams ran back into the dugout and ducked through the runway door to get himself a drink of water.

The fans were on their feet again, deafening the air with their cheers. A good four or five minutes passed before anybody worried about getting the game underway again.

When Ted ducked back into the dugout, he put on his jacket and sat down at the very edge of the bench, alongside Mike Higgins and Del Baker. The players, still on their feet anyway, crowded around him, urging him to go out and acknowledge the cheers.

The fans were now chanting, "We want Ted . . . we want Ted . . . we want Ted." Umpire Johnny Rice, at first base, motioned for Ted to come out. Manager Mike Higgins urged him to go on out. Ted just sat there, his head down, a smile of happiness on his face.

"We wanted him to go out," Vic Wertz said later, "because we felt so good for him. And we could see he was thrilled, too. For me, I have to say it's my top thrill in baseball."

But another player said: "I had the impression—maybe I shouldn't say this because it's just an impression—that he got just as much a kick out of refusing to go out and tip his hat to the crowd as he did out of the homer. What I mean is he wanted to go out with the home run, all right, but he also wanted the home run so he could sit there while they yelled for him and tell them all where to go."

Mike Higgins had already told Carroll Hardy to replace Ted in left field. As Clinton came to bat, with two men out, Higgins said: "Williams, left field." Ted grabbed his glove angrily and went to the top step. When Clinton struck out, Ted was the first man out of the dugout. He sprinted out to left field, ignoring the cheers of the fans, who had not expected to see him again. But Higgins had sent Hardy right out behind him. Ted saw Carroll, and ran back in, one final time. The entire audience was on its feet once again, in wild applause.

Since it is doubtful that Higgins felt Williams was in any great need of more applause that day, it is perfectly obvious that he was giving Ted one last chance to think about the tip of the hat or the wave of the hand as he covered the distance between left field and the dugout.

Ted made the trip as always, his head down, his stride unbroken. He stepped on first base as he crossed the line, ducked down into the dugout, growled once at Higgins and headed through the alleyway and into the locker room.

He stopped only to tell an usher standing just inside the dugout: "I guess I forgot to tip my hat."

To the end, the mirror remained intact.

After the game, photographers were permitted to go right into the clubhouse, but writers were held to the 15-minute rule. One writer tried to ride in with the photographers, but Williams leveled that finger at him and said: "You're not supposed to be here."

Somehow or other, the news was let out that Ted would not be going to New York, although there seems to be some doubt as to whether it was Williams or Higgins who made the announcement. The official Boston line is that it had been understood all along that Ted would not be going to New York unless the pennant race was still on. The fact of the matter is that Williams made the decision himself, and he did not make it until after he hit the home run. It would have been foolish to have gone to New York or anywhere else, of course. Anything he did after the Boston finale would have been an anticlimax.

One of the waiting newspapermen, a pessimist by nature, expressed the fear that by the time they were let in, Ted would be dressed and gone.

"Are you kidding?" a member of the anti-Williams clique said. "This is what he lives for. If the game had gone 18 innings, he'd be in there waiting for us."

He was indeed waiting at his locker, with a towel wrapped around his middle. The writers approached him, for the most part, in groups. Generally speaking, the writers who could be called friends reached him first, and to these men Ted was not only amiable but gracious and modest.

Was he going for the home run?

"I was gunning for the big one," he grinned. "I let everything I had go. I really wanted that one."

Did he know it was out as soon as it left the bat?

"I knew I had really given it a ride."

What were his immediate plans?

"I've got some business to clean up here," he said. "Then I'll be covering the World Series for *Life*. After that, I'm going back to Florida to see how much damage the hurricane did to my house."

The other players seemed even more affected by the drama of the farewell homer than Ted. Pete Runnels, practically dispossessed from his locker alongside Ted's by the shifts of reporters, wandered around the room shaking his head in disbelief. "How about that?" he kept repeating. "How about that? How about that?"

As for Ted, he seemed to be in something of a daze. After the first wave of writers had left, he wandered back and forth between his locker and the trainer's room. Back and forth, back and forth. Once, he came back with a bottle of beer, turned it up to his lips and downed it with obvious pleasure. For Ted, this is almost unheard of. He has always been a milk and ice-cream man, and he devours them both in huge quantities. His usual order after a ball game is two quarts of milk.

Williams remained in the locker room, making himself available, until there were no more than a half-dozen other players remaining. Many of the writers did not go over to him at all. From them, there were no questions, no congratulations, no good wishes for the future. For all Ted's color, for all the drama and copy he had supplied over 22 years, they were glad to see him finally retire.

When Ted finally began to get dressed, our man went over and said: "Ted, you must have known when Higgins sent you back out that he was giving you a final chance to think about tipping the hat or making some gesture of farewell. Which meant that Higgins himself would have liked you to have done it. While you were running back, didn't you have any feeling that it might be nice to go out with a show of good feeling?"

"I felt nothing," he said.

"No sentimentality? No gratitude? No sadness?"

"I said *nothing*," Ted said. "Nothing, nothing, nothing!"

As our man was toting up the nothings, Ted snarled, "And when you get back there tell them for me that they're full of . . ." There followed a burst of vituperation which we cannot even begin to approximate, and then the old, sad plaint about those 12 years of merciless persecution.

Fenway Park has an enclosed parking area so that the players can get to their cars without beating their way through the autograph hunters. When Ted was dressed, though, the clubhouse boy called to the front office in what was apparently a prearranged plan to bring Williams' car around to a bleacher exit.

At 4:40, 45 minutes after the end of the game and a good hour after Ted had left the dugout, he was ready to leave. "Fitzie," he called out, and the club-house boy came around to lead the way. The cameramen came around, too.

The locker-room door opens onto a long corridor, which leads to another door which, in turn, opens onto the backwalks and understructure of the park. It is this outer door which is always guarded.

Waiting in the alleyway, just outside the clubhouse door, however, was a redheaded, beatnik-looking man, complete with the regimental beard and beachcomber pants. He handed Ted a ball and mentioned a name that apparently meant something to him. Ted took the ball and signed it.

"How come you're not able to get in?" he said. "If they let the damn newspapermen in, they ought to let you in." Walking away, trailed by the platoon of cameramen, he called out to the empty air: "If they let the newspapermen in, they should let everybody in."

He walked on through the backways of the park, past the ramps and pillars, at a brisk clip, with Fitzie bustling along quickly to stay up ahead. Alongside of Williams, the cameramen were scrambling to get their positions and snap their pictures. Williams kept his eyes straight ahead, never pausing for one moment. "Hold it for just a minute, Ted," one of them said.

"I've been here for 22 years," Ted said, walking on. "Plenty of time for you to get your shot."

"This is the last time," the cameraman said. "Co-operate just this one last time."

"I've co-operated with you," Ted said. "I've co-operated too much."

Fitzie had the bleacher entrance open, and as Ted passed quickly through, a powder-blue Cadillac pulled up to the curb. A man in shirt sleeves was behind the wheel. He looked like Dick O'Connell, whose appointment as business manager had been announced the previous night.

Fitzie ran ahead to open the far door of the car for Ted. Three young women had been approaching the exit as Ted darted through, and one of them screamed: "It's him!" One of the others just let out a scream, as if Ted had been somebody of real worth, like Elvis or Fabian. The third woman remained mute. Looking at her, you had to wonder whether she would ever speak again.

Fitzie slammed the door and the car pulled away. "It was him," the first woman screamed. "Was it *really* him? Was it *him?*"

Her knees seemed to give away. Her girl friends had to support her. "I can't catch my breath," she said. "I can hear my heart pounding." And then, in something like terror: "*I can't breathe.*"

Attracted by the screams, or by some invisible, inexplicable grapevine, a horde of boys and men came racing up the street. Ted's car turned the corner just across from the bleacher exit, but it was held up momentarily by a red light and a bus. The front line of pursuers had just come abreast of the car when the driver swung around the bus and pulled away.

There are those, however, who never get the word. Down the street, still surrounding the almost empty parking area, were still perhaps 100 loyal fans waiting to say their last farewell to Ted Williams.

In Boston that night, the talk was all of Williams. Only 10,454 were at the scene, but the word all over the city was: "I knew he'd end it with a home run . . ." and "I was going to go to the game but—"

In future years, we can be sure, the men who saw Ted hit that mighty shot will number into the hundreds of thousands. The wind will grow strong and mean, and the distance will grow longer. Many of the reports of the game, in fact, had the ball going into the center-field bleachers.

The seeds of the legend have already been sown. George Carens, an elderly columnist who is more beloved by Ted than by his colleagues, wrote:

"Ted was calm and gracious as he praised the occupants of the Fenway press penthouse at home plate before the game began. Afterwards he greeted all writers in a comradely way, down through his most persistent critics. In a word, Ted showed he can take it, and whenever the spirit moves him he will fit beautifully into the Fenway PR setup."

Which shows that people hear what they want to hear and see what they want to see.

In New York the next day, Phil Rizzuto informed his television audience that Ted had finally relented and tipped his hat after the home run.

And the *Sporting News* headline on its Boston story was:

SPLINTER TIPS CAP
TO HUB FANS AFTER
FAREWELL HOMER.

A New York Sunday paper went so far as to say that Ted had made "a tender and touching farewell speech" from the home plate at the end of the game.

All the reports said that Ted had, in effect, called his shot because it was known that he was shooting for a home run. Who wants to bet that, in future years, there will not be a story or two insisting that he *did* point?

The legend will inevitably grow, and in a way it is a shame. A man should be allowed to die the way he lived. He should be allowed to depart as he came. Ted Williams chose his course early, and his course was to turn his face from the world around him. When he walked out of the park, he kept his eyes to the front and he never looked back.

The epitaph for Ted Williams remains unchanged. He was sometimes unbearable but he was never dull. Baseball will not be the same without him. Boston won't be quite the same either. Old Boston is acrawl with greening statues of old heroes and old patriots, but Ted has left a monument of his own—again on his own terms—in the Children's Cancer Hospital.

He left his own monument in the record books too. For two decades he made the Red Sox exciting in the sheer anticipation of his next time at bat.

He opened his last season with perhaps the longest home run of his career and he closed it with perhaps the most dramatic. It was typical and it was right that the Williams Era in Boston should end not with a whimper. It was entirely proper that it should end with a bang.

So, the old order passeth and an era of austerity has settled upon the Red Sox franchise.

And now Boston knows how England felt when it lost India.

The Mick

Mickey Mantle, the only Hall-of-Famer to have been named after another (Mickey Cochrane, the catcher) was the greatest switch-hitter in the game of baseball. Bothered continually by nagging leg injuries in his later career, the New York Yankee record-setter was forced in 1969 to end his eighteen-season career with the Yankees. Physical pain and the frustration of not being able to do the simple baseball tasks knocked him out of spring training.

Casey Stengel put it all in perspective when he said sadly, "He was the best one-legged player that I ever saw play the game."

With good legs and a somewhat injury-free career, Mantle might have completely rewritten the record books. Instead, the country boy from Spavinaw, Oklahoma, who took New York by storm in the early fifties and held command longer than most mayors, never achieved his true greatness. Could Mickey Mantle have been the best in the history of the modern game is the question that arises at every winter session of the Hot-Stove League. Like other issues brought up for debate at these impromptu meetings, no one can ever know the real answer.

Mantle's record 565-foot blast out of Washington's Griffith Stadium in 1953 was a clue to his strength, while his membership in the select Triple-Crown Club three years later—some say this was his best of all seasons—points to his all-around skills. He led the leagues that year with 52 homers, 130 ribbies, and a .353 batting average.

Mantle will always be remembered by fans for the furious home-run battle that he waged—and lost—with teammate Roger Maris in 1961. The two were hot on Babe Ruth's 1927 record pace until Maris pulled ahead in the second week of September and went on to top the immortal Ruth's record by an asterisk. He had 61 homers for a 161 game season. Mantle finished the race with a career-high 54 homers and an abscessed hip.

Many former athletes whose careers have been cut short by injury are often prone to ask themselves, "Why me?" "Why couldn't I have had someone else's legs?" or "If only my elbow didn't start to hurt, I could have gone further." This select group of fallen heroes, many of whom were kept from reaching their full potential but whose spirits were stronger and tougher than their brittle bodies, would be led by one, Mickey Charles Mantle.

In 1961, Mantle had cartilage removed from his right knee. He had the same operation the following year. The year 1955 was marked by a severe groin pull; 1956 by a seriously sprained left knee; 1957 by a sore shoulder. In 1959 it was a broken finger; in 1961 hip pain; in 1963 a broken left foot; in 1965 surgery on his shoulder. But he was also slowed down by many leg problems.

On March 1, 1969, Mickey Mantle could not go on any longer. The press gathered for spring training in Fort Lauderdale rushed over to the Yankee Clipper Hotel to hear Mantle's announcement.

"I'm not going to play any more baseball. I was really going to try to play, but I didn't think that I could. I have had three or four bad years in a row and, as a result, received the greatest disappointment of my career by falling under .300 as a lifetime average. I was actually dreading playing another season. I just can't play any more and I know it. . . ."

And so the curtain came down on the career of Mickey Mantle. Other young men, more physically equipped and in better health, will come to the big leagues and make a run at Mantle's records; and someday they will be toppled, for that is the nature of the game: to do better than your predecessors. But for one who saw "The Mick" and cheered his every move, the nagging question will always remain: What if he had had a career free of serious injuries?

The Man with a Dream

As a teenager, Hank Aaron started his baseball career playing shortstop for the Indianapolis Clowns, a touring black team that called the Midwest its headquarters and every small town from Bangor to Tallahassee its home. It was a tough

Mickey Mantle

life—living, sleeping, and eating on a bus—but Aaron had a dream he wanted to fulfill.

At the end of the 1952 season, when Hank signed on with the Boston Braves for $10,000, his days of passing the hat with his teammates after the game were finally over. Four years later he had established himself as a star on the rise in the major leagues. In this third season with the Braves, he had a .328 batting average—tops in the National League that year (.25 points behind Mickey Mantle). The following season, Aaron was awesome. He smacked 44 balls out of the parks to lead in the home-run category, and his 132 RBIs were also best in the league. Aaron was to lead in the RBI category a record four times, one short of the major-league record shared by Babe Ruth and Lou Gehrig.

Twenty-three years after Aaron left the Clowns, Al Downing of the Los Angeles Dodgers wound up and pitched to Number 44, Hank Aaron, in a nationally televised game. The time was 9:07, Eastern Time. It was 63 degrees and an overcast, drizzly April 28, 1974.

Hammerin' Hank drove Downing's ball for a home run 400 feet out into Atlanta's left-field bullpen, and 54,000 fans erupted into cheers. Babe Ruth's 714 career-home-run record had just been eclipsed; a milestone had been achieved, a myth shattered, and a national hero toppled, but still the people cheered. When Hank Aaron hit number 715, a lifelong dream to be the top long-ball hitter in the major leagues had been achieved. He stood smiling at home plate after rounding the bases, and the thunderous applause poured down on him like rain. Hank Aaron, the poor boy from Mobile, Alabama, was a happy man.

Achievements

- 16 grand slams; tied with Babe Ruth, seven short of Lou Gehrig.
- 661 career home runs as an outfielder; leads the National League by a landslide.
- 47 home runs in 1971; Atlanta Braves club record.
- 3,771 hits in career, second to Ty Cobb by 420.
- 755 lifetime home runs at the rate of one for every sixteen times at bat; the best in baseball history.
- Led the National League eight times in total bases: 1956 (340), 1957 (369), 1960 (334), 1961 (358), 1963 (370), 1967 (344), 1969 (332).
- Top batter in the National League in 1956 (.328) and 1959 (.355)
- National League home-run leader 1957 (44), 1963 (44), 1966 (44), 1967 (39).

UMPIRES

The Men in Blue

Though sticks and stones his bones may crack
  And bottles innundate his back
The harshest names
From men and dames
Won't jar his self-possession.

Though folks call him "Jesse James"
And "crook" and "yegg" and suchlike names,
And say he's blind,
  He doesn't mind.
Now what is his profession?
                    —*The Baseball Magazine*, January 1926

Baseball umpires are not like ballplayers. Although they must worry about balls and strikes, they are not at all affected by base hits, batting averages, fielding errors, or league standings. The winner of the Most Valuable Player award has had no bearing on their profession, and their interest in the outcome of the World Series is like any other American's.

In many respects, baseball umpires can be likened to the black-smocked judges who preside in our courts of law. They must both follow the laws as they are written and they must above all be impartial. Like the judge, the umpire's job is to keep the proceedings under control and to see their "case" to completion.

Umpires are self-reliant, but in 1876 the rules stated: "Should the umpire be unable to see whether a catch has been fairly made or not, he shall be at liberty to appeal to the bystanders, and to render his decision according to the fairest testimony at hand."

This antiquated form of sportsmanship no longer holds true. The umpire is totally on his own and in plain view of thousands of fans in the ball park. Every call he makes is carefully analyzed not only by players and spectators at the park but by second-guessing fans watching the game at home on television.

Regardless of instant replay, beer bottles, and catcalls, the umpire must be strong-willed and ready to stand behind his decisions. There is no turning back once a call has been made. Umpiring is a thankless job that is only best appreciated by the umpire's immediate family, if he still has one after being on the road for weeks without being able to get home.

The umpire must be both rule-enforcer and peacekeeper, and when things get a bit unsavory in the stadium—the umpire is the usual target—a knowledge of fisticuffs or some form of Oriental defense is an asset. South American *futbol* refs have been known to have been killed in the line of duty by unruly mobs. Luckily for the baseball umpire, the most that Americans toss at them are insults.

Catfish. For some the name means a large scaleless fish, the type with cat-like whiskers about a rather large mouth. For Bill Klem, the greatest umpire in the history of the major leagues, the word catfish was all he needed to hear to get fired up. Even if he saw a player or a manager mouth the word, his face would darken with rage. The name was actually given Klem when he umpired in the American Association in 1904. During a game, he called a play that didn't sit too well with Columbus manager Bill Clymer. "You old catfish!" he yelled at Klem. "You can't talk, smile, or do anything but move your gills." The simple sobriquet stuck, and Klem was labeled for life.

Bill Klem umpired in the National League from 1905 to 1941, working behind the plate through five no-hitters and officiating in eighteen World Series. A myth has grown up around Klem about how he never made a bad call, "never missed one in his heart." This points out the type of man he was, and it was his implicit honesty that made him one of the greatest ever to don an umpire's suit.

Klem had a unique tactic for dealing with raging managers or angry players. He would simply drag his spiked shoe in the dirt, making a rough line. If a player or manager crossed it he was automatically ejected from the game. No one ever dared cross Klem's line, and his umpiring went on without too many disputes.

Klem did the most to help change the working conditions for his fellow officials. Getting dressing facilities for after the game was his first step. A startled National League commissioner, Harry Pulliam, wanted to know why umpires needed their own changing rooms.

"It's embarrassing to be on a streetcar in uniform after the game, especially when the home team has lost," retorted an incensed Klem.

Not only was it embarrassing, it was also dangerous.

Following his retirement from active service in 1941, Klem became chief of the National League's staff of umpires, a post he held until his death in 1951. The Hall of Fame inducted him two years later, along with Tommy Connolly of the American League—the first umpires ever to be enshrined in the Hall.

Some Umpires of Note

Charles Rigler, one of the premier umpires of the National League, officiated in ten World Series between 1910 and 1930. He is usually credited with being the first to raise his right hand to indicate strikes. Rigler may have been the first umpire to do so, but back in 1902, Cincinnati coaches were already using the hand signals that umpires use today, for the benefit of William (Dummy) Hoy, the deaf outfielder and .292 slugger who couldn't hear the calls of the umpire.

George "Watch" Burnham was a rookie umpire in the early 1880s who was often derided for his terrible officiating. Of his performance in Chicago it was written, " . . . More unjust decisions in Chicago in three days than all the errors made in Chicago by all the umpires all season."

Managers hated to see Burnham show up at the ball park to work a game. But it seems that Burnham was not deemed all *that* bad an official. On July 25, 1883, the supposedly unpopular official was presented with an inscribed gold watch by appreciative Cleveland fans. Chiseled inside the timepiece was *Presented to George Burnham by his Cleveland friends, July 25, 1883.*

Only much later was it discovered that Burnham, in an effort to attain a modicum of popularity, had paid for the watch, written the inscription, and orchestrated the entire presentation ceremony!

For punching plate-umpire *Frank Dascoli* in 1948, Chicago Cub catcher Dewy Williams was hit with one of baseball's weirdest fines. Williams was fined $100 by the league office and suspended for five days. This was not to be a short vacation for Williams. He was ordered to serve his five-day sit-out in the Cincinnati dugout in full uniform and ready to play! Should anything happen to Ray Lamanno, the team's only other able-bodied catcher, Williams was to go into the game and take his place. For each game that he played, another day would be added to his suspension.

Bill Klem had a run-in with Frankie Frisch that was more amusing after the game than during it, for sure. Frisch was the manager of the Pirates from 1940 to 1946 and was just as much a battler as a manager as he had been as a

Bill "Catfish" Klem

Give Him a Chance

Hall of Fame infielder for the Giants and Cards (1919–37). In his first year with Pittsburgh, he became so worked up during a game that when he felt Klem had called one wrong against the Bucs, he pretended to faint; and before thousands of startled Pittsburgh fans and players, he fell on the ground near the dugout.

Klem, the plate umpire, came running over when he saw what had happened. Immediately realizing what Frisch was up to, he bent over and whispered to the striken manager, "If you ain't dead, Frisch, then you're out of the game."

Ralph Houk is better known as a former New York Yankee catcher, coach, manager, and general manager, but from 1955 to 1957 he was the head man of the Denver team in the American Association. In his final year there he guided them to the Little World Series title, which was a portent of what would happen when he stepped up to the Yankees.

Houk had a terrible temper and was put on probation several times for the general abuse he dished out to umpires. Nevertheless, on one particularly bad call he stormed out of the dugout and stalked the home-plate ump. Eyeball to eyeball with the man, Houk prefaced his remarks to the man in blue by saying, "I'm not allowed to cuss you out any more, but I just thought you might like to know that I passed a kennel on the way to the game and your mother is all right."

Now Guess

Who is it the fans all hate?
Who should be kept outside the gate?
Who someday will meet an awful fate?

Who makes decisions that are awful now?
Who likes to hear the players jaw?
Who gets the goat of John McGraw?

Who thinks he's it without a doubt?
Who calls a man safe when he should be out?
Who doesn't know what he's talking about?
—*The Baseball Magazine*
February 1909

Hammurabi's "eye for an eye, tooth for a tooth" code of laws is updated here. The following clipping dated August 22, 1929, was found at the Library of the Baseball Hall of Fame in the file labeled *Violence.*

Punishment to Fit the Crime

If a spectator is apprehended and identified as having thrown pop bottles at an umpire, bind him to a stake and let the umpire throw bottles at him.

If a pitcher dusts off the batters until it has become a nuisance and a menace to health, give the batters the privilege of dusting off the pitcher.

If an infielder deliberately spikes a base runner, seize the infielder and give to the base runner the right to caress the infielder with the ticklish side of a horse radish grater.

If a fielder trips a base runner deliberately, roll the offending fielder on a barrel from home plate to center field and return. . . .

MANAGERS

Connie Mack

He was born Cornelius McGillicuddy in relative poverty in 1862, but when he died ninety-three years later he had come to own the majority of the Philadelphia A's and was better known to generations of baseball fans and players as Connie Mack, Mr. Baseball.

When Mack was nine years old, he spent the summer working in a cotton mill running errands. It was there that he started to play a cut-down version of baseball called four-old-cat, a sandlot game more akin to cricket than any other ball game. In his later teens he started playing "real baseball"—the catcher still caught the ball on a bounce then—in a field in the Central Massachusetts League. Soon after, Mack took a big gamble both socially and financially when he signed on with Meriden in the Connecticut State League. He was a twenty-two-year-old catcher in a sport that attracted all forms of gambling and corrupt players. Player wages were met by passing the hat after the ball game, and if someone came up short in his pay, the manager tried to make it up in the next game. Mack already had a good-paying job in a shoe factory, and his decision to make a career in the sport he loved was a difficult one because his mother was against it. After Mack promised her he wouldn't smoke, drink, or curse like the other ball players, she gave him permission to become a pro ball player.

Mack certainly did not stand out in the National League when he played for Washington, Buffalo, and Pittsburgh for a ten-year span ending in 1896. The 1893 season with Pittsburgh was his best at bat—he sported a .325 average—but his lifetime total is a mere .251. Still, Connie Mack earned his reputation on the ball field. As the shrewd nonplaying manager of the Philadelphia A's for a record fifty consecutive years, Mack's team won nine American League pennants, participated in eight World Series, and won five of them (1910, 1911, 1923, 1929, 1930).

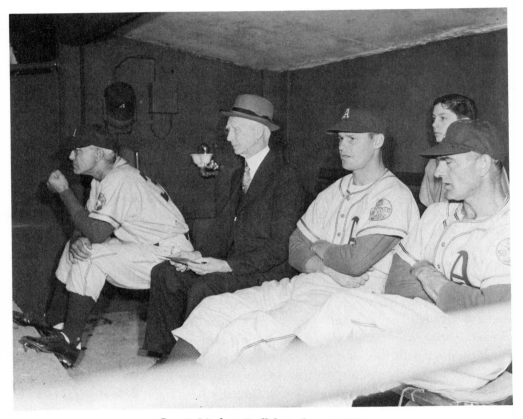

Connie Mack at Griffith Stadium (1950)

Mack was a quiet and reserved man who never wore a baseball uniform while managing the club. Instead, he would sit in the dugout dressed in a three-piece suit and direct the players on the field with a scorecard he always carried in his hand.

Hall-of-Famers Rube Waddell, Eddie Collins, Charles "Chief" Bender, Frank "Home Run" Baker, Eddie Plank, Mickey Cochrane, Al Simmons, Herb Pennock, Lefty Grove, and Jimmie Foxx all were Mack men and played chief roles in winning twenty-four Series games for their leader.

Many have said that Mack kept a tight hand on the team's purse strings, and in comparison to a few other teams, notably Chicago and New York, maybe he did. In 1910, however, he assembled the fabled "$100,000 infield," which consisted of former schoolboy sensation Stuffy McInnis, Columbia University's Eddie Collins, Jack Barry at shortstop, and Frank Baker at third. Mack didn't pay the amount that was part of their nickname; they were just worth that much money on the open market.

Mack later broke up the amazing infield after easily winning the American League pennant by eight and a half games in 1914. Their loss to the "Miracle Braves" in four straight Series games did not change his mind on the sale of the players. Fans were not coming to the games, he said, because the A's rarely lost. No one wanted to pay to watch perfection.

Mack's players were versatile, both adept at hitting as they were in the field. This is difficult to find today in a game where specialists seem to abound. There are batters who do well against lefty pitching, and there are men who can steal a base in domed stadiums better than in big-city stadiums built after 1957. In 1910 and 1913, Mack's men showed their versatility. They had to. In those ten World Series games, Connie Mack never made a substitution! No relievers or pinch hitters entered the game. Chief Bender was the A's ace, winning two of the games of the 4–1 sweep in 1910 and two more in the four-game sweep three years later.

Connie Mack was already a legend when he was inducted into the Hall of Fame in 1937, but he had no intention of stopping just because baseball wanted to honor him. He managed for thirteen more seasons. The victories were more difficult to come by in later years, but then he didn't have the stars like he used to. Even in his seventies, Mack admitted that managing a baseball team was still fun and exciting. "I'd die within two weeks if I ever left baseball," he used to say. Mack was well-loved, and no one liked to hear him talk like that, but he knew himself too well.

The city of Philadelphia and the sports world lost a great man when Connie Mack died on Febuary 8, 1956, a short fifteen months after he sold the Philadelphia A's and left baseball for good.

A Manager's Guidelines

Joe McCarthy was manager of the New York Yankees from 1931 to 1946. His teams won eight American League pennants and seven World Series titles (1932, 1936, 1937, 1938, 1939, 1941, and 1943) in that time. With great players on his team like Babe Ruth, Tony Lazzeri, Lou Gehrig, and Joe DiMaggio, success at managing was not too difficult to come by; but McCarthy had previously managed the lowly Chicago Cubs from last place in 1925 to the World Series in 1929, so he did know a bit of baseball himself.

Included here are his guidelines, penned by McCarthy himself. Each stems from personal experience, no doubt, and each is still as meaningful today as it was a half century ago.

1. Don't throw the ball before you catch it.
2. Take your bat off your shoulder if you want to hit .300.
3. Outfielders throwing the ball behind the runner lock the barn after the horse has been stolen.
4. Keep your head up and you might not have to hold it down.
5. When you start to slide, slide. He who changes his mind may change a good leg for a broken one.
6. Look ahead, not backward on the bases. Remember what happened to Lot's wife.
7. Don't throw the ball to the base after the runner is there. A ball in the hand is safer than one in the air.
8. Touch all bases. That's what they are there for.
9. Don't find too many faults with the umpire. You can't expect him to be as perfect as you are.
10. Nobody became a good player by walking after the ball.
11. Don't quit; the game isn't over until the last man is out.
12. A pitcher hasn't anything if he hasn't control.

THE TEAM DOCTOR

A Beantown Medicine Man

Dr. Arthur Pappas has been team physician for the Boston Red Sox since 1977. "There are no positions in baseball, where if a player isn't one hundred percent physically fit he could play and not detract from the overall performance of the team. Baseball is a game of reflexes and timing. An injury, even a small one, is enough to throw off a player's entire game."

In Spring 1979, sitting in the lobby of his office just across the street from Children's Hospital in Boston, the quiet-spoken man talked about his job of treating baseball players. "They're entertainment people," said the good doctor, "and their treatment makes the news.

"Some players go through a career and never have a major injury, while others may be injury-plagued one year and free the next. I have come to assume that some players can go for long stretches without any major physical problems. When fans think of injuries to baseball players, they normally think of the pitcher with the bad arm. The demands on the arm for any athlete in a throwing sport, particularly for the pitchers, are just so abnormal and so intensive that when they continue to ask the body to tolerate that stress it frequently reacts by breaking down. I don't know whether it is the type of ball thrown by a pitcher that can spell arm trouble. Most pitchers have the same repertoire of pitches. The major difference though, seems to be in the flexibility of their bodies, their maintenance, and their general conditioning.

"As I become more involved with baseball, I become more impressed with the fact that a pitcher has to be 100 percent or he can't pitch. One little change in his motion will be enough to change control, velocity, and what he is trying to do with the ball. The entire throwing motion in pitching is abnormal. Throwing is not just elbow and forearm. It starts in the spine and goes through the shoulder and then down the arm. If there is any alteration in the throwing motion, you are going to have pain and loss of performance. Whenever a pitcher sets out to change a throwing style, or if a coach encourages it, you can probably anticipate some medical problem soon.

"It probably used to be true that baseball players were the least conditioned of all professional athletes, but I think that this has all changed. Over the past year or two I've noticed that players have become more aware of conditioning and nutrition. Well-conditioned ball players would never pass an endurance test of the highest grade, but I think that when you are looking at a ball player who is in shape you are seeing a man with eye-hand coordination, reflexes, and quickness of moves that are as great if not greater than any other professional athlete.

"The range of injuries for ball players [is] very much the same for each player on the team. Most baseball injuries are related to upper-extremity problems rather than lower-extremity problems, such as those you find in football. The lower-extremity problems I do see are all related to baserunning: sliding, double plays, and things like that. Ankle and knee problems are common. But the majority of injuries are related to the upper extremity. Some are acute, such as one force causing an injury. Many others are caused by repetitive use or overuse of a particular muscle or muscle group. Doctors know the mechanics of throwing, and we can analyze the different phases of a pitch, but we really don't know the influence of individual muscle forces. Then, too, we don't know how some people make it to the major leagues, what makes one player better than another.

"Medicine has changed in thirty years in a general sense, but so far as what you do specifically in treating players, I'm not sure things have changed that much at all. Now we have more modalities, a few more tricks, different shots, perhaps some exercises, but if you were to ask if there have been major changes in treatment to ball players in the past three decades, I'd have to say no. We just don't have a good scientific basis to understand what makes one player good and another player not so good. What we have seen in baseball is players starting to realize that conditioning will make them better. We try to encourage this and help to formulate specific stretching exercises.

"The lifestyle, the living pattern, of a pro baseball player is a difficult one. Once the players take the field in the beginning of March, they are essentially playing ball every day until the first of October. Some games are in the afternoon and some at night. When they are on the road they may stay in one place for three or four days, and then they pack up and leave. One trip that the Sox made this year started off with a game in Boston. Right after the game they had to catch a flight to Seattle, where they had a game the following day. Once the game was finished there they had to get back to the airport to get a flight back to Boston for a game the next day. Those two trips across America in the space of three days, with three games sandwiched in between the time zones, takes a lot out of the players both mentally and physically.

"When a player is on the road, he usually arrives in a new town in the middle of the night. He will then sleep until noon. When he finally wakes up, he'll usually have a big breakfast. He's tired. He's lost somewhere up to three hours time in flight. Shortly after he finishes eating, he will head for the park. If it's a night game, he has to be at the park by 3:30. He has to dress, warm up, and be ready to play. The player hasn't eaten much before the game, so afterward he may have something to eat in the clubhouse. By that time it is midnight.

"Most players are bored. They are tired. Some are perhaps looking for a little action somewhere. Physically, most are ready to go back to the hotel and go to sleep.

"The lifestyle of a baseball player has led many into alcoholism and drug abuse. After going through the baseball routine for three or four months, it starts to catch up with some of the players. Once it's midnight he may sit down and have a few beers and start talking to people. The hours quickly pass, and before he knows it's morning. People who live this way, whether they be truck drivers or baseball players, ask themselves the same question many times: "How do I get myself up for what I have to do?" This is how greenies became popular. Uppers or something artificial was used to get the players ready for yet another game.

"Drug-taking is not as prevalent today as it was ten years ago, because there has been a concerted effort on the part of organized baseball to become involved in drug- and alcohol-abuse programs for ball players. Don Newcombe has headed a program and put in a tremendous amount of time making players aware of what his experiences were and how drugs and alcohol influenced his performance and why.

"Loneliness may be a factor in the big leagues, but simply, many of the players are just bored. It's a drag. Then there is the problem of the high-performance athlete, the superstar. Once he leaves his circle of friends and goes on the road, he can't just go into any average restaurant and expect to eat a meal undisturbed like everyone else. A superstar's life is not his own, and he is hounded by fans wherever he goes.

"Baseball is not really a violent life, but there are a different series of demands that are placed on the player's lives. It's not that they are hard drinkers or late-night men, but their life pattern does not permit a normal life when they are on the road. The demands on their lives from their ball club down to the fans make their lives difficult."

BALL PARKS

Cow Pastures to Space Domes

Ball parks of old, those not of steel, concrete, artificial turf, and all-enclosing steel roofs, have quickly disappeared from the major leagues. In the National League, only the Chicago Cubs play in an authentic "old" park. Wrigley Field, first opened in 1893 and later expanded in 1916, has neither lights for night games nor an automatic scoreboard. Men still sit behind the board and change the score manually the way it was always done.

Building new parks with artificial turf and other trappings of modernity took away the science involved in the special "tailoring" of fields. Ned Hanlon, the manager of the early Baltimore Orioles (1891–98) and the Brooklyn Dodgers (1899–1905) was the acclaimed master of this handiwork. Going simply on appearances, Hanlon looked like a real Milquetoast, yet despite his innocent mien it was Hanlon who thought up and instigated such practices as lowering the pitcher's mound whenever Christy Mathewson of the Giants came to pitch.

"Hanlon knew that I used a lot of speed when I first broke into the League, getting some of it from my elevation on the diamond," said Mathewson in his book *Pitching in a Pinch*. "He had a team of fast men who depended largely on a bunting game and their speed in getting to first base to win. With me fielding bunts out of the hollow, they had a better chance of making their goal. Then pitching from the lower level would naturally result in the batters getting low balls, because I would be more apt at misjudging the level of the plate."

Hanlon proved to be the master of deceit. He had standing orders with all his players to trip runners, to push them out of bounds, and if all this failed, to hold them by their pants as they rounded the base. Hanlon's boys won the National League pennant in 1894, 1895, 1896, 1899, and 1900.

Connie Mack, the Philadelphia A's patriarch, was also one to alter the fields when he had to, always making sure that extra water was added to the base paths before a game to slow down opposing base stealers. Once, in a morning workout session prior to an afternoon game, Mack had the groundskeeper raise the level of the pitcher's mound two feet for the benefit of Hall of Fame pitcher Rube Waddell, who used the extra height to help his speed. Rube was one of the greatest pitchers in the American league and notched 349 strikeouts in 1904. On this particular turf-building day, however, there were to be no strikeouts by the great Rube; he failed to show up for the game, lingering instead at a favorite tavern. Needless to say, Mack's plan backfired, and he paid for his trickery by gloomily watching his team get shelled in the game.

Adding soap to the dirt on the pitcher's mound so that unknowing pitchers would dry their hands in it and get slippery palms was another trick from the early days. So was letting the outfield grass grow to ankle height or better. Extra baseballs were then left in strategic spots and thrown into play at key moments.

Weak-hitting clubs would sometimes paint the walls or fences in the outfield a pale color. This way, when strong-slugging teams came to the park they would have trouble seeing the ball as it came out of the bright background created in the outfield. The light background would not bother the home team since they couldn't hit too well anyway!

An old trick used by almost every team was to take a new ball that the ump had tossed into play and pass it around the infield. As each fielder got the ball he would spit tobacco juice on it and rub it with dirt. The ball quickly came to match the color of the darkening afternoon sky, a boon to the pitching staff and a real problem for batters.

With the introduction of the ball park, the game of baseball changed from simply a Sunday afternoon diversion from work—a true sport—and evolved into a full-scale business. As the game progressed in keeping with the nation's economic growth, so too did the ball parks. Playing grounds moved from the initial open lot of amateur times, to the fence-encircled wooden stadiums, then to the concrete-and-steel facilities of the twenties, thirties and forties.

The superstadiums came next. Candlestick Park in 1960 was the first. Then the Houston Astrodome quickly followed as the phenomenon of the sixties, with Seattle's Kingdome the marvel of the seventies. The Astrodome was completed in 1965, and for the first time it made bad weather no longer an excuse and rainchecks quickly became obsolete. The "Eighth Wonder of the World," with its permanent temperature of 72 degrees, came with an 800-ton, 474-foot-wide computer-operated scoreboard that exploded like a Fourth of July celebration whenever something spectacular happened on the field.

Rising inflation and differences in priorities have driven stadium-building

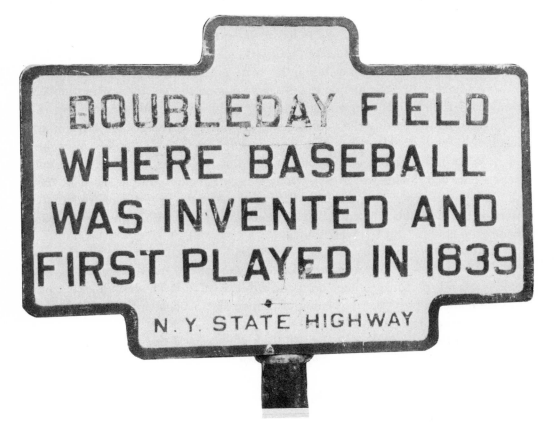

Doubleday Field, Cooperstown, N.Y.

Unidentified Ball Park

Elysian Fields, Hoboken, New Jersey

costs upward, but it is still a shock to think that the entire Yankee Stadium, the "House That Ruth Built" in 1923, cost $2 million, the same price as the Astrodome scoreboard.

Of Ebbets Field and the Polo Grounds

Many old ball parks have been demolished to make way for newer and bigger stadiums. In the case of the Polo Grounds and Ebbets Field in New York, once the homes of the Giants and Dodgers respectively, both were leveled for apartment projects after both teams left the city for the West Coast.

Opened April 9, 1913, Ebbets Field housed the wildest baseball fans and one of the zaniest baseball teams to date. Superfan Hilda Chester would always come to the games with a large banner that read "Hilda is here," and once the game started she would make good use of the two large cowbells she carried in with her.

The 1939 Dodger season is remembered by many, not so much for the Dodgers' low finish in the standings but for the on-field attack of umpire George Magerkurth, a former boxer, by an equally large assailant. It was learned later that the attack was planned, plotted, and carried out not out of anger because of Magerkurth's shortcomings as an ump, nor because of the Dodgers' loss to the Braves that day; it was done solely as a means to sufficiently distract the fans while an accomplice in the bleachers went through their pockets for wallets and other items of worth!

The right-field wall at Ebbets was a sight to see—as wild and bizarre as the Dodger loyalists, most of whom started to exercise their vocal cords on the first pitch and continued the exercise until they got home later that day. The wall was 20 feet high and topped off by a screen to protect apartment windows on Bedford Avenue that were too often being smashed by powermen Jacques Fournier, Floyd "Babe" Herman, and Adelphia Bissonette. The wall, a concave structure, was the bane of many visiting outfielders, who could only stand and watch in frustration as weakly hit balls wildly caromed off the wall for stand-up triples.

Near the wall, next to the scoreboard that advertised Schaefer beer, was a sign that advertised a dare from clothier Abe Stark to hit the sign and win a suit. No batter ever made good on Stark's long-standing offer, since the sign was so low that all balls were easily caught before they could come close to hitting the target.

Colorful players and managers are interwoven in Brooklyn Dodger history. Wilbert "Uncle Robbie" Robinson was manager of the team from 1914 to 1931, watching them win league pennants in 1916 and 1920. "Just get up there and hit the ball" was how he gruffly replied to one newcomer to the organization who wanted to know what the Dodgers' hitting signals were.

Casey Stengel was also with the Dodgers (1934–36), as was The Lip, Leo Durocher, who managed the Bums from 1939 to 1946 and won the pennant in 1941, only to lose the Series to the Yankees 4 games to 1.

During their stay in Brooklyn, the Dodgers went to the World Series a total of nine times. They lost eight times, six of those defeats coming at the bats of the hated Bronx Bombers, the Yankees.

Babe Herman, the leader and founding member of Brooklyn's daffiness boys, came to the team in 1926. In only his first year under Uncle Robbie, Herman became the only player in major-league ball who "tripled into a double play." This amazing event came about in a game against the Boston Braves. With the bases loaded and one out, Herman smashed a line drive off the right-field wall, knocking in John Deberry who was on third. Dazzy Vance, who was on second base, pulled up halfway between home and third because he thought Herman's fly ball had been caught; so he went back to third base.

Chick Fewster was confused. He had been on first base headed for third, but when he saw Vance heading back to third, he just stopped in his tracks. In the meantime, Herman was running with his head down, trying to get as many bases possible out of the hit. He ran past Fewster and slid into third base—at the same time that Vance slid in from the other side.

The Dodger fans stared at this comedy in disbelief, not knowing what was going on in front of their eyes. The Braves, meanwhile, refused to be duped by Herman. Eddie Taylor, the Braves third baseman, took the relay throw from the outfield and tagged both Herman and Vance. When confused umpire Ernie Quigley gave no sign as to who, if any, were out, Taylor reversed the order of tags and touched the Brooklyn runners a second time. Again Quigley didn't say anything.

Doc Gautreau came running in from center field. If Taylor couldn't get them out, then he would go after Fewster, who was standing near second base. He grabbed the ball from Taylor and went running after him. The chagrined Fewster was finally tagged "out" in front of the bullpen in right field.

When the smoke cleared and some order returned to the game, it was decided that the inning was over. Fewster was out for leaving the base path and Herman, well, he was out for passing Fewster. "I thought Fewster was going to score" was all Herman had to say in his defense.

In 1924 the Dodgers had a heated series with their other hated rivals, the New York Giants. The game was sold out, and thousands of fans stood outside

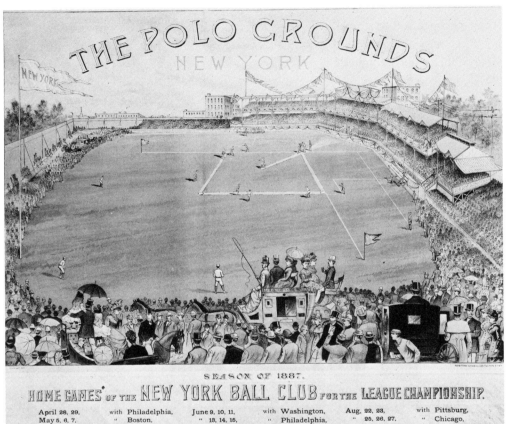

The Polo Grounds, New York, N.Y.

the gate trying to get in. Finally they tore down a telegraph pole and used it as a battering ram to smash through the center-field gate. They then took their positions along the outer rim of the outfield.

On one play, Hack Wilson went back for a fly ball; the crowd parted, allowing Wilson to catch the ball. It was a sporting gesture that few onlookers could believe. Then, like a clam, the crowd closed up again, engulfing the Giant outfielder. When Wilson was finally spit out back on the field he was missing his glove, his sunglasses, and the ball!

June 15, 1938, was a night to remember in Brooklyn. Ebbets Field was outfitted with lights, and the first night game was played against the visiting Cincinnati Reds, The Reds did not make the Dodgers look good in their evening debut, and Johnny Vander Meer was the worst offender. Just four days after pitching a no-hitter against the Boston Braves, twenty-four-year-old Vandy masterminded a 6–0 no-hitter against the Dodgers.

Vander Meer performed a pitching feat never achieved before—18 consecutive innings of no-hit baseball.

Just as Brooklyn was one borough of many different nationalities, a melting pot of creeds and colors, so too were the Dodgers. The Bums were everybody's team, and it was only fitting that Jackie Robinson start with the Dodgers in 1947. Helped by the reception that he received in Brooklyn, baseball's first black player led the league in base stealing, hit .297, and was named Rookie of the Year in the National League. The Dodger fans embraced Robinson, and it was this warm reception that smoothed the way for other black players who followed.

The World Series was first televised in 1947. The Dodgers took it on the chin, losing to the Yankees in seven games. Winning the pennant but losing the Series seemed to be the Dodgers' fate. The Brooklyn fans were loyal—the popular joke was that 15,000 would come to Ebbets Field just to see why they turned the lights on. They were finally rewarded for their fealty in 1955 in the fifty-fourth World Series. In the seventh and final game, behind the 2–0 shutout pitching of Johnny Podres, joy and jubilation came to Brooklyn. After losing five previous Series to the Yankees, they finally topped them in their sixth meeting and were the champs of baseball.

All that is left of Ebbets Field today are memories. On September 24, 1957, the Dodgers beat the Pirates 3–0 before 6,673 diehards. Ebbets, once one of the most famous fields of baseball, is gone. So too are the Dodgers—Roy Campanella, Pee Wee Reese, Duke Snider, Clem Labine, Carl Furillo, Carl Erskine, Sandy Koufax, Gil Hodges, Jim Gilliam, Don Hoak. These were the last players in the park for the Dodgers in 1957. They packed their bags and left Brooklyn forever.

The Dodgers are gone from Flatbush, but they are never far from the hearts of the people who still remember "dem bums."

After a close game, Jim Mutrie, manager of the New York National League Baseball Club, was heard to exclaim, "My big fellows! My giants! Newspaper writers picked up Mutrie's cry. No, they didn't rename the team the "Big Fellows." They settled on "Giants," and the name is with us to this day.

Eddie Stankey, Leo Durocher, Sal "The Barber" Maglie, Bobby Thomson, Dusty Rhodes, Christy Mathewson, Rube Marquard, Mel Ott, Johnny Mize, Carl Hubbell, Willie Mays. Giants, each one of them, and all great names who made the Polo Grounds a New York institution.

Polo Grounds history is built around John McGraw and Christy Mathewson. Mathewson, "Big Six" as he was known to his admirers, helped make strikeout pitching and superb control Giant trademarks. Always out to improve his financial lot, Mathewson also pioneered "checkbook journalism" in sports by demanding payment for interviews before he would talk to reporters.

John McGraw was Mr. Giant. Although less imposing physically than Mathewson, McGraw made his five feet seven inches and 150 pounds seem like a lot more. In 1902, Little Napoleon was persuaded to leave his managing job in Baltimore and take over the Giants. Only if his terms could be met, he told Giant owner Andy Freedman, would he come to New York. This included getting rid of any players he wanted to and bringing in his own men; "Iron Man" Joe McGinnity, Roger Breshnahan, and others.

Freedman agreed, and McGraw did just what he had promised. The Giants moved from last place to pennant winners in 1904. Thanks to Christy Mathewson's three scoreless games against Philadelphia, the Giants won the World Series in 1905.

McGraw stayed thirty years with the Giants, winning a total of ten league pennants and three World Series championships. He was the greatest manager the game has yet to see.

The Polo Grounds was known as the softest home-run touch in the National League. The last Polo Grounds was never actually a polo field but acquired the name from the Giants' original field, which was one in 1883. The new ball park was opened in 1891 in upper Manhattan, and since people were still in the habit of saying "I'm going to the Polo Grounds to see the Giants play," the name was kept.

A fire in April destroyed the double-decker horseshoe stands, but they were quickly rebuilt out of concrete and ready for use two months later.

The Polo Grounds squatted below a piece of land called Coogan's Bluff. This location caused a crimping on the outfield dimensions and necessitated

Fenway Park, Boston

Night Game at Fenway Park, Boston

pulling in the foul poles. The right-field pole was only 257 feet from home plate, the left-field pole was 279, and the center-field pole was 482. Defense in the outfield called for clever fielders, especially in right and left, where fly shots came off the walls like ricocheting billiard shots.

The Polo Grounds was a home-run hitter's paradise. The Yankees played in the park from 1913 to 1923 until their park was ready, and Babe Ruth proved to be a popular tenant. Joe Jackson was another. Thought to be the game's most natural slugger, Jackson put on a hitting exhibition for the fans when he hit the first ball over the Polo Grounds roof. This fond memory of Jackson would stay with Giant fans until it became known that Jackson was involved in the Black Sox fixing scandal of 1919, the worst attack ever on the integrity of the game.

Other memorable hitters who visited the park included Yankee strongboy Tony Lazzeri. On October 2, 1936, in the third inning of the World Series, he smashed a grand slam home run that brought despair to the hearts of Giant followers. They were even more embarrassed when the Yankees went on to win the game 18–4. But grand slams were Lazzeri's speciality. On May 24, in a game against the Philadelphia A's, he had a grand slam in the second inning and another in the fifth to lead the Yankees to a 25–2 slaughter.

The Polo Grounds was the scene of numerous noteworthy incidents. During the heat of the Giants' pennant drive in 1908, it was in the Polo Grounds that Fred Merkle failed to touch second base as the winning run crossed home plate for the Giants. The Polo Grounds was also the site of the greatest strikeout story in the history of the All-Star Game. On July 10, 1934, King Carl Hubbell, the Giants' left-handed screwball specialist, set down five consecutive Hall of Famers and brought the Polo Grounds fans to their feet in cheers.

In the first inning of this annual game between the game's greatest players, Charlie Gehringer started out with a single to center field. Boston's Heinie Manush, the first ball player ever ejected from a World Series (he snapped an umpire's bow tie in 1933) walked on Hubbell's next pitches.

Hubbell had pitched 46⅓ scoreless innings the previous year and ended up with an earned run average of 1.66. The King was a pitcher to be feared, and the 50,000 spectators gathered for the game knew it. With no outs and baseball's "Murderers' Row" of Babe Ruth, Lou Gehrig, and Jimmie Foxx coming up, the King would really be pushed to the limit of his pitching ability.

To everyone's amazement, Babe Ruth watched three screwballs go whizzing by and was thumbed out. Lou Gehrig didn't fare any better. He went to join Ruth on the bench after four pitches. Double X, Jimmie Foxx, Philadelphia's representation in the game, was next up. Foxx had won the triple crown the year before with 48 homers, 163 RBIs and a .356 batting average. Gehringer and Manush were sure that Foxx would be able to advance them. The first pitch was called a ball, but the next three screwballs were strikes, and Jimmie Foxx was out.

It took ten pitches, and three of the major leagues' most powerful hitters went down—an incredible feat that may never be equaled. Al Simmons and Joe Cronin went down in the second inning, and it wasn't until Bill Dickey was able to get a single that Hubbell's magic spell was broken. After he finished his pitching duties for the day, Hubbell went to the sidelines to the sounds of a thunderous ovation. The National League went on to lose the game to their American League rivals, but that fact has faded in history. Said Joe Heydler, the league president who was at the game, "It was the greatest feat I have witnessed in more than sixty years of baseball viewing."

The Polo Grounds had other great moments, like the scene of New York City's annual Civil War, the battle between the Giants and Dodgers, and the accompanying squabbles between their partisans.

It was October 2, 1951. The time: 3:58 P.M. In the ninth inning of the last game of the National League season, Ralph Branca of the Dodgers pitched to Bobby Thomson, the Giants' Glasgow-born outfielder. The resulting "shot heard round the world" scored three Giant runs and gave the Giants a surprising 5–4 upset victory over the Dodgers and the National League pennant.

The delirious crowd flowed onto the field and mobbed their heroes. After falling behind the Dodgers by 13½ games in mid-August, Thomson's home run capped a pennant drive that had the entire city captivated in the summertime drama. The Giants fans rejoiced while the Dodger fans mourned. And it all happened in the Polo Grounds. Although the Giants would lose the 1951 Series to the Yankees, thousands of fans will never forget Thomson's Polo Grounds homer.

The year 1954 was the last glory year for the Giants. They snatched the Series from Cleveland 4 games to 0. Three years later it was all over. Claiming financial troubles and poor fan support, the Giants bade farewell to their fans and left for San Francisco. The once proud Polo Grounds, site of so much baseball history, drama, and excitement, fell victim to the wrecker's steel ball. Jackhammers and blasting caps finished off the job, and the stadium was ignominiously leveled to make way for a city housing project.

SUPERSTITIONS

Look, how the world's poor people are amazed
At apparitions, signs, and prodigies,
Whereon with fearful eyes they long have gazed,
Infusing them with dreadful prophesies.
          —William Shakespeare, *Venus and Adonis*

The Giants' Faust

In the midst of the 1911 baseball season, things could not have been going any worse for Manager John McGraw's Giants. His pitchers were getting tagged for hits in every game, and all hopes for winning the pennant were being crushed by the realities of having one of the poorer records in the National League.

At midseason, the Giants were in Saint Louis on a western swing. One day a strange man in his early thirties approached McGraw in the lobby of Planter's Hotel and proceeded to tell him a bizarre tale. His name was Charles Victor Faust and he had recently paid five dollars to a fortune-teller in Kansas City to find out what he should do with his life. The gypsy told Faust that he was destined for greatness as a pitcher for the New York Giants.

The ever-believing Faust took the *zingara* at her word and left to find fame and fortune with McGraw's team. Now that he had tracked them down in Saint Louis, he was ready for his tryout. McGraw had nothing to lose, since he desperately needed someone to spark his pitching staff. If anything, the hayseed would lift the team's spirits.

After watching Faust throw only a few times, McGraw was certain of two things: first, that Faust had been taken for five dollars in Kansas City, and second, that Faust was wasting his time trying to be a pitcher. The Giants on the sidelines laughed as Faust went through his contorted windup and delivery. To

Velvet Tooth Picks Advertisement

everyone's surprise, McGraw did not send Faust away. Instead, he invited him into the dugout to watch the game.

Strangely enough, the Giants won that day and snapped a long string of losses. With Faust in the dugout in the following games, the Giants didn't lose any either. Faust soon grew tired of sitting on the bench with the Giants. The fortune-teller had said he was to become a pitcher, and he wanted his turn. When McGraw wouldn't let him in a game, he packed his bags and left just as mysteriously as he had appeared.

Nothing much was said about Faust after he left, nor was the connection made between the winning streak and the presence of Charles Victor Faust in the dugout.

A few weeks later, Faust took to the road and traveled in boxcars to New York City. Once again filled with a determination to pitch for the Giants, he headed up to the Polo Grounds and went straight to the office of John McGraw.

The Giants had been losing steadily since Faust's disappearance, and McGraw was in no mood to see Faust. He left word to have the unkempt and unwanted Faust barred from the premises. That day, as the Giants were going down to another defeat, Faust was taking a job in vaudeville as a stagehand. The Giants dropped their next three games before they heard from Faust again.

McGraw seemed to sense something in Faust, and he agreed to take Faust with the team on their next road trip. The Giants did seem to win when Faust was with them, so why not have him along for good luck, thought McGraw.

The Giants lost only four games on their trip and according to Christy Mathewson had "one of the greatest ever trips."

Faust became the Giants' good-luck omen, and McGraw made wise use of his strange abilities to turn close defeat into victory. In one extra-inning contest, with runners on base and threatening to score, McGraw sent Christy Mathewson to the bullpen to get Faust to come sit in the dugout. The plan worked. The rally stopped, and in the next inning the Giants went on to win.

Later that season, Charles Faust was signed to a contract as a thirty-one-year-old rookie. The record books show that the Marion, Kansas, native, born in 1880, pitched in two games for the Giants for a grand total of two innings. He allowed two hits and two runs for a 4.50 ERA.

Faust's Giants won the 1911 pennant, and there wasn't a man on the team who would not say that it wasn't because of Faust's amazing presence.

No one is exactly sure what happened to Faust during the World Series that year against the Philadelphia A's. Maybe he was kidnapped as he once was in Saint Louis. In both cases, he wasn't around when the Giants needed his good-luck potion. Just as Saint Louis had beaten the Faustless Giants after he was kidnapped, so too did the A's, taking the Series 4 to 2.

It was clear that it was simply Charles Faust's presence in the dugout that instilled in the Giants both the confidence and the competence they needed to win games. McGraw even declared to the press, "I give Faust full credit for winning the 1911 pennant for me."

Historically, just as man has always relied on good-luck charms—a rabbit's foot, a four-leaf clover—when he is confronted with uncertainty, so, too, have major-league ball players relied on that "something extra." Baseball is a game structured around uncertainty. Can a pitcher continue to throw strikes? Will the batter be able to hit the ball the next five times up? Even now, when players are drafted according to highly technical computer printouts and high-priced scouting services, players still rely on superstition to help them with their game. Baseball, more than any other sport, still carries with it remnants of earlier men who believed that if you went too far out in the ocean you'd fall off the world.

Charles Faust was the Giants' good-luck charm for one season. When he didn't show up in 1912 or in subsequent seasons, the players looked for some new ritual, person, or thing to help them win. They must have found it in 1917, because they won the pennant that year. In 1921 and 1922 they certainly had something going for them. They won the Series both times.

And Charles Victor Faust? Well, in 1914 he moved to the Pacific Northwest and was soon legally declared insane. Maybe they viewed things a bit differently out there than in New York. In 1915, he died in Fort Steilacoom, Washington. He was thirty-five years old.

Some Common and Not-so-Common Baseball Superstitions

Christy Mathewson claims that in 1912 the Philadelphia A's had a hunchback ball boy they kept for good luck. The previous year he had been voted a half share in the World Series pot for helping them to a 4–2 victory over the Giants.

John McGraw hired a driver to come to the Polo Grounds front gate with a wagon filled with empty barrels when a slumping player went 4 for 5 at bat after seeing such a wagon near the field.

It's a bad omen for anyone to say to the pitcher in the eighth inning, "Come on now, only six more men left."

Ty Cobb used to have a habit of going to the ball park the same way every day and putting his uniform on the same way each time. In 1909, one day after he went 4 for 5 in a game, he almost came to blows with the Detroit Tigers trainer because he had moved Cobb's towel from one peg and put it on another. Cobb went hitless that day and vowed never to let the trainer near his clothes again.

George Stallings was the manager of the 1914 "Miracle Braves" that went from eighth place on July 19 to win the National League crown and then sweep the Series from the Philadelphia A's. Stallings had a peculiar habit that most players in the league soon became aware of. He disliked small sparrows and other little birds that would come to peck at bits of bread in front of the Braves dugout, so he would always fill his pockets with pebbles to throw at the bad-luck omens. Opposing players were sure to leave grain in front of the dugout whenever the Braves came to play. They weren't too successful in 1914.

Never step on the baselines when coming in from the field at the change of an inning.

Never change socks during a hitting streak.

No black cats allowed in the dugout.

Step on a base when leaving or heading out to the field.

A broken bat means a hitless streak coming up.

Never mention to a pitcher that he has a no-hitter in progress.

Seeing a cross-eyed girl is even worse than breaking a mirror. The remedy to get back good luck is to remove your baseball cap and spit in it.

For each hairpin found in the ball park the batter will get one base hit.

Never allow bats to cross over each other on the rack. If they do, the next batter will strike out.

New York Giant Bobby Thomson wore the same socks for seventeen days, culminating in the "homer heard round the world" against the Dodgers in 1951.

In 1929, Lefty O'Doul of Philadelphia was called "the Man in the Green Suit" because he wouldn't change or wash his uniform all year for fear of bringing bad luck. He hit .398 that season.

Yes, even the Japanese. After a Saint Louis Cardinal goodwill visit to Tokyo, Japanese players started to bless themselves before they took a swing in the batter's box. If Stan Musial and teammates did it and got hits, then one enterprising Japanese club felt it was worth a try. They went on a fifteen-game winning streak.

The Detroit Tigers last won the American League pennant in 1968. That's when they last had their specially colored infield ball to warm up with for good luck.

A Harvard-educated chairman of a New England prep school eats pistachio ice cream before Red Sox home games. He claims that it helped the Sox to the pennant in 1946 and 1967.

Lou Brock of the Saint Louis Cardinals never steps on second base on the way to the outfield. He claims that the last time he did the other team scored a run that inning.

Red Sox catcher Carlton Fisk feels it is bad luck to be in the dugout during the playing of the national anthem. He thinks that if he is he will have a poor game.

A razor cut or nick means a missed fly on the field.

Beware of left-handed barbers.

Spilled coffee on the tablecloth means bad luck for seven days.

Dropped knife? Beware of wild pitches!

If the starting pitcher sees a hunchback before the game, he must immediately borrow someone else's shirt for the game.

If a player finds his sock is inside out, he shouldn't change it or the team will lose.

Seeing a white horse and hearing the ringing of a bell is the worst omen.

Don't ever swing at the first pitch.

John "Chief" Meyers believed that each bat possessed one hundred hits. He would immediately change once his bat was worn out.

In pregame practice, Johnny Evers of the Chicago Cubs would stop his batting practice if he was hitting well so he could save his hits for the game.

The Philadelphia A's upset the Chicago Cubs in a five-game Series in 1910, because Eddie Collins and his mates started eating pineapple, the "wonder fruit." Collins, who had a lifetime Series average of .328, hit .429 in the 1910 Series, rapping out four doubles in the process.

The great slugger Joe DiMaggio would swing two bats when he was in the on-deck circle. Before he stepped into the batter's box he would rub his right foot in the dirt behind his left heel. Then, he would rub dirt in his hands, tap the bat on the plate, wiggle the bat, and then he was ready for the first pitch!

"I only have one superstition. I make sure to touch all the bases when I hit a home run."—Babe Ruth.

BLACK HISTORY

Blacks in Baseball

The end of the Civil War and Abraham Lincoln's Emancipation Proclamation did little to alleviate the de facto segregation that existed in America. It was glaringly evident on the sports field, perhaps the true mirror of a country's social system, where it was a rarity to find blacks and whites mixing for any form of athletic competition—something akin to what world powers decry when they refer to South Africa's government-mandated, racially separate sports programs.

This being the case, waiters at the Argyle Hotel in Babylon, Long Island, banded together in 1885 and formed their own baseball team. This was to be the first all-black baseball squad ever assembled in the nation. They were a talented bunch, and the next year these food-serving ball players knocked off the best team in America, the Cincinnati Red Stockings.

This victory was to be the Argyle's last major one, for the following spring the great Cap Anson of Chicago, the first player to get 3,000 hits, refused to take the field against a Newark, New Jersey, team that featured Canadian pitching sensation George Stovey. Stovey's skin color was black, which was certainly evident, and he forced Anson to show his true colors—which turned out to be of racist hue: brilliantly red-necked and lily white.

Anson's refusal to play a racially mixed team touched off a chain reaction. The thinking went along the lines that if Anson, one of the pioneers in baseball, wouldn't play with blacks, then neither would any other white players. For blacks, the door to baseball was closed and remained so for the next sixty years. It took Branch Rickey and Jackie Robinson to crash the cruel barriers in the late 1940s. Ol' Cap Anson must have been somersaulting in his grave.

Jackie Robinson was a powerfully built athlete from Pasadena, California, whose skills in the athletic arena—football, baseball, track, basketball—did not

Hank Aaron

go unnoticed by UCLA. He accepted a scholarship there and quickly set about record-setting.

In the autumn he was UCLA's leading ground-gainer on the football team. Switching to basketball, Robinson led the league in scoring. In track and field he was also a standout. Unlike older brother Mack, who was a sprinter who finished second behind Jesse Owens in Adolph Hitler's 1936 games, Jackie was not very fast. Although he was later fast enough to lead the National League in stolen bases on two separate occasions, while at UCLA he concentrated on the broad jump. Again, as in the other sports, he set a conference record. Squeezed in with all this activity was his infield duty with the Bruin baseball team.

Shortly after Robinson was released from the army in 1945, he signed on with the Kansas City Monarchs, a barnstorming baseball team in the Negro Leagues. The money wasn't too bad—$100 a week—and it gave him a chance to stay active in sports. This was all a black ball player could hope for during those times. One year later, things changed dramatically for Robinson. Invited to come to New York City by Branch Rickey, Brooklyn Dodger team president, he found himself confronted with the most serious decision in his life. Rickey had been scouring the country for baseball talent regardless of color. The Dodgers had not won the pennant since 1941, and the cigar-chomping president was under extreme pressure to get his team back in contention. Jackie Robinson, the .345-slugging first baseman of the Monarchs, was the man Rickey felt could turn things around for his team. Happily, he was proved to be correct.

Starting for the Dodgers in 1947, the year he was to win Rookie of the Year honors at first base, and continuing for nine more seasons, Robinson helped the Dodgers to six National League pennants and one World Series title. In 1949, the year he led all National League sluggers with a .342 batting average (.2 percentage points from topping George Kell of Detroit for major-league honors), he was picked as the league's Most Valuable Player.

Branch Rickey had selected wisely when he chose this century's first black major-leaguer. Robinson was a trailblazer for other blacks who were soon to follow him into organized baseball. Being the first in anything is not an easy task, but for Jackie Robinson, the task of being the first black major-league ball player in the modern era was especially difficult. He was challenged to fights on many occasions by white players who wanted to make him lose his cool and be thrown out of the game. He was insulted, his life was threatened by anonymous callers, and in the early goings even his own teammates were against him. Luckily, Robinson lived through it all, carrying with him the enormous burden of being black in a segregated game, of trying to be the best when so many were waiting, hoping for him to fail. The Hall of Fame opened its doors to Jackie Robinson in 1962.

Black Firsts

First black professional baseball player:
Bud Fowler played for the team in New Castle, Pennsylvania, from 1872 until Cap Anson voiced his protests about black participation in professional baseball in 1887.

First black major-leaguer:
Moses Fleetwood Walker, catcher for Toledo in the American Association in 1884, hit .251 in 41 games with his club. His career ended three seasons later, following the Anson Proclamation.

First black major-leaguer of the twentieth century:
Jackie Robinson, Brooklyn Dodgers, 1947.

First black pitcher in the major leagues in the twentieth century:
Dan Bankhead was signed by Brooklyn in 1947. The twenty-six-year-old from Empire, Alabama, appeared in six games for the Dodgers that season as a mop-up man. He started off his major-league career in spectacular fashion. In his first game with the Dodgers on August 26, 1947, he poled the ball over the wall for a home run, becoming the sixteenth batter in major-league history to have such a debut.

First black manager in organized baseball:
In 1951, Sam Bankhead, cousin of Dan Bankhead, became the manager of the Farnham, Quebec, team in the Provincial League.

First black manager in the major leagues:
Frank Robinson broke into the major leagues as a player with Cincinnati in 1956 and tied the record for home runs by a rookie with 38. In 1961 he was voted National League Most Valuable Player, an honor he won again while with Baltimore in 1966; thus he became the first player ever to win the award in two leagues. That same year he also won the Triple Crown with a .316 batting average, 122 RBIs, and 49 home runs. In 1975, the slugging ball player became the first black manager in the history of the major leagues when he was signed by the Cleveland Indians to be playing-manager.

First black umpire in organized baseball:
Thirty-five-year-old Emmett Ashford of Los Angeles left his job in the post of-

fice to begin work as umpire in the Southwest International League in 1951. In 1966, almost two decades after Jackie Robinson had opened the major leagues for blacks, Emmett Ashford finally got his chance in the big leagues when he was selected to join the regular staff of American League umpires. He retired in 1971 when he reached the league's mandatory retirement age of fifty-five.

WOMEN

Women in Baseball

Manager of Flora Ball Team, Dear Sir:

I have read of your ball team as being champions of northern Indiana, and Flora being a country town, I would like very much to be a part of your team. I have played with a number of lady ball clubs and am considered the equal of the average country player. Besides, a lady in your club would prove an attraction and would justify your team paying the salary I would ask—$80 per month and expenses. I will sign for the entire season and I will play at home or travel. My position is center field. Please let me know at once, as I have other engagements pending.

M. E. Phelan, June 12, 1903

Baseball has never been strictly a men-only affair. In 1890, less than fifteen years after the National League started play, the first all-women team in the United States was organized. Women had already been involved in playing baseball to a small extent, but they had never organized and formed teams.

In the early 1900s, a team called the Bloomer Girls was started. This popular attraction toured the country, principally playing exhibition games against local town nines. "Bloomer Girls" was a misleading name, since many times the team had as many as three men in the starting lineup. There is not any record of fan protest at the sham, and the fans enjoyed watching the distaff side trying to swing for the fences.

Amanda Clement of Hudson, South Dakota, never played for the Bloomer Girls. She would have made a welcome addition, since she could throw the ball 275 feet, a distance most women would find difficult to reach even with two tosses. In 1903, the spunky fifteen-year-old stood behind the plate and umpired her first men's baseball game, becoming the first female umpire in the United

YOUNG LADIES' BASE BALL CLUB NO. 1.
(Copyrighted.)

EFFIE EARL, S. S. EDITH MAYVES 3 B. ALICE LEE, L. F. ROSE MITCHELL, R. F. ANGIE PARKER, 2 B.
MAY HOWARD, CAP AND P. ANNIE GRANT, C. F., KITTIE GRANT, 1 B. NELLIE WILLIAMS, C.

First Women's Baseball Team (1890)

States. For six years, Clement traveled the western baseball circuit, officiating in as many as fifty games a season.

It wasn't until 1971 in the midst of the women's liberation movement that a woman tried to get behind the plate again. After finally gaining the credentials to be an umpire, Bernice Gera of New York officiated in only one minor-league game and then called it quits. Abused by spectators, players, and managers alike, Gera found baseball umpiring to be a less than ideal working situation, so she abruptly quit. Shortly after her quick departure, she filed a $25 million damage suit against organized baseball, claiming among other things total discrimination against women umpires.

Phil Rigney did his best to promote women's baseball. The spirited owner of the Chicago Cubs inaugurated in 1943 the AAGBL, the All-American Girls Baseball League. This midwestern league lasted for twelve seasons and at the height of its popularity had six active teams: the Fort Wayne Daisies, the Milwaukee Chicks, the South Bend Blue Sox, the Kenosha Comets, the Racine Belles, and the Rockford Peaches. Some of the woman players were widely praised for their skills, and some were even compared with none other than Babe Ruth.

Wally Pipp, the New York starting first baseman who unwittingly gave up his position to bench-warming Lou Gehrig in 1925 because of an upset stomach, was an ardent Peach supporter. "Lady players will be in the major leagues within two to five years," said Pipp. Pipp's enthusiasm might have gotten the best of him that day, but coming from a major-leaguer who was the initial spark for one of baseball's most incredible records—Lou Gehrig's 2,130 consecutive games played—he should be allowed a little tongue-in-cheek.

THE JAPANESE

In the near future, it is quite possible that American major-league baseball teams will be playing in the larger cities of Japan. This would all be part of baseball's westward expansion.

In the following story, excerpted from the book *The Chrysanthemum and the Bat,* author Robert Whiting describes the history of *bēsubōru* madness in Japan. Although baseball came many centuries after *sumo,* the number-one spectator sport in the country, baseball is quickly making inroads and will soon be the most watched sport in Japan.

Major-league baseball in Japan? Remember, Tokyo is less than eleven hours away from Candlestick Park.

Outdoor Kabuki

by Robert Whiting

The big Seiko clock above the electronic scoreboard in center field read 6:20—thirty minutes before game time. The two-tiered 50,000 seat Korakuen Stadium was already filled to overflowing. In the special "jumbo stands" down the left and right field foul lines, policemen were urging standing-room ticketholders to move a little closer together so that even more people could be packed in to see the game.

The *sushi, sake,* and *hotto dogu* vendors had sold out their first loads and were hurrying back for refills before the aisles became completely clogged with fans.

Behind both dugouts, camera crews from two major networks were setting up their equipment to televise the game. In the press box, sportswriters from Japan's five major sports dailies were getting ready to report the evening's contest.

As a soft female voice announced the starting pitchers, the ticket windows outside the massive stadium closed, causing hundreds of irate fans to storm the gate. One old man was trampled in the rush and carted off to the hospital.

The event was a game between the two teams tied for first place in the Central League—the Yomiuri Giants of Tokyo and their traditional rivals from Osaka, the Hanshin Tigers. It was the first day of June and the season was only seven weeks old.

Each spring when the cherry blossoms come into bloom, the Land of the Rising Sun starts its annual love affair with the game of baseball. Almost overnight, Japan is transformed into a nation of starry-eyed pitchers, catchers, and home-run hitters; a nation of *bēsubōru* nuts.

White-collar workers grab the company ball and bat at lunchtime and head to the nearest park for a quick game of work-ups under the noonday sun. Delivery boys park their motorcycles between noodle deliveries and pull fielder's gloves from back pockets for a leisurely game of "catch-ball" in the nearest alley.

Platform conductors in train stations practice shadow swings with their red signal flags or work on their pitching deliveries with discarded candy wrappers, while those with enough time throng to the nearest "batting range" for 100 yen worth of swings against a mechanical curve-ball pitcher. And all across the five main islands of the tiny nation thousands of diamonds are filled with aspiring sluggers, ready to fight it out for the prestige of wearing that school uniform.

Each season, millions of fans pour through the turnstiles to see their favorite teams in action—from the little leagues all the way up to the professionals. The sport is so popular that even high school and college games draw capacity crowds.

The annual ten-day national high school championship tournament at Koshien Stadium in Osaka draws over 400,000 and is, in Japan, an event equal in significance to the Stanley Cup playoffs in hockey or the World Cup finals in soccer. There is hardly a TV set in any house, coffee shop, or tearoom around the nation that is not turned on NHK (Japan's government owned TV network) to see the continuous nine-to-six live daily coverage of the tournament.

College teams, such as those in Tokyo's glamorous Big Six University League, are followed with the fervor that Americans usually reserve for Saturday afternoon collegiate football. The semiannual three-game series between Tokyo's traditional crosstown rivals, Keio and Waseda, for example, draws well over 60,000 spectators per match and commands a nationwide TV audience. For sheer spectacle, this event outdoes a Michigan–Ohio State football game. Karate-chopping cheerleaders and raven-haired pom-pom girls lead a stadium full of frenzied students wildly screaming *"ganbare"* (Let's go) in unison. A series win for Waseda touches off a wild night of merrymaking in the narrow twisting sidestreets of Shinjuku (Tokyo's version of Greenwich Village) that is reminiscent of Times Square on New Year's Eve. A Keio win brings a similar fate to the downtown area of the Ginza.

The national obsession with *yakyu* (field ball), as it is commonly known, hits its peak when the glamor boys of Nippon—the professionals—take the field. Each year, nearly twelve million *bēsubōru* fanatics turn out to watch the twelve teams of Japan's two professional leagues, the Central and the Pacific. While two and a half million—or one out of every four spectators—flock to Korakuen Stadium to see the darlings of Japan, the Yomiuri Giants—the oldest, winningest, and most popular team in the country.

For those who stay home, there is a pro game on national TV nearly every night during the season. On weekends, a fan can plop down on his straw mat floor with his bottle of *Kirin* or *Asahi* beer and, with a flick of the dial, choose from two and sometimes even three games being broadcast simultaneously.

Baseball has become a fixture in Japanese life since it was first introduced in 1873, some twenty years after Commodore Perry and his "Black Ships" visited the island nation and thus ended more than two centuries of isolation. An American named Horace Wilson, a professor at a Tokyo university, is recognized as having first taught the game to the Japanese. Initially played by Kimono-clad youths in sandals, the game has flourished on a high school and collegiate level from the turn of the century. There were detractors, however, like critic Inazo Nitobe, an educator who later became an official of the League of Nations. He called baseball "a pickpocket's sport . . . in which the players are tensely on the lookout to swindle their opponents, to lay an ambush, to steal a base. It is, therefore, suited to Americans, but it does not please Englishmen or Germans."

The first professional league in Japan was not officially established until 1936, two years following a tour of American major-league all-stars led by Babe Ruth, Lou Gehrig, and Lefty O'Doul.

Before that visit, few Japanese believed professional baseball could succeed in their country. The sport was undeniably popular—Big Six college games drew enormous crowds. But tradition-bound Japanese were expected to remain loyal to favorite college teams, leaving the pros with no one to cheer them on. Furthermore, monetary considerations would, it was argued, so dilute the purity of the sport that right-thinking people would turn away in disgust.

These dark prophecies proved false, however. So overwhelmingly popular were the American stars, particularly the 39-year-old Ruth (who walloped 13 home runs in the 18 games he played in Japan), that in 1935, Matsutaro Shoriki, owner of the prestigious *Yomiuri Shinbun* (Japan's largest daily newspaper and the sponsor of the tour) decided to form a pro-baseball team of his own, the Tokyo Giants. A year later, several other firms followed suit and Japan's first professional league was born. By 1940, there were nine teams.

With the coming of Pearl Harbor, baseball took a back seat to Japan's all out drive for victory. By 1944 the season had dwindled to a mere 35 games, with only six teams contending for the pennant. It hardly mattered, for by this time baseball, like every other aspect of Japanese national life, had become a tool in the fanatical war effort. The Tokyo Giants were renamed *"Kyojin Gun,"* or "Giant Troop." (It was as if the New York Yankees had been dubbed the "Yankee Battalion.") Such English baseball terms as "strike" and "ball" imported from enemy America were scrapped for the Japanese *"yoshi"* and *"dame"* (good and bad). A shortstop became a *"yūgeki"* (freelancer) and when a runner slid into home plate the umpire would pronounce him "alive" or "dead" (*ikita* or *shinda*) instead of "safe" or "out."

In 1945, the year of Tokyo fire bombings and the Japanese surrender, play was suspended altogether. But when the occupation forces under Douglas MacArthur moved into Japan, baseball quickly recovered. In 1948 eight teams played a total of 105 games. MacArthur himself, recognizing the Japanese love for this alien game, personally issued the order to clean up Korakuen Stadium, home of the Tokyo Giants. The ball park had been used as an ordnance dump during the war.

Baseball thrived so well in the early postwar years that by 1950 two leagues were formed. That year, there were 15 teams but the number eventually dropped to 12, six teams in each league. Meanwhile the game's popularity soared, surpassing even traditional Japanese sports like *sumo* wrestling.

Today baseball is unquestionably Japan's favorite sport. The teams in the Pacific and Central Leagues each play a 130-game schedule and the two pennant winners meet in October in the Japan Series, the Oriental version of the American World Series.

Three of Japan's 12 pro ball clubs make their home in Tokyo, four in Osaka, and one each in Nagoya, Fukuoka, Kawasaki, Hiroshima, and Sendai. Most teams are owned by business firms and exist primarily for public relations purposes. This results in some rather unlikely names. The *Taiyo Whales* of Kawasaki are owned by the Taiyo Fishery Co. and the *Yakult Swallows* of Tokyo are the property of a major health food company. The *Hankyu Braves*, the *Nankai Hawks*, the *Kintetsu Buffaloes*, and the *Hanshin Tigers* (all of Osaka) are owned by private railways. Others include the *Lotte Orions* of Sendai (chewing gum), the *Chunichi Dragons* of Nagoya (newspapers), the *Yomiuri Giants* of Tokyo (newspaper/TV), the *Hiroshima Toyo Carp* (owned jointly by the citi-

Roy Campanella with Japanese Players

zens of Hiroshima and Toyo Kogyo—a major automobile manufacturer), and the *Nippon Ham Fighters* of Tokyo. The *Taiheiyo Club Lions* of Fukuoka are privately owned, but have a primary advertising contract with the Taiheiyo Club Corporation, a major land developer.

The professionals stock their teams with college and high school standouts in an annual draft. And the players, often stars in their own right, sometimes command large bonuses.

Baseball owes much of its status as the premier sport in Japan to an enlightened media that not only knows the game, but also understands how to make it interesting. Japanese TV and radio announcers working in teams can elevate the most routine encounter between a pitcher and a batter into a moment of high drama. Between pitches—and throughout the game—sportscasters discuss the comparative strengths and weaknesses of the man at the plate and the man on the mound: "This pitcher usually tires after seventy pitches and he has already thrown seventy-four. . . . Notice how the batter has widened his stance? (*Camera shot of stance*) He wasn't doing that a month ago. I think that's why his batting average has fallen. He is not putting his hips into his swing and he is also taking his eyes off the ball. . . . Let's take a look at that last pitch in slow motion. See how the pitcher's leg came down too soon? That is why the pitch was high . . ."

Announcers discuss previous encounters between the pitcher and the batter. With the help of computer records, they predict, sometimes with amazing accuracy, what pitch will be thrown and what the batter is likely to do in a given situation: "Watanabe has a .220 lifetime average batting against this pitcher Suzuki; however, he is .314 against him this season. What do you think accounts for the difference? / Well let's see. Suzuki used to retire him on a high outside slider. However, this season Watanabe has learned to punch that particular delivery to the opposite field. / What do you think Suzuki will use this time? / It is difficult to say, but, with two out and a runner on second, I don't think he will use the slider. In my opinion he will throw an inside fastball at the chest. Look how Watanabe is crowding the plate. It would be easy to get him with that pitch. / If Suzuki throws an inside fast ball, I think Watanabe will try to foul it off and wait for a better pitch. / Maybe so, but, since Watanabe is batting second tonight, it might be a good idea for him to reach first and let Kobayashi try to drive the runs in. / I don't think so. Kobayashi has the power, but his lifetime batting average against Suzuki is less than .100. He is lefthanded and Suzuki is lefthanded. / Yes, but . . ."

And so it goes, sometimes seemingly forever. There is never enough time between pitches for Japanese announcers to say all they have to say. They are often accused of talking too much, and their frequent mistaken predictions are a standing joke. But the interest and excitement they can generate in a slow moving game is truly amazing.

On televised games in the States, if a pitcher shakes off a sign three or four times and steps off the mound, boredom ensues. The announcer will talk about the wonderful dinner he had the night before, discuss his latest fishing expedition, or welcome a group of visiting firemen—anything except what is going on down on the field.

In Japan, when a pitcher keeps shaking off a sign, the tension mounts. The announcer pays attention. He becomes more excited: "He shook the sign off again! What do you think he wants to throw? Ah! He just shook it off a third time! / I think the pitcher wants to throw his fast ball and the catcher wants him to come in with a curve? / Why? / Because in a similar situation last month . . . etc."

When a batter keeps fouling off a 3–2 pitch with a runner in scoring position on second base, the typical U.S. announcer will run down the league standings, report on the top ten batters, or tell the viewer about the Goodyear blimp. In Japan, the announcer tells the viewer *why* the batter keeps fouling off so many pitches. The fan learns that the rightfielder has a weak arm and that the batter is waiting for an outside pitch he can poke to right.

When a player slides into base, the Japanese TV baseball viewer (or listener) gets lessons on how to slide. He learns whether the slide was a good one or not. When an infielder makes a play, the fan gets advice on playing the infield in various situations. He gets lessons on how to bat, how to pitch, how to throw, how to steal signs, and how to manage a team.

Thanks to excellent TV coverage the Japanese fan cannot help become involved in the details of the game as he is drawn into the intricacy of each play. Games in Japan last nearly three hours on the average, much longer than games in the U.S. Yet, in Japan, the broadcasts somehow never seem as dull or as long as they do in the States.

Japan is a baseball fan's paradise. And the baseball addict who must have his regular dose of baseball news, capped off by a night game, is indeed fortunate to be born there. Consider the day of an average baseball nut—a Tokyo *salariman* who is, no doubt, a Giants fan.

Oh his way to work he stops at the newsstand in front of his train station. Here he has a choice of five major daily sports newspapers: *Chunichi Sports, Hōchi Shinbun, Nikkan Sports, Sports Nippon, Sankei Sports,* as well as *Daily Sports.* (There are none in the United States.) Each paper sells for 50 yen (15 cents a copy) and it tells him every conceivable thing he might want to know about the previous night's baseball activities.

As the "platform pusher" wedges him into the already packed morning express, he eagerly scans the headlines: GIANTS SLASH TIGERS! "Ah! My team won." Crammed against the door of the train and unable to turn around, he struggles to unfold his paper and prepares to enter the separate reality of baseball.

Sub-headlines quickly summarize the story: GIANTS OPEN UP TWO-GAME LEAD OVER TIGERS IN TIGHT C.L. PENNANT RACE. WIN ON "SAYONARA" HIT IN 12TH INNING. OH BLASTS 40TH HOME RUN. HORIUCHI STRUGGLES TO VICTORY. NOTCHES 13TH WIN OF YEAR ON "GUTS" ALONE. HURLS 179 GRITTY PITCHES. And next to the large photo showing the Yomiuri Giants leftfielder scoring the winning run in the 8–7 victory, he finds the details of the game:

31 August, Showa 48. Korakuen Stadium. Yomiuri Giants vs. Hanshin Tigers. Season record: Giants 10 wins; Tigers 10 wins; 1 tie. Starting time: 6:50. Attendance: 50,000. Final score: Giants 8, Tigers 7. Extra-inning game, 12 innings. Winning pitcher; Horiuchi; 13 wins, 14 losses, 36 games. Losing pitcher: Wako; 2 wins, 4 losses, 16 games. Home runs: Oh (3 runs 1st inning) 40 (Enatsu); Horiuchi (3 runs—7th inning) 2 (Wako); Kirkland (3 runs—5th inning) 17 (Horiuchi); Toi (2 runs—8th inning) 6 (Horiuchi); Tabuchi (2 runs—8th inning) 33 (Horiuchi).

The August moon hung forlornly in the sweltering summer mist over Korakuen Stadium as ace Giant pitcher Horiuchi trudged wearily off the mound. He stopped once and turned to glance at the clock over the huge electronic scoreboard out in centerfield. The hands had just passed ten o'clock.

Horiuchi was thinking the same thought that was running through the minds of everyone else in the park: Would the game reach the 13th inning before the 10:10 curfew? Could the Giants score the winning run in the bottom of the 12th? Would the game end in a tie? As Horiuchi confessed later: "I wanted the time to run out. Their clean-up trio would be leading off the top of the 13th. I could see that the ball had heavy eyes. It wouldn't do what I wanted it to. . . . Anyway, all I was thinking of was a tie."

At 10:10 the game would be three hours and twenty minutes old and would not enter a new inning. Pitching with two days rest, Horiuchi had gone the full 12 innings and had thrown 179 grueling pitches. He was tired and wanted the game to end. Everyone was in agreement. Coach Makino instructed, "I don't want to go into the 13th inning." Everyone knew what he meant. The Giants would play for time.

Horiuchi, batting eighth in the Giant lineup, led off the bottom of the 12th inning. The Giant bench continuously called him back for advice. To stall for time, he kept changing bats, stepping out of the box, knocking the dirt from his shoes, putting resin on his hands, conferring with the third-base coach and stroking his bat. After Horiuchi struck out, centerfielder Shibata came to bat. Shibata alone used up five minutes at the plate. The clock then passed 10:10. The Giant bench breathed a sigh of relief. The Giants could not lose this game now.

Shibata drove the next pitch into left field for a single. The Giants were beginning to hear the sounds of a "sayonara" hit. With two out and Shibata on second as a result of

Doi's grounder to third, Takada came up and blasted Wako's first pitch into shallow center. Shibata rounded third and rushed into home plate with the winning run.

The Giants, who had been content to tie, saw a victory come tumbling their way, magically appearing out of the humid summer night. Takada's comrades in the dugout on the first-base side emptied onto the field to welcome home their hero, who had blasted the "*sayonara*" hit.

Said the happy Takada: "When I hit the first pitch thrown by Wako in the 10th inning and grounded out to third, it was a *shūto bōru* (screwball). I had an idea he might be throwing the same pitch again, so I was ready. I was just trying to meet the ball." And so, with this determined spirit, Takada settled the question that had been on everyone's mind for three hours and twenty-four minutes, this hot summer night of August 31.

Horiuchi, in his typical manner, frequently exasperated the Giant fans during the game. He was given a 3–0 lead in the first inning, when Oh lined a 1–2 low-outside fastball into the leftfield stands for a three-run home run, and in the third inning was presented with another run. But, in the fifth inning, with two men on, the erratic young hurler gave up a home run to the black foreigner Kirkland and allowed the Tigers to tie the score.

Whenever it looked as though the Giants would win, Horiuchi would do something to throw the game in doubt. He indeed lived up to his nickname of "Bad-Boy Taro." To his credit, however, he did pitch out of several tight spots from the eighth inning on. So perhaps this grueling 12 inning, 179 pitch win is evidence that Horiuchi is regaining some of the fighting spirit he had last year when he won 26 games.

As the train makes another stop and the platform pusher shoves a few more passengers in, our baseball fan, barely able to move, delves deeper into his 16-page paper. SPIRITLESS DRAGONS LOSE FIRE—FACE MAJOR SHAKE-UP. "They'll need it." CARP SINK INTO C.L. CELLAR. "What's new?" BRAVES SLICE NIPPON HAM. HAWKS FLY LOW—DROP THIRD IN A ROW. THE FOREIGNER COMES THROUGH—REPOZ BLASTS "SAYONARA" HOME RUN. "Hummm."

"This looks like a good story. THE COWARDLY PITCHER: DOWN AFTER ONLY 46 PITCHES."

The performance of Hanshin's ace pitcher, Enatsu, last night was shameful. It was even more shameful because the Tigers started him to satisfy the fans' expectations. The spiritless pitching of this twenty-game winner has seriously damaged Tiger chances in the pennant race. True, it may be said that he had only two days rest and was tired. But, the same was true for his pitching rival Horiuchi. Furthermore, this season, the Tiger star had a record of 8–2 when starting with two days rest, while Horiuchi was an abysmal 0–3 before last night's game. It would seem that Enatsu would be far superior.

But, he wasn't. Consider the first inning. Enatsu gave up a walk, a sacrifice, and another walk. There were runners on first and second, and one out. Then C.L. home-run leader Oh blasted Enatsu's first pitch into the left-field stands. The Giants led, 3–0. Enatsu's listless pitching continued into the third inning. Giant batters hit his half-hearted balls for another run and Enatsu was taken out of the game.

And that is not all. Enatsu's remarks in the locker room were not those of a man aware of the crucial importance of this encounter. For example, he said casually, "You say that I was beaten by Oh. Well, Oh has 40 home-runs. The one he hit off me tonight was just one of the forty home-runs that man has hit this season. When he came up in the third inning, I put him out on a fly to right, didn't I? I am just an ordinary human being. I'll try to do better in my next start against the Whales."

Well, of all the nerve! I must say that Enatsu may be ordinary, but the four runs he surrendered may be the catalyst that will turn his Tigers into ordinary cats. The Tiger batters came through quite splendidly. But, unfortunately, their ace let them down.

With two days rest, Horiuchi pitched, erratically, desperately and frantically. But, he showed his true fighting spirit by throwing 179 agonizing pitches. Enatsu threw only 46 pitches and returned quickly to relax in the baths of the Midori Inn. In my opinion, that is the difference between the fighting spirit of Enatsu and Horiuchi.

The train pulls into Tokyo Station and our friend hurries to his office in Marunouchi, Tokyo's business center.

Comfortably seated at his desk, with a cup of green tea before him, he opens his paper again. After glancing to see who won the best player and fighting spirit awards for last night's games, he turns to the statistics with a tinge of anticipation. And, what statistics!

Ten-column box scores on each game. (Those in U.S. papers are usually six columns or less.) Times at bat, runs scored, hits, RBIs, strikeouts, walks, sacrifices, stolen bases, errors, and adjusted seasonal batting averages. Down below are nine-column boxes for the pitchers: Innings pitched, number of batters faced, number of pitches thrown, number of hits allowed, strikeouts, walks, runs surrendered, earned runs surrendered, and adjusted season ERAs. And if this is not enough, our fan can turn to the inning-by-inning batter-by-batter account of what happened in each game.

If he still has time before his boss catches him loafing, he can pore over the standings that show how each team is doing against every other team in the league. This data includes the total number of games each team has played, total wins, losses, ties, percentages, home runs, runs scored, runs allowed, and team batting and pitching averages.

During his mid-morning break, he can study the upcoming schedule detailing who is playing whom, when, and where for the next ten games. Or he can read a summary of how each team has performed for the last ten games.

At lunch, over fish, rice, and *misomiso* soup, he can discuss the previous night's game with his colleagues and pick up any details of the encounter his newspaper might have missed (improbable as it may be).

During his afternoon break, he returns to his paper to review individual batting and pitching performances. There he finds the following statistics for the top thirty batters in each league: Batting average, games played, unofficial times-at-bat, official times-at-bat, runs scored, hits, home runs, total bases, RBIs, strikeouts, walks, sacrifices, and stolen bases. And for the pitchers: ERA, games pitched, hits allowed, home runs surrendered, strikeouts, walks, runs allowed, and earned runs allowed.

If there is a lull in the late afternoon, he can sneak a look at what the managers had to say about the games the night before, in the *Kantoku No Hanashi* (The Manager Speaks) section of the paper. The following are examples of what he might find.

(On winning three in a row):

I can't believe it. I think they were in worse condition than we were. I don't know what happened. I tried a number of new strategies in this series, and I think I learned something. But, I also think they learned something. So I don't know what will happen next time.

(On losing seven in a row):

I apologize to the fans for this disgrace. I just hope we will get better. I don't know what has come over my pitching staff. They have lost their fighting spirit.

(On an upcoming series with the Giants):

I have formulated a plan to overcome the Giants. We will defeat the Tigers three in a row in our upcoming series, and then we will win three of our four games with the Giants. I cannot reveal the details of my plan at this moment.

(On being in last place):

This cannot continue. Our baseball is a product that we are selling to our fans. No matter how low we sink in the standings we must strengthen our resolve and play to the utmost of our ability for the rest of the season. It is a professional responsibility we have. My men must try harder tomorrow. I will hold a meeting to discuss the matter with them. My humble apologies.

After this, our fan may well take a quick look at what the players had to say.

(A pitcher on his disappointing defeat):

I'm sorry. I wanted to throw my curve ball, but they were aiming for it, so I had to go with my *shūto bōru* (screwball). Unluckily, my *shūto* was too sweet and so they hit me. I will do my best to redeem myself in the future.

(A pitcher on pitching while sick and winning):

I tried to pitch at *mai-pēsu* [my pace] all throughout the game. It was very painful, but fortunately my slider was razor sharp. I was lucky to win. From now on I am not going to think about my health anymore. I vow to think solely about pitching to help the team win the championship for our fans.

(A pitcher on his six-hit shutout):

I do not want to be rude to the Lions, but I have the fullest self-confidence when I am pitching against them. I have no inclination to lose against them. It was very easy.

(A pitcher on getting his 20th win):

My condition was not good tonight, but I had to win at all costs, so I struggled desperately. I gained these 20 wins because of the manager and my teammates. I was filled with dread that I would not be equal to the task at hand. I pitched with all my might. It was very painful, but I am deeply satisfied with this game and with this season. I will now aim for the best pitching percentage in the league.

(A pitcher upon winning his third game in a row):

I have pitched over 200 balls in the past three days. But I am not tired. I have only been pitching in this league for three years, and I am not thinking of the long run. I want to play for a long time, but the important thing at the moment is a man's spirit. I have not been pitching long in the professionals, so there is no depth to my pitching. I am young and my mind has not developed yet. However, I will pitch as the team wants me to pitch and vow to do my best.

(A batter on his prolonged batting slump):

I don't know what is wrong. I am seeing the ball well. I feel I am in good condition. I am eating well and my bowel movements are regular. I must ask the batting coach for guidance.

(An outfielder on dropping a fly ball to lose the game):

Damn it! I had the ball right in my hands. And it just popped out again. I am really ashamed of myself. I truly apologize to my teammates and to the fans.

After this, there is still the baseball gossip in the gossip column (*Eto Files For Bankruptcy. Harimoto Arrested in Drunken Brawl—Out For Two Weeks*) as well as all the latest college, high school, and industrial league baseball news.

After work, our fan stops to buy a copy of *Bēsubōru*, a popular weekly magazine. A typical table of contents might include the following:

1. I Owe My Career To My Mother—She Did My Homework For Me While I Practiced Baseball.
2. The Change in Bad-Boy Taro. Could It Mean Another Pennant For The Giants?

3. How I Keep My Batting Eye—I Only Read Comic Books.
4. Oh Sets His Sights On Aaron: What Breaking Hank Aaron's Home-Run Record Will Mean To Sadaharu Oh.
5. America's Unforgettable Baseball Games.
6. Heartbreak Column: Yōshida Tries To Forget The Pain.
7. Why Nagashima Hides In The Dugout.
8. The Garlic *Shochu* Craze (drink made from distilled sweet potatoes): How It Gives The Players Vim And Vigor And Keeps The Fans Away.
9. What It Means To Be A Yomiuri Giant.
10. *Tears And Laughter In Baseball:* When A Backache Becomes Too Much To Bear.
11. *Foreign Topics:* Streaking In Major-League Parks.
12. *The Daimyō* (Lords) Of Professional Baseball.
13. The Dilemma Of The Lions And Monster Frank Howard: Is He Worth The Money?
14. Dr. Baseball: Clete Boyer Of The Whales.
15. Fiction: The Seven Samurai Of Baseball.
16. *Baseball Diet Corner:* Snakes, Frogs, And Other Energy Foods.
17. The World Series And Japan.
18. Rookie: Fresh Ham Of Nippon Ham.
19. The Burning Ace Of The Burning Dragons.
20. The Pen-Pal Corner (where one finds such letters as the following):

If you are a girl and you consider yourself the number-one fan of the Nankai Hawks, why don't you write to me and we can exchange opinions. For I am the number one fan of Nankai in Sakai City.
Kenji Wakisaka (16) (male)

I have been a very faithful fan of Lotte for seven years. I am waiting for letters from girls all over Japan who are especially interested in the Pacific League.
Toshio Tarui (19) (male)

I am a fan of Chunichi, Lotte, Hanshin, high school baseball, university baseball, Elton John, and Morio Kita (a contemporary writer). Please, someone, write to me.
Mitsue Uchiumi (15) (female)

Returning home, our fan nods to his wife as he walks through the door, takes a quick bath, and changes to his *yukata* (a casual summer robe). He hastily downs his dinner of fish and rice and is ready for more baseball.

From 6:30 to 7:30, he listens to the game on radio and then switches to watch all the action live on his Sony color TV. Then, at precisely 8:56, he hears the announcer say: "We deeply regret this, but unfortunately our broadcast time has once again expired. It is deeply disappointing to us, but thank you for tuning in. The results will be reported on the sports news at 11:10. We will be back on the air tomorrow night at the same time."

In Japan, for some inexplicable "aesthetic" reason, games are invariably telecast for one hour and 26 minutes, no matter who is playing. This can be infuriating, especially when in the 9th inning, with the score tied and bases loaded, the game goes off the air.

With a groan, our fan returns to his radio and listens to the last few innings. After the game he watches the sports news so he can see that home run he missed when the TV broadcast was shut off.

Tired, and perhaps even sated, he then crawls between the *futon* (Japanese bedding) laid on the floor by his patient but baseball-weary wife and goes to sleep.

THE PRESS

The Dilution of Memorable Events
by Leonard Koppett

The subject came up in an oblique way. It was in a Yankee dressing room after Elliott Maddox had hit a ninth-inning double to win a game, and someone mentioned how long Maddox had been a bench-rider at Detroit before he came to New York and got more of a chance to display his talents, especially as a center fielder.

The thought arose that it must have been pretty tough for anyone to displace a center fielder as good as Mickey Stanley, who happened to be playing for Detroit at the time—and the thought of Mickey Stanley triggered another— the utter forgetability of unforgettable events.

After all, Mickey Stanley performed one of the most remarkable accomplishments in all major league baseball history. An established outfielder by trade, he suddenly switched to shortstop, with virtually no experience, for the 1968 World Series and helped the Tigers win it.

At the time, it was hailed as a remarkable event—a brainstorm, perhaps, on the part of Manager Mayo Smith; a fantastic pressure to put on one player; a dazzlingly successful move designed to get an extra bat into the lineup since Ray Oyler, the regular shortstop, had hit .135 (honest, one hundred and thirty-five) during the regular season. Any way you looked at it, it was a mind-boggling arrangement that would be associated with Stanley's name forever.

And when's the last time you heard anyone talk about it?

That, after all, was only six years ago, [1974] and Stanley has been playing regularly—in center—ever since.

And once you do mention Stanley's excursion at shortstop, most fans' faces light up and they say, "Yeah, I remember that. Wasn't that something?" But on its own momentum, the whole thing is virtually forgotten.

Or take the rarest of all baseball accomplishments, the unassisted triple play. Bill Wambsganss of Cleveland pulled one off in the 1920 World Series—the only time it's happened in a Series—and appropriately became a perpetual quiz question. Then in 1923, it was done by George Burns of the Boston Red Sox, and Ernie Padgett of the Boston Braves, and in 1925 by Glenn Wright, the Pittsburgh shortstop.

By the time Jim Cooney of the Cubs executed one on May 30, 1927, it must have started to seem pretty routine. At any rate, when Johnny Neun of the Tigers got one the very next day, the New York Herald-Tribune found it worthy of a one-sentence, bottom-of-the-page filler-type item. (One can see the head of the copy desk marking the wire copy for a small head and musing, "Heck, this same thing happened yesterday.")

But for 40 years after that, no one made an unassisted triple play, and all the years that I was beginning to follow baseball, from the 1930s on, Neun was universally identifiable as "the man who made the last unassisted triple play." And it wasn't just a trivia question. It was an inescapable identification wherever Neun showed up.

Then, one day in 1968 (July 30, if you must know), Ron Hansen, playing for the Washington Senators, pulled an unassisted triple play.

Okay, you knew that. But what's the last time it came up in talk?

Quick now, what's the best pitching performance ever in a single game? Harvey Haddix, right? He pitched 12 perfect innings against the Milwaukee Braves for Pittsburgh in 1959. Sure, he lost in the 13th, 1–0—but no one else, before or since, has gone through an opposing batting order four times, through 36 consecutive batters, without letting anyone reach base. The fact that his own team never scored, so that the game could end, takes nothing away from what Haddix did. But it's almost forgotten.

I'm sure you can think of many comparable situations, in many sports, that were absolutely incredible when they occurred, truly once-in-a-lifetime—that have completely receded from general awareness.

Now it just so happens (as usual in this space) that I think there's a not-so-trivial reason for this.

There's simply too much going on in sports for any immortal event to retain its immortality. Not only that, but we live in a television age, conditioned to short attention spans. We've been taught, maybe against our wills and maybe not, that no matter what happens—a man walking on the moon, a war, a political speech or a wild championship sport event—it will be followed 15 seconds later by a station break and a new program making just as determined a bid for our attention.

There is a great loss in this, a loss of common heritage and shared values (and that, of course, is a world wide trend on many levels more important than sports). The fact is that until the last decade or so, if you said "Merkle's Boner" to a baseball fan, he almost always knew what you were referring to. If you talked about Roy Riegels running the wrong way in the Rose Bowl, you got a spark of recognition from people who weren't born when those events took place.

The blurring of such common memories—and therefore, a degree of impoverishment of the overtones today's events could have—is essentially the price we pay for two things, expansion and television.

The effect of expansion is obvious enough. When there were only 16 baseball teams, and perhaps 12 pro football teams, and six big league hockey teams, it was within the grasp of a dedicated fan to be fairly familiar with the principal figures in each sport. When the major league scene encompasses, as today, some 120 teams with at least 2,000 "regulars," each involved in six months of competition or more, it's impossible to follow it all.

Expansion, in the sense of historical events, is inescapable in the time dimension. Whatever happened in the 10th World Series automatically seemed more memorable, at the time, than what happened in the 60th, with 59 previous series already available for our awareness.

Then TV, which gives eye experience and reduces the need for reading, cut down on the digestion of events and creates a loss of context. All of this may explain the loss of "fan loyalty" and why only "hot" events sell.

THE COMMISSIONER

Judge Kenesaw Mountain Landis

Baseball has had five commissioners, but Judge Kenesaw Mountain Landis is unquestionably the man that made the position the powerful one it is today.

Landis was named after a mountain where his father was hit by a cannonball during the Civil War. Although small and frail in appearance, Landis's rulings and pronouncements carried the weight and power associated with his unusual name.

Landis came to baseball in 1921, when the sport was mired down in its lowest moral point in history. He immediately stated the demands he wanted met if he took the job. The owners agreed, and Landis set about cleaning up baseball.

Evidence had been submitted that six of the nine starters and two reserves on Charles Comiskey's Chicago White Sox had conspired with New York gambling czar Abe Attell to throw the 1919 World Series to the Cincinnati Reds. Lengthy civil court proceedings were started, and although the eight "Black Sox" players were cleared by the court of any wrongdoing, Judge Landis, who had once fined Standard Oil $29 million for swindle, took his own stand in the name of baseball. Landis barred the eight men from organized baseball for the rest of their lives.

"Shoeless" Joe Jackson was certainly affected the most by the judge's decision, because throughout the entire proceedings he didn't seem to know what was going on. Although he was supposedly paid off by the gamblers, not the $20,000 he was promised, he still came up with 12 hits and a Series-high .375 batting average. Included in that bundle was a home run and three doubles, which must have made the heavy rollers back in New York sweat blood. The White Sox put on a show in their sixth game. Playing in Cincinnati, they won a

Judge Landis

"Shoeless" Joe Jackson

5–4 extra-inning game that took some of the embarrassment out of their shocking 9–1 opening-game defeat.

Still, the Sox lost the Series 5–3, and soon afterward baseball lost Joe Jackson, one of its greatest hitters.

Jackson was the illiterate baseball player from South Carolina who sometimes signed "X" for his signature. Instead of becoming one of the most prolific hitters in the game, Jackson was tossed out after fourteen seasons with a .408 season in 1911 and a .356 lifetime average. He ended his days behind the counter of a South Carolina liquor store, selling spirits and trying to hide from curious customers the fact that he was once the greatest hitter in the game.

Judge Landis didn't stop with the Black Sox. During his twenty-four-year reign as the sports world's most powerful figure, he was to suspend Babe Ruth for barnstorming, expel Jimmy O'Connell and Cosy Dolan of the New York Giants for a bribe scheme, fine Connie Mack for an illegal player swap, and liberate minor-league players that had been illegally tucked away on farm teams.

When Judge Landis passed away in 1944 at the age of seventy-four, he had succeeded in raising baseball to an incorruptible and dignified plateau. He restored America's confidence in the game and set the strong standard for other commissioners to follow.

Landis was elected to the Hall of Fame four weeks after his death.

Major-League Baseball in One Hundred Years

by Bowie K. Kuhn

Fifth Commissioner of Major Leagues

1969–

Baseball is fundamentally the same game it was seventy-five or eighty years ago. The strike zone has been altered, and the height of the pitcher's mound has been changed, but for the most part the game has not changed. In one hundred years I don't think the basics of the game will change very much—the game works quite well.

It is on the periphery that we probably will see immense changes in the next century. As our lifestyle and lives change, I can foresee more indoor parks. That could lead to many changes in baseball. Perhaps the biggest change would

Commissioner Bowie Kuhn

be in scheduling. Baseball could have an indoor season and an outdoor season. Who knows what advancements will be made with the playing surfaces. And the stadium features! Your imagination can really run away with the possibilities, and each one would be a convenience for the fans.

In the future, too, managers undoubtedly will have the added advantage of new technology, probably to the point of having a computer at their side in the dugout.

The biggest change may be in baseball's geographical pattern. I would not guess at this time what that pattern will be except to say I feel confident that the major leagues will be largely international in scope. I think all continents could well have teams, and I look for the rosters to be heterogeneous; Japanese and Chinese players with teams in other countries, and vice versa.

THE GREATEST EVER

In 1969 a survey of baseball fans, baseball writers, and sportscasters was taken by the major-league offices to select by position the greatest players of the first one hundred years of major-league baseball. By polling a sufficient number of knowledgeable baseball people, it was felt that the question, "Who are the greatest players?" would be settled.

The results of the poll were announced at the Centennial Baseball Dinner on July 21, 1969. See if you agree with the poll.

The Finalists

First Base

George Harold Sisler
The Saint Louis slugger hit safely in 41 consecutive games in 1922. A lifetime .340 batter, he set the major-league record of 257 base hits in 1920. Fielded at .987. Most Valuable Player in 1922. Hall of Fame 1939.

Stanley Frank Musial
A three-time National League MVP (1943, 1946, 1948), this Saint Louis first baseman was tops in double plays in 1957—his seventeenth year with the Cards. He retired seven seasons later with a .331 lifetime batting average and .989 fielding percentage. Hall of Fame 1969.

Stan Musial

Jackie Robinson

Henry Louis Gehrig

Gehrig's 2,130 consecutive games as the New York Yankees' first baseman speaks for his great skill and determination. American League MVP in 1927, 1931, 1934, 1936. A lifetime .340 batter and a .991 fielder. Hall of Fame 1939.

Second base

Charles Leonard Gehringer

Charley Gehringer was the Detroit Tigers' dependable second sacker for eighteen consecutive seasons (1925–42). He helped the Tigers to three American League flags (1934, 1935, 1940) and hit .321 in the 20 Series games he appeared in. A lifetime .976 fielder and .321 batter. Hall of Fame 1949.

Edward Trowbridge Collins

Eddie Collins came into the big leagues with Philadelphia in 1906, and after spending twelve years with the White Sox he returned and finished his twenty-five-year career with Connie Mack's Philadelphia A's. On September 11, 1912, the super-fast Collins stole six bases in one game, a record; eleven days later he duplicated the feat. Collins fielded at .969 and was a .333 lifetime slugger. MVP in the American League in 1914. Hall of Fame 1939.

Rogers Hornsby

The Rajah was a National League fixture for nineteen seasons. In 1924 he had 24 home runs for Saint Louis and a batting average of .424. The acclaimed greatest right-handed batter in history increased his long-ball hitting to 39 round-trippers the following season and sported a .403 batting average. For five seasons, from 1921 to 1925, his batting average was .397, .401, .384, .424 (the tops in baseball history), and .403—an average of .402 for those years. Hornsby had a lifetime .957 fielding average and a .359 batting mark. Triple Crown in 1922 and 1925. MVP in 1925 and 1929. Hall of Fame 1942.

Third base

Harold Joseph Traynor

Opposing batters knew better than to try and bunt against Pittsburgh's quick-starting, rifle-armed Pie Traynor. For seven seasons he topped the National League in putouts. Played in two World Series with the Pirates (1925, 1927) and batted .293. A lifetime .945 fielding percentage and .320 hitter. Hall of Fame 1948.

Jack Roosevelt Robinson

Jackie Robinson was as feared as a batter as he was as a glovesman. In one World Series game in 1952, the Dodgers' top slugger was walked a record four times by the Yankees. Rookie of the Year in 1947 and National League MVP in 1949. Lifetime .311 batsman, .983 fielding average. Hall of Fame 1962.

Brooks Robinson

Baltimore Oriole Golden Glove man Brooks Robinson was still an active player at the time of the poll. MVP in the American League in 1964. Tops for league third basemen in putouts in 1958, 1960, and 1964. Played in the World Series with Baltimore in 1966 and 1969. A future Hall of Famer.

Shortstop

John Peter Wagner

Dependable Pirate slugger Hans Wagner came into the National League from Louisville in 1897. From 1897 to 1913, the game's greatest all-around player hit .300 or better. His .381 was his career high (1900). A .946 fielder and a .329 batter. Hall of Fame 1936, one of the original five inductees.

Joseph Edward Cronin

The American League standout as shortstop for more than fifteen seasons was feared at the plate. As a pinch hitter in 1943, Joe established the American League record for home runs by hitting five that year. A .953 fielder and a .302 slugger. Hall of Fame 1956.

Ernest Banks

Banks was still active at the time of the poll, but his solid glovework and batting had already helped establish him as "Mr. Cub." Ernie slammed 3 home runs in one game on August 4, 1955, and was the leading home-run hitter in 1958 and 1960 in the majors. A future Hall-of-Famer.

Outfield

Joseph Paul DiMaggio

The Yankee Clipper holds the major-league record for a 56-consecutive-game hitting streak set in 1941. The slugging star led the Yanks to ten American League titles. Joe had 46 homers in 1937 and topped the leagues in batting in

Babe Ruth

Babe Ruth's Locker

1939 with .381, his highest career mark. League MVP in 1939, 1941, and 1947. A .978 fielder and a .325 lifetime batter. Hall of Fame 1955.

George Herman Ruth

More words have been written about Babe Ruth than any other American sports figure. Originally a pitcher (lifetime 2.28 earned run average for 163 games), Ruth went on to establish the home run as a major attraction in big-league baseball. His 60 homers in 1927 in a 154-game season is a record that may stand the test of time. Author of 16 grand slams in 2,503 lifetime games; scored 177 runs in 1921, the all-time major-league record. American League MVP in 1923. A .968 fielding average, .342 slugger. Hall of Fame 1936.

Theodore Samuel Williams

Ted Williams was the last major-leaguer to hit over .400 (.406, 1941). The Boston Red Sox slugger led the American League in total bases six times (1939, 1942, 1946, 1947, 1949, 1951). He was so feared as a hitter that he led the league in bases on balls eight times (1941, 1942, 1946, 1947, 1948, 1949, 1951, 1954) and was walked intentionally 33 times in 1957! In 1957, Williams tied the major-league record by hitting three home runs in one game on two separate occasions. He was American League MVP in 1946 and 1949. A .974 fielder and a .344 batter. Hall of Fame 1966.

Tyrus Raymond Cobb

Ty Cobb, the Georgia Peach, was the first man selected to Baseball's Hall of Fame in 1936. His lifetime batting mark of .367 is the highest ever in major-league history. In 1911, the Detroit Tiger dynamo batted a career high of .420 and won the Chalmers Award, early baseball's equivalent of the MVP award. From 1905 to 1926, he played with Detroit, stealing a career-high 96 bases in 1915 (892 lifetime). Helped Detroit to three pennants, 1907, 1908, 1909. Batted over .300 in every year except his rookie season in 1905 (.240). Fielding average, .961.

Tristram Speaker

The Gray Eagle was the MVP in the American League in 1912, the year that he had his highest batting average, .383. The Boston outfielder made two unassisted double plays from the outfield in the 1918 season and started a unique form in playing his position. His shallow positioning in the field made him more like a fifth infielder and was the reason he was able to race to second base to work the pickoff play with the catcher. Tris was a lifetime .344 hitter over a twenty-year career that ended in Philadelphia in 1928. Fielding average, .970. Hall of Fame 1937.

Willie Howard Mays

Willie Mays was still active at the time of the poll. Mays came to the Giants in 1951 as a fence-busting minor-leaguer with less than 120 games experience in organized ball. He hit 20 homers in his first season (batting .274) and helped the Giants win an amazing pennant battle from the Dodgers. Mays was a clever fielder and showed his versatility in the 1954 World Series by snagging a Vic Wertz drive that is still the most talked about fielding effort in World Series history. National League MVP in 1954 and 1965. All-Star selection 1954 to 1969. Powered four home runs in one game (1961), three homers in one game (1961 and 1963), and had 52 in one season (1965). Elected to the Hall of Fame in 1979.

Catcher

William Malcolm Dickey

Bill Dickey was the New York Yankee starting catcher from 1929 to 1946 and played a key role in seven successful World Series championships during that time. He batted .438 in the 1932 battle with Chicago and .400 in the 1938 Series, again against Chicago. In ten of eleven seasons, Dickey batted over .300, with .362 in 1936 his high point. A .980 fielder and .313 hitter. Hall of Fame 1954.

Gordon Stanley Cochrane

Mickey Cochrane played the bulk of his thirteen-year career with Connie Mack's Philadelphia A's and went to the World Series in 1929, 1930, and 1931. In 1934 and 1935 he went to the Series with the Tigers. Cochrane's most productive year at bat was 1932. That season he had 23 homers, 112 ribbies, and a .293 batting average. He suffered a skull fracture in the 1937 season and was knocked out of the game at the age of thirty-four. American League MVP in 1928. Lifetime batting .320. Hall of Fame 1947.

Roy Campanella

Campy came to the Brooklyn Dodgers in the 1948 season and quickly established his position on the club by taking part in a league-high 12 double plays for catchers. He was the National League MVP in 1951, 1953, and 1955. The

Cy Young

Christy Mathewson

Willie Mays

Walter Johnson

hard-hitting backstop had a career-high 41 homers in 1953, along with 142 ribbies. Had 3 home runs in one game (1950). Campanella established the World Series record by throwing out two men in the first inning of the 1952 Series. Had a .995 fielding average with the Dodgers in five World Series. An auto accident in January 1958 left him paralyzed, tragically ending his playing career at the age of 36. Lifetime fielding average, .980, lifetime batting, .276. Hall of Fame 1969.

Right-handed Pitcher

Walter Perry Johnson

Big Train's career with the Washington Senators stretched from 1907 to 1927; he pitched an American League record 802 games. In 1913 he had his career season high of 36 victories, 12 of them shutouts. In all, Johnson had 416 victories, 113 shutouts. The two-time MVP (1913 and 1924) was perhaps one of the game's fastest pitchers. His 1.14 earned run average 1913 was his best mark. Hall of Fame 1936.

Denton True Young

Cy Young won a record 511 major-league games in twenty-three seasons. "More than you'll ever watch in a lifetime," he liked to say. At the turn of the century, when relievers and specialists were unheard of, Cy Young pitched an arm-stretching 75 games. In 1901 he went 33-10 and in 1903 he went 32-10. In his career with four clubs, Young pitched 7,377 innings; nine of these were "perfect," on May 5, 1905, against Philadelphia. Cy engineered two victories in Boston's 5-game-to-3 victory over Pittsburgh in the first World Series in 1903. Hall of Fame 1937.

Christopher Mathewson

Big Six won a record 373 games in his National League stint with the New York Giants. In his first year in the major leagues he went 0-3 (1900). The following season he got unwound and went 20-17, the first of thirteen 20-plus winning seasons that he would have in his career. In 1908, Matty was 37-11 and left 259 batters standing at the plate on the third strike. His amazing control of the ball was the talk of the major leagues. Christy had 2,505 career strikeouts and only 837 bases on balls. Led Giants to four National League pennants. Went 5-5 in World Series play, striking out 48 and walking 10. ERA 1.15 in Series. Hall of Fame 1936.

Left-handed Pitcher

Robert Moses Grove

Lefty Grove's major-league debut with Connie Mack's Philadelphia A's in 1925 was inauspicious. His 116 strikeouts were tops in the league, but his 131 walks were also the league's highest. Grove posted a disappointing 10-12 mark that year but came back two seasons later to explode for 20 victories. The next six seasons he never had less than 20 wins a year. In 1931, his 31-4 helped the A's to the pennant, but his 16 fans in 26 innings of play that Series was not enough to keep the Cards from taking the Series 4 games to 3. Grove had 300 career victories and 140 losses, for a .682 winning average. Hall of Fame 1947.

Sanford Koufax

Sandy Koufax was the game's top strike-thrower. In three seasons he had more than 300 strikeouts (1963, 1965, 1966), establishing the major-league mark. His 382 mark in 1965 was the best ever in major-league history. Koufax played for the pennant-contending Dodgers and was always under pressure to win. He responded in the World Series by throwing 15 strikes on the October 2, 1963, game against the Yankees. Koufax pitched four no-hitters in his career, a National League record. His 11 shutouts in 1963 was also a record for left-handed pitchers. Cy Young Award winner in 1963, 1965, 1966. MVP in 1963. Hall of Fame 1972, the youngest ever selected, at thirty-six years old.

Carl Owen Hubbell

King Carl was the star of the Giant pitching staff for sixteen years, dazzling batters with his tricks, striking them out with his infamous screwball. When he left the game after the 1943 season, he had won 253 games and lost 154, for a winning average of .622. He played for three Yankee World Series championship teams (1933, 1936, 1937) and had an ERA of 1.79 for his 50⅓ innings of work. Best remembered for striking out Ruth, Gehrig, and Foxx in the 1934 All-Star Game. In 1933, Hubbell pitched 46 consecutive innings without allowing a run to score; went 23-12 that year, ten of the victories being shutouts. MVP in 1933 and 1937. Hall of Fame 1947.

Manager

Joseph Vincent McCarthy

Marse Joe took over as Yankee skipper in 1931, following a short stay and one pennant with the Chicago Cubs. McCarthy went on to guide the Yanks to eight

American League flags and seven World Series titles before he left the team in 1946. Great players such as Ruth, Gehrig, Lazzeri, Gomez, and DiMaggio helped bring McCarthy nothing less than a fourth-place finish in his fifteen years with the team. Hall of Fame 1957.

John Joseph McGraw

Little Napoleon ruled the New York Giants like no other major-league manager would dare. His autocratic style that went so far as setting off-field habits for the players turned in handsome dividends. From 1904 until he retired in 1932, the Giants won 10 pennants and 3 World Series titles (1905, 1921, 1922). In defending his players, he battled with umpires often. Famed arbiter Bill Klem was McGraw's favorite target, and in 1928 the two almost came to blows. McGraw actually fought with Ty Cobb and former friend, Wilbert Robinson. Hall of Fame 1937.

Charles Dillon Stengel

Casey Stengel came to managing from the playing ranks where he had a lifetime .284 average and 60 homers as an outfielder for the Dodgers, Phillies, Giants, and Braves. In 1934, Stengel became manager of the Dodgers. He moved to Boston in 1938 and took over the floundering Braves. As was the case in Brooklyn, Stengel had to fight to keep the team out of the league cellar. In his later years Stengel was rewarded with better teams, much better. He took over the Yankees at age fifty-nine (in 1949), and for the next five seasons he was rewarded with five World Series titles. Before he left the Bombers in 1960, the Yanks had won two more Series and three more pennants. The Old Professor (he was given a degree by the University of Mississippi for coaching the baseball team) was whimsical, comical, kind, and a keen judge of talent. In 1962, at the age of seventy-two, Stengel became the first manager of the N.Y. Mets and stayed with them for four seasons before retiring from the game. He was named Manager of the Year in 1949, 1953, and 1958. Hall of Fame 1966.

Babe Ruth

The Greatest Player Ever in the First One Hundred Years of the Game.

"If someone beats my record [home run] I want him to do it under the same conditions that I operated."

THE GREATEST EVER

BABE RUTH

JOE DiMAGGIO   TY COBB

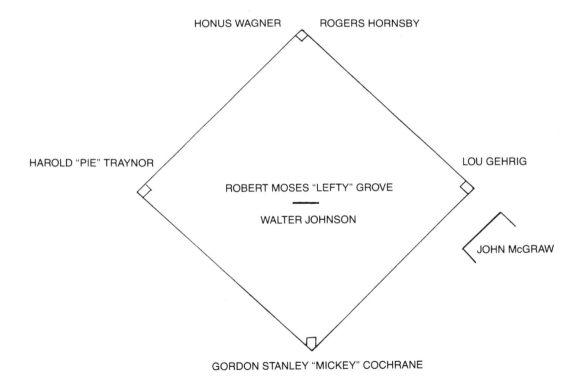

HONUS WAGNER   ROGERS HORNSBY

HAROLD "PIE" TRAYNOR   LOU GEHRIG

ROBERT MOSES "LEFTY" GROVE
———
WALTER JOHNSON

JOHN McGRAW

GORDON STANLEY "MICKEY" COCHRANE

GLOSSARY

Since its earliest days, baseball, more than any other native sport, has had—or invented—certain words or expressions to suit the needs of the game. Although baseball is rich in humorous, colorful, vigorous, and decidedly apt words and idioms, the etymology of many of these has unfortunately been poorly documented, lost, or so disputed that their exact sources will never be known.

Included here are some of the more common terms from baseball terminology over the years, compiled especially for *A Baseball Album* by a lexicographer friend who wishes to remain anonymous.

apple: a baseball.

backstop: the catcher.

bag: first, second, or third base.

Baltimore chop: a batted ball that takes an extremely high bounce after it hits the ground, usually on or near the plate. So called because early Baltimore Spider players, especially Wee Willie Keeler, used this tactic frequently.

banjo hit: a ball that "plunks" off the bat and falls between the infield and outfield but is not hit high enough to be called a "Texas Leaguer."

banjo hitter: a player who cannot hit a long ball.

barnstorm: to go about the country playing exhibition games in small towns and rural districts. Popular in early baseball after teams left spring training camps and headed north; a means of gaining extra money and publicity. According to A. G. Spalding, the first barnstorming tour was in 1860 when the Excelsiors of Brooklyn played in several cities of central and western New York.

beanball: ball thrown close to or at a batter's head, or "bean," to intimidate him.

bearing down: to give total concentration and maximum effort in a crucial moment of the game.

beauty: a ball called for a strike that should have been hit by the batter out of the ball park.

bleeder: a lucky one-base hit, usually a softly hit grounder.

blooper: a lucky hit that just makes it out of the infield.

bonehead: a dumb player or a player who makes a "stupid" play.

boner: a dumb play.

boot: an error.

box: the pitcher's mound; stems from earlier times when the pitcher threw from a specified area 45 feet from the plate, outlined in the shape of a box.

bullpen: an area adjoining the outfield where reserve pitchers warm up. The term possibly originated at the turn of the century when Bull Durham tobacco signs were placed on the outfield fences of most ball parks. The signs were 25 feet high and almost 40 feet long, and $50 was given to any player who was able to hit one. Since pitchers generally warmed up in front of the signs, the area became known as the bullpen.

bunt: to tap the ball lightly so it doesn't leave the infield. Credit for invention goes to Tim Murnane, National League player from Boston (1876–77). Murnane came up with the idea after hitting a feeble shot that rolled up to the pitcher's mound. Murnane went home and made a flat bat that he practiced with to gain proficiency at bunting. The bunt was referred to as a freak play in accounts of 1888 and did not take on its importance in game strategy until much later.

busher: a novice, a raw recruit.

butterfingers: a player who lets an easily hit ball drop through his fingers.

change of pace: a pitching method of fooling the batter by alternating fast and slow deliveries.

charley horse: a pulled muscle, generally the thigh; a common baseball injury. According to Walter McCredie, a minor league coach, the term originated in 1889 in Sioux City, Iowa.

The Sioux City team had an old white horse named Charley. Although he could hardly walk, he was used to pull a rig to drag the diamond before the games. His legs were so bad that it would take sometimes as long as thirty minutes to do the job. Thereafter, when a player came up with a limp, someone would say, "Here comes Charley." This was later changed to "You have a Charley in your leg," and finally "You have a charley horse."

choke: to grip the bat several inches from the bottom.

chucker: pitcher; generally a fastball specialist.

circus catch: a sensational catch.

cleanup batter: The fourth batter in the lineup; generally the player who will drive in all the men on base, thereby cleaning up the bases.

clinker: an error.

clothesline: a hard-hit, low line drive.

crab: a player who is always complaining or finding fault.

crank: a baseball enthusiast; a fan.

cripple: a ball that is pitched when the count is 3-0, 2-0, 3-1; a player who takes advantage of the pitch at this time is known as a "cripple shooter."

crooked arm: a left-handed pitcher.

cyclops: a player who wears eyeglasses.

diamond: the infield playing surface; so-called because it looks like the mineral.

down the alley: describing a perfectly pitched ball that is called for a strike.

drag bunt: a bunt aimed at first base by a left-handed hitter.

duster: a beanball; a pitching tactic in which a ball is deliberately thrown at a batter to move him away from the plate. Generally causes the batter to fall to the ground to avoid being hit.

eagle eye: a sharp eye; a fine ability for judging a pitched ball.

fan: a follower of a team; an enthusiastic spectator; first coined by Tim Sullivan, manager and scout in the early 1880s. Derivative of fanatic. Also means to strike out.

far corner: third base.

fat one: a pitch right over the plate deemed easy to hit.

fielder's choice: fielder handles a ground ball and throws to a base other than first, attempting to retire an advancing runner already on base, rather than the batter. Batter is charged by the scorer as hitting into a fielder's choice and is given an official "at bat" and no hit.

fireman: a relief pitcher called into the game during an emergency.

foot in the bucket: batting position in which the front foot is positioned toward the foul line—or the water bucket in the dugout—instead of toward the pitcher.

free ticket: a base on balls.

fungo stick: a thin bat used for hitting fly balls in practice.

glass arm: a weak-throwing pitcher.

goat: a postgame sobriquet for a player whose poor performance or error cost the team the game.

gopher ball: a pitch that is easy to hit; from "go for."

grandstand player: a player who makes easy plays look difficult.

grapefruit league: exhibition games held during spring training.

groove: the height in the strike zone at which the batter is best able to hit the ball.

handcuff: a hard hit that goes through the infielder's hands opposite the glove side.

high hard one: a fastball that arrives above the batter's waist.

hill: the pitcher's mound.

hit-and-run: an offensive play in which a runner advances on a pitch that a batter hits into territory vacated by the fielder moving to cover the base.

hit the dirt: to slide or drop to the ground to avoid a pitched ball.

hold out: to refuse to sign a new contract. To refrain from reporting to the team. Charles Sweeney, second baseman of the Cincinnati Reds, was perhaps baseball's first holdout. In the 1869 season he was paid $800, which he thought was insufficient the following year. He held out for $1,000 and didn't report to the team until he was paid that sum.

hook: curveball; one of a variety of sliding techniques.

horse collar: going hitless for the day.

hot corner: third base.

hot dog: a player who is overtly ostentatious in his playing mannerisms.

Houdini: a trick pitcher.

ice it: to make a play that decides the game's outcome.

iron man: a workhorse pitcher; a durable player.

jockey: a player who rides the opposition.

jughandle: a curveball.

junk artist: a pitcher who throws slow or off-speed pitches.

keystone base: second base.

knuckleball: a specialty pitch thrown by using fingernails, fingertips, or knuckles to grip the ball; the pitched ball does not rotate and is strongly affected by air currents. Very difficult to catch.

lay it down: make a sacrifice hit.

leadoff: the first batter in the lineup.

long strike: a long ball that just barely goes foul.

look it over: to take time in choosing a pitched ball to hit.

meal ticket: a team's most successful player.

Mexican standoff: a tie game.

moxie: courage.

nightcap: the second game of a doubleheader that is finished during the night.

pick off: to catch a runner off base by a quick throw from either the pitcher or the catcher.

pinch hitter: a substitute batter.

rabbit ball: a ball with extra "hop"; first introduced in the major leagues in 1910. The ball was slightly altered in manufacture by the introduction of cork, allowing the ball to travel significantly farther when hit.

rain check: invention of Abner Powell (1888) of New Orleans, a former pitcher and minor-league club owner. It was his idea to make a ticket with a detachable section that would be redeemable for admission to another game if the first game was canceled due to rain.

rhubarb: a mix-up, a confused situation; a controversy. First popularized by Walter Lanier "Red" Barber, the colorful major-league broadcaster with the Cincinnati Reds, Brooklyn Dodgers, and the New York Yankees.

ribbies: abbreviation for "runs batted in."

scatter arm: pitcher with good speed but lacking in control.

seventh-inning stretch: the time between halves of the seventh inning in which fans customarily get up and stretch. Brother Jasper of Manhattan College in The Bronx is credited with originating the stretch in 1882. Since he was the college baseball coach and also the prefect of discipline, he exerted control over the students who came to all home games at the Polo Grounds. He always cautioned the students not to leave their seats or move around until the game was over. One day in 1882 he noticed that the students were becoming restless at a home game, so he announced to the fans that they could take a few moments to move around and stretch when Manhattan was coming up to bat in the seventh inning. The practice was continued for all other Manhattan home games and was eventually picked up by Giant fans.

shine ball: a baseball that has been doctored, usually with talcum powder; probably invented by Dave Darforth in 1915 while pitching for Louisville in the American Association. Oil was used on the field to control the dust problem, and the innovative Danforth discovered that by rubbing the oil-and-dirt-covered ball on his trouser leg the ball became smooth and shiny and hopped when he pitched it.

shoestring catch: a hit ball caught at shoe-top height.

slugger: a long-distance hitter.

slump: a losing streak or temporary loss of batting eye.

snake: curveball.

southpaw: a left-handed pitcher; term originated in the late 1890's when it was common practice for ball fields to be laid out so that the batter faced east, away from the setting sun in the west. Thus, first base would be on the southern side, and since a left-handed pitcher throws from this side, he has acquired the "southpaw" moniker.

spitball: a pitched ball on which secretion, saliva, or sweat had been placed. Invented by George Hildebrand, Providence outfielder. Burleigh Grimes, who retired at the end of the 1934 season (270 lifetime victories), was the last of eighteen players allowed to throw spitballs legally. The spitball was outlawed in 1920.

squeeze play: an intricate play, rarely used in games; the runner on third heads for home plate on the pitch. The batter then bunts the ball away from the runner and allows the runner to score. The origin of the term is uncertain. Joe Yeager (d. 1937), who played with Brooklyn in 1898, is credited with being the inventor, although two Yale students used it against Princeton in 1894.

tee off: to hit a long, hard ball.

Texas Leaguer: a looping hit that drops safely between the infield and the outfield; the ploy originated in minor-league parks in the Texas League.

tools of ignorance: catcher's equipment.

walk: a base on balls.

waste one: a tactic of throwing wide to a catcher with the idea that the base runner on first will try and steal second, the catcher would then have an ideal opportunity to throw him out. Also, a pitching strategy of throwing wide to a batter who has an unfavorable count against him; the theory is that the batter will chase a bad ball.

whiff: to strike out.

wing: a pitcher's throwing arm.